TEST ANXIETY

THE SERIES IN CLINICAL AND COMMUNITY PSYCHOLOGY

CONSULTING EDITORS
Charles D. Spielberger and Irwin G. Sarason

TEST ANXIETY
Theory, Assessment, and Treatment

Edited by
Charles D. Spielberger, Ph.D.
University of South Florida

Peter R. Vagg, Ph.D.
University of South Florida

Taylor & Francis
Publishers since 1798

USA	Publishing Office:	Taylor & Francis 1101 Vermont Avenue, N.W., Suite 200 Washington, DC 20005-3521 Tel: (202) 289-2174 Fax: (202) 289-3665
	Distribution Center:	Taylor & Francis 1900 Frost Road, Suite 101 Bristol, PA 19007-1598 Tel: (215) 785-5800 Fax: (215) 785-5515
UK		Taylor & Francis Ltd. 4 John St. London WC1N 2ET Tel: 071 405 2237 Fax: 071 831 2035

Kevin Roan
For permission

TEST ANXIETY: Theory, Assessment, and Treatment

1 2 3 4 5 6 7 8 9 0   BRBR   9 8 7 6 5

This book was set in Times Roman by Harlowe Typography, Inc. The editors were Christine Williams and Kathleen Baker. Cover design by Michelle M. Fleitz. Printing and binding by Braun-Brumfield, Inc.

A CIP catalog record for this book is available from the British Library.

∞ The paper in this publication meets the requirements of the ANSI Standard Z39.48-1984 (Permanence of Paper)

Library of Congress Cataloging-in-Publication Data

Test anxiety : theory, assessment, and treatment / edited by Charles
    D. Spielberger, Peter R. Vagg.
        p.   cm. — (the series in clinical and community psychology,
    ISSN 01460846)
    Includes bibliographical references and index.

    1. Test anxiety.   2. Students—Psychology.   3. Anxiety—Treatment.
I. Spielberger, Charles Donald, date.   II. Vagg, Peter Robert.
III. Series.
    [DNLM: WM 172 T3418 1995]
LB3060.6.T47   1995
371.2'6'019—dc20
DNLM/DLC
for Library of Congress
                                                                95-14242
                                                                CIP

ISBN 0-89116-212-7
ISSN 0146-0846

Contents

Contributors

BENJAMIN ALGAZE, University of South Florida, Tampa, FL, USA
SCARVIA B. ANDERSON, Educational Testing Service, Atlanta, GA, USA
WILLIAM D. ANTON, University of South Florida, Tampa, FL, USA
SAMUEL BALL, Educational Testing Service, Carlton, Victoria, Australia
JEFFREY R. BEDELL, Florida Mental Health Institute, Tampa, FL, USA
TUCKER M. FLETCHER, University of South Florida, Tampa, FL, USA
JESS H. GHANNAM, The University of Michigan, Ann Arbor, MI, USA
HECTOR P. GONZALEZ, University of South Florida, Tampa, FL, USA
PETER G. GLANZMANN, Johannes-Gutenberg Universität, Mainz, Germany
VOLKER HODAPP, Der Heinrich-Heine-Universität Düsseldorf, Germany
JOHN JAMIESON, Lakehead University, Ontario, Canada
MARK C. KLISCH, University of South Florida, Tampa, FL, USA
LOTHAR LAUX, University of Bamberg, Germany
E. MICHAEL LILLIBRIDGE, University of South Florida, Tampa, FL, USA
HERBERT A. MARLOWE, Florida Mental Health Institute, Tampa, FL, USA
JAMES D. PAPSDORF, The University of Michigan, Ann Arbor, MI, USA
JOHN C. PARKER, IV, Grossmont Psychological Associates, La Mesa, CA, USA
WILLIAM I. SAUSER, JR., Auburn University, Auburn, AL, USA
CHARLES D. SPIELBERGER, University of South Florida, Tampa, FL, USA
PETER R. VAGG, University of South Florida, Tampa, FL, USA

Foreword

Test anxiety. The very words reverberate in people's innermost beings. Who has not suffered from test anxiety in some situation? Since the earliest research studies, anxiety has been identified as a major variable affecting performance. However, the relation between anxiety and performance is not a simple one. Anxiety usually has negative effects; but the nature of the task, the way individuals handle their anxiety, and the interactions of anxiety with other personality characteristics and with situational variables—all of these factors make research on anxiety endlessly fascinating.

I first dealt with anxiety in a study carried out in 1946, the results of which we felt were clearly influenced by the interaction of our experimental conditions with student anxiety. My first attempt to reduce anxiety was so simple and effective that it seemed almost too good to be true. In the early 1950s, several of my teaching fellows suggested that we might help students who had high test anxiety by providing an opportunity for them to write comments about questions on the multiple-choice answer sheets we used for course exams. The results clearly showed a positive effect on performance, primarily on the last half of the test, with particularly favorable effects for students high in anxiety.

After replicating these results a couple of times, we tried to find other ways of dealing with the problem of students with high test anxiety, but from that time on, we found *we* were the ones who were frustrated, as one attempt after another ran into difficulties. For example, we thought that giving students open-book examinations would help, but test-anxious students still performed more poorly than those with low anxiety. We then tried giving students take-home tests, but once again, those students with high test anxiety did more poorly. It seemed that no matter what we did in our efforts to help anxious students improve their grades, our interventions seemed to benefit other students more.

We discovered that it was not enough to help test-anxious students stop worrying during examinations because their anxiety not only interfered with their test performance, but also had adverse effects on studying before the test. They spent as much, or even more, time than other students in studying, but the methods they used were less likely to produce better learning. Their preferred strategies, memorization and repetition, were not conducive to developing understanding or the ability to apply their knowledge to more complex situtations. We first tried giving 2 hours of study habits instruction and found no effects; then we tried 4 hours with still no effects; then 6 hours with no effects. Only after we instituted a full semester course, "Learning to Learn," did we actually produce favorable results for students high in test anxiety.

In most of our test anxiety research, as well as in much of the research carried out by others, the focus has been on interventions and their effects on test anxiety and performance. The unique contribution of the Spielberger and Vagg book is that it examines the *processes* that mediate the effects of interventions on anxiety and performance. *Test Anxiety: Theory, Assessment, and Treatment* represents a major step forward in research in this field. This book has made a major contribution to my own thinking, and I am confident that it will be useful to many others—those dealing with the practical problems of helping test-anxious students as well as investigators doing research in the area.

W. J. McKeachie
Ann Arbor, Michigan
November 1994

Preface

Aptitude and achievement test scores, as well as academic performance, are increasingly used in evaluating applicants for jobs and admission into educational programs. Consequently, examination stress and test anxiety have become pervasive problems in modern society. The adverse effects of test anxiety often lead to substantial underestimation of an individual's ability and to reduced access to educational and occupational opportunities. Beause of the serious consequences of test anxiety, it is not surprising that educators, counselors, psychologists, and psychiatrists have developed a broad array of treatment programs designed to reduce test anxiety. These therapeutic interventions have included such diverse treatment components as biofeedback, desensitization, cognitive behavior modification, rational–emotive therapy, and study skills training.

To understand the therapeutic impact of specific treatment interventions on test anxiety and academic performance, a comprehensive theory that encompasses the antecedents, correlates, and consequences of test anxiety is required. Because worry and emotionality have been identified as the major components of test anxiety, an adequate theory must recognize and differentiate between the influence of these two distinctive components on test performance. The theory also needs to specify the impact of worry and emotionality on the cognitive, affective, and physiological processes that mediate their effects on attention, concentration, and information processing. In addition, a comprehensive theory must take into account study habits, attitudes, and test-taking skills because these correlates of test anxiety have substantial influence on how adequately students prepare for, and how well they perform on, examinations.

In early test anxiety treatment studies, therapeutic interventions were directed primarily toward reducing the anxiety experienced by test-anxious students during examinations. Common sense suggested, and empirical research findings verified, that test anxiety adversely affects the performance of many students. Therefore, reducing anxiety should improve test performance and thus facilitate academic achievement. Although most of the early test anxiety treatment studies were successful in reducing the anxiety that students experienced during examinations, improvement in course grades and academic achievement was rarely found.

The treatment of test-anxious university students was systematically investigated in a series of studies in collaborative research programs at the University of South Florida (USF) and the University of Michigan (UM). The empirical findings from five previously unpublished USF and UM test anxiety outcome studies are described in detail in Part III of this volume. Developments in test anxiety theory, and in the assessment of test anxiety, that have evolved from these studies are also presented by the contributors to this volume. The editors and the authors of 11 of the 14 chapters participated in the USF and UM test anxiety treatment programs.

The chapters in Part I review and evaluate advances in the theory and measurement of test anxiety. In Chapter 1, Spielberger and Vagg present a Transactional Process Model that identifies the most important factors that influence worry and emotionality. They also discuss the major determinants and internal processes that mediate the effects of worry and emotionality on academic performance. A comprehensive "state-of-the-art" review of test anxiety measures is presented by Anderson and Sauser in Chapter 2. In examining the validity of test anxiety measures, they provide critical insight into the meaning of the construct. In Chapter 3, Bedell and Marlowe describe several measures that have been frequently used in research on test anxiety, and they evaluate the convergent, divergent, and predictive evidence of the construct validity of these measures. Hodapp, Laux, and Glanzman examine the definition of test anxiety as a situation-specific trait in Chapter 4 and report recent research findings on the construction and validation of a new test anxiety scale.

The chapters in Part II examine the antecedents, correlates, and consequences of test anxiety. Anton and Lillibridge present in Chapter 5 case studies of six test-anxious students. Noting that a wide range of factors appears to contribute to the etiology of test anxiety, they conclude that it is not possible to identify a single, specific set of psychological antecedents. In Chapter 6, Papsdorf, Ghannam, and Jamieson report eye movement patterns and finger temperature elevations of test-anxious students, which they interpret as evidence that interhemispheric competition interferes with attention, concentration, and test performance. Noting a number of similarities between mathematics anxiety and test anxiety, Anton and Klisch in Chapter 7 contend that cognitive and behavioral treatments should be effective in helping students deal with these problems. Although high anxiety generally has a negative impact on performance, Ball observes in Chapter 8 that for some students anxiety actually facilitates performance on important examinations such as the Scholastic Aptitude Test.

Five USF and UM test anxiety treatment studies are reported in Part III of this volume. The treatment components in these studies, described in detail in Chapters 9–13, used a variety of therapeutic procedures designed to reduce worry, emotionality, or both in test situations. The efficacy and locus of impact of each treatment component used in these studies are examined in Chapter 14 in the context of the Transactional Process Model presented in Chapter 1. Cognitively focused treatments were generally more effective in reducing test anxiety, its worry and emotionality components, and trait anxiety than were treatments that targeted emotionality.

This volume will be of interest to educators, counselors, and psychologists who are called on to help students deal with examination stress and a wide range of academic problems. Vocational and rehabilitation counselors who are likely to encounter evaluation anxiety in their clients will find the contents of this volume useful for assessing these problems and for making appropriate referrals for treatment when indicated. Clinical psychologists and psychiatrists who provide services to a wide range of clients with a variety of performance anxieties will also benefit from a more comprehensive understanding of the nature of test anxiety, it adverse effects on performance, and the therapeutic techniques that have proved effective in its treatment.

We would like to express our gratitude to Professors Wilbert J. McKeachie and James D. Papsdorf of the University of Michigan, and to our colleagues in the UM and USF psychology departments for serving on the thesis and dissertation committees of the students (now colleagues) who worked with us in test anxiety programs. We also wish to thank Dr. William D. Anton, director of the USF Counseling Center for Human Development, not only for his contributions to the research program, but also for making the resources of his center available to us. For their expert technical and clerical assistance in processing the manuscripts for this volume, we are indebted to Dianne Gregg, Staci Martin, Jennifer Pagnotta, and Eric Reheiser, and especially to Virginia Berch and Karen Unger of the USF Center for Research in Behavioral Medicine and Health Psychology.

Charles D. Spielberger
Peter R. Vagg

I

TEST ANXIETY, THEORY, AND MEASUREMENT

1

Test Anxiety: A Transactional Process Model

Charles D. Spielberger and Peter R. Vagg
University of South Florida, Tampa, Florida

In the test-conscious culture of the second half of the 20th century, people's lives are greatly influenced by test performance. Therefore, it is not surprising that anxiety during examinations (or test anxiety) has become a pervasive contemporary problem (Hembree, 1988; Pekrun, 1992; I. G. Sarason, 1980, 1983; I. G. Sarason & Sarason, 1990; Schwarzer & Jerusalem, 1992; Spielberger, 1962, 1972b, 1976, 1980; Tobias, 1992). For some students, test anxiety is so disturbing that they must seek professional assistance to help them cope with its debilitating effects. Consequently, psychologists, counselors, and educators have become increasingly concerned with understanding the intense emotional reactions that many students experience during examinations, and these concerns have stimulated the development of effective therapeutic methods for the treatment of test anxiety (Allen, 1971, 1972, 1973; C. H. Brown, 1938a; C. H. Brown & Gelder, 1938; Hagtvet & Backer-Johnsen, 1992; Schwarzer et al., 1987, 1989; Spielberger et al., 1976, 1979; Spielberger & Weitz, 1964).

Early research on examination stress and the evolution of test anxiety as a psychological construct are considered in this chapter. The relation between test anxiety and state and trait anxiety is then examined, and a conception of test anxiety as a situation-specific personality trait with worry and emotionality as its major components is outlined. Approaches to the measurement of test anxiety are also briefly reviewed and evaluated. Finally, a Transactional Process Model is proposed as a conceptual framework for analyzing and evaluating (a) the effects of examination stress on the internal emotional and cognitive processes that influence test anxiety and (b) the adverse effects of worry and emotionality on information processing and academic achievement.

EARLY RESEARCH ON EXAMINATION STRESS AND TEST ANXIETY

Fear and anxiety were clearly recognized as significant aspects of human behavior in ancient Egypt, the Old Testament, and in Greek and Roman literature. Rollo May (1950/1977) traced the historical roots of most current conceptions of anxiety to the philosophical and theological views of Pascal in the 17th century and Kirkegaard in the 19th century. From a biological perspective, Darwin (1872/1965) considered fear to be a universal characteristic in both animals and humans that has evolved over countless generations as an adaptive response to dangerous situations. Manifestations of fear, according to Darwin, included heart palpitations, trembling, increased perspiration, dryness of the mouth, and other physiological and behavioral reactions that would now be recognized as resulting from activation of the autonomic nervous system.

In contrast to Darwin's emphasis on the observable biological and behavioral manifestations of fear, Freud (1895/1924, 1936) focused on anxiety, which he regarded as the subjective experience associated with fear reactions. He defined anxiety as "something felt," an unpleasant emotional state. In addition to trembling, disturbances in respiration, and biological manifestations similar to those described by Darwin, Freud proposed that anxiety states consist of feelings of tension, apprehension, and nervousness. Freud also distinguished between "objective" anxiety, in which the emotional response is proportional to a real danger in the external world, and "neurotic" anxiety, in which the intensity of the emotional response is much greater than the objective danger. In neurotic anxiety, the person responds to an internal danger emanating from unacceptable sexual and aggressive impulses that had been repressed.

In what appears to be the first empirical investigation of test anxiety, published in 1914 in the *Journal of Biological Chemistry,* Folin et al. reported that approximately one out of five medical students showed evidence of glycosuria (i.e., sugar in the urine) after a stressful examination; none of these students showed any trace of glycosuria before the examination. Similar findings were reported by Walter B. Cannon (1929) in his classic book *Bodily Changes in Pain, Hunger, Fear and Rage,* which led Cannon to conclude that academic examinations provided an ideal situation for investigating the effects of real-life stress on physiological reactions.

The noted Russian physiologist Alexander Luria (1932) was perhaps the first investigator to call attention to individual differences in the emotional reactions that students experience in test situations. Luria classified medical students who became excited and disorganized during examinations as "unstable"; those who remained relatively calm, with well-coordinated speech and motor reactions, were considered "stable." More than 60% of the students classified as unstable were judged to have "neuropathic symptoms," as compared with only 16% of the stable students. These findings were interpreted by Luria as evidence that academic examinations evoked intense emotional reactions (test anxiety) in unstable (i.e., neurotic) students, for whom such situations elicited "unmanageable stress."

Between 1932 and 1937, test anxiety received a great deal of attention from German investigators. The first book on test anxiety (Neumann, 1933) was published during this period, along with a number of papers on its etiology and treatment (e.g., Redl, 1933; Stengel, 1936; Weber, 1934). Conceptualized in the context of psychoanalytic theory, test anxiety was assumed to result from traumatic childhood experiences. Unfortunately, this research was never translated into English and has subsequently received little attention in the test anxiety literature.

C. H. Brown and his colleagues, in a series of studies at the University of Chicago (C. H. Brown, 1938a, 1938b; C. H. Brown & Gelder, 1938; Fiedler, 1949; Hastings, 1944; Waite, 1942), systematically investigated individual differences in test anxiety. The Chicago group developed the first psychometric scale for identifying test-anxious students, finding that students with high scores on this scale were nervous before examinations and performed more poorly than those who were relatively calm. The potentially serious consequences of test anxiety were also noted by C. H. Brown (1938a, 1938b), who attributed the suicides of two university students to worry over approaching examinations.

McKeachie (1951) conducted a number of studies in an effort to find ways to reduce the negative impact of anxiety on students' classroom test performance. He observed that "while anxiety may be a valuable motivating force, it inhibits performance if it cannot be resolved" (p. 157). In his pioneering research, McKeachie found that anxious students performed better on multiple-choice examinations when given the opportunity to write comments about the questions, and attributed this improved performance to a reduction in anxiety for students who could "dispel or channelize some of the tensions built up by tests" (p. 156).

McKeachie and his colleagues also reported evidence that anxiety during examinations was not the only determinant of the performance decrements of test-anxious students. Differences in ability and inadequate study habits were also important in explaining the poor performance of test-anxious students (Lin & McKeachie, 1970). In a more recent study, Naveh-Benjamin et al. (1981) observed that poor test-taking skills appeared to be a major determinant of the worry cognitions that contributed to the performance decrements of test-anxious students.

Whereas McKeachie's research focused on modifying test situations to help students reduce anxiety during examinations, S. B. Sarason and his co-workers identified specific examination conditions that caused high test-anxious students to perform more poorly than did low test-anxious students (Doris & Sarason, 1955; Mandler & Sarason, 1952; S. B. Sarason et al., 1960; S. B. Sarason et al., 1952). These investigators convincingly demonstrated that evaluative instructions and failure feedback interfered more with the performance of high test-anxious students than with that of low test-anxious students. However, high test-anxious students did relatively better on examinations in which evaluation stress was minimized.

This line of research was further advanced by I. G. Sarason (1958a, 1960, 1961, 1965), who reported that high test-anxious students performed more poorly when achievement was emphasized. In situations designed to allay anxiety, high test-anxious students showed improved performance, whereas low test-anxious students actually performed less well (I. G. Sarason, 1958a). In subsequent research, I. G. Sarason (1975b, 1984) found that test-anxious students were more self-critical and more likely to experience task-irrelevant worry responses that interfered with performance during examinations than students low in test anxiety. Because these negative, self-centered worry responses were incompatible with good performance, the high test-anxious students also did more poorly on learning tasks, and on intelligence and achievement tests, than did low test-anxious students.

TEST ANXIETY AND STATE–TRAIT ANXIETY

In the early studies of examination stress (e.g., Cannon, 1929; Folin et al., 1914), test anxiety was inferred from the physiological responses (e.g., glycosuria) that students experienced during stressful examinations. Thus, test anxiety was implicitly defined as functionally equivalent to the physiological arousal associated with activation of the autonomic nervous system (Spielberger, 1966a, 1972a). Such definitions typically ignored the experiential qualities of the emotional states that were experienced during examinations. Definitions of test anxiety that emphasize physiological arousal also fail to take into account individual differences in anxiety proneness as a personality trait that influence the perception and appraisal of examinations as more or less threatening.

In the context of Lazarus's (1966; Lazarus & Averill, 1972) conception of stress as a transactional process, Spielberger (1966a, 1972a, 1975, 1976) distinguished between the stress associated with examination situations (stressor), the subjective interpretation of a test as more or less threatening for a particular person (threat), and the emotional states that are evoked in test situations. The concepts of *stressor* and *threat* denote significant components of a temporal sequence of events during an examination that result in the evocation of an anxiety reaction:

$$\text{Stressor} \rightarrow \text{Threat} \rightarrow \text{S-Anxiety}$$

The emotional state (S-Anxiety) experienced during examinations consists of feelings of tension, apprehension, nervousness, and worry and associated physiological arousal resulting from activation of the autonomic nervous system. The intensity of this S-Anxiety reaction will vary as a function of the degree of perceived threat, which depends on a number of factors, such as the nature of the test questions, the student's general ability and aptitude in the subject matter area, how diligently he or she has prepared for the examination, and individual differences in test anxiety as a personality trait.

Trait anxiety (or T-Anxiety) refers to relatively stable individual differences in anxiety proneness, that is, to differences in the disposition to perceive a wide range of situations involving evaluative stress as dangerous or threatening and to respond to such situations with more or less intense elevations in S-Anxiety. Measures of individual differences in T-Anxiety, which can be assessed by determining the frequency that S-Anxiety reactions have been manifested in the past (Spielberger, 1983), provide an estimate of the probability that anxiety states will be experienced in stressful evaluative situations in the future. Test-anxious students are generally higher in T-Anxiety, tend to perceive examinations as more dangerous or threatening than individuals low in T-Anxiety, and experience more intense levels of S-Anxiety when taking tests (Spielberger, 1980).

Because test-anxious individuals respond to examinations with more frequent and more intense elevations in S-Anxiety, test anxiety can be viewed as a situation-specific anxiety trait (Spielberger et al., 1978). Consequently, during examinations individuals high in test anxiety, compared with those who are low in this situation-specific trait, are more likely to experience (a) more frequent and intense elevations in S-Anxiety, (b) greater activation or arousal of the autonomic nervous system, and (c) more self-centered worry cognitions and test-irrelevant thoughts that interfere with attention and performance (Spielberger, 1972b; Spielberger et al., 1978).

MAJOR COMPONENTS OF TEST ANXIETY: WORRY AND EMOTIONALITY

Liebert and Morris (1967) were first to conceptualize test anxiety as having two major components, *worry* and *emotionality*. Their definition of emotionality primarily in terms of the physiological reactions evoked by evaluative stress is similar in many respects to S-Anxiety as described above. However, the physiological changes resulting from arousal of the autonomic nervous system are emphasized in this definition, and less attention is given to the qualitative feelings that are associated with autonomic activation. The worry component of test anxiety, as described by Liebert and Morris (1967), is "primarily cognitive concern about the consequences of failure" (p. 975). Research findings reported by Morris and Liebert (1969) indicated that worry was associated with performance decrements on tests and other intellectual tasks. In contrast, they found little or no relation between emotionality and performance.

On the basis of a comprehensive review of the test anxiety literature, Wine (1971) concluded that the performance decrements of test-anxious students were primarily due to the worry cognitions experienced by these students during examinations. She suggested that the attention of high test-anxious individuals is diverted from task requirements by distracting worry cognitions such as self-criticism and by other task-irrelevant thoughts. According to Wine (1971), "the high test-anxious person responds to evaluative conditions with ruminative, self-evaluative worry, and, thus, cannot direct adequate attention to task-relevant variables" (p. 99).

I. G. Sarason (1972) has suggested a similar explanation of the adverse effects of worry on test performance, observing that high test-anxious individuals were more self-centered and self-critical than low test-anxious individuals and were therefore more likely to experience personalized, self-derogatory worry cognitions that interfered with task performance. According to I. G. Sarason (1975a), "the highly test-anxious individual is one who is prone to emit self-centered interfering responses when confronted with evaluative situations" (p. 175). Sarason also noted that "whereas the less test-anxious person plunges into a task when he thinks he is being evaluated, the high test-anxious person plunges inward" (p. 393). High test-anxious students not only experience the attentional blocks noted by Wine, but may also fail to appropriately interpret informational cues that are readily available to them.

Covington (1984) also directly attributed the poor performance of test-anxious students to the averse effects of worrying during examinations. According to Covington, "During testing, anxious students worry that they are falling behind, scold themselves for forgetting the answers, and fearfully recall similar, previous test situations that ended in disaster. Such intrusive worry inhibits all but the simplest, automatic responses" (p. 39).

In the context of the state–trait distinction, now widely accepted in anxiety research, Spielberger et al. (1978) have conceptualized test anxiety as a situation-specific form of T-Anxiety, with worry and emotionality as major components. During examinations, high test-anxious persons respond to the evaluative threat inherent in most test situations with greater elevations in S-Anxiety, which is essentially equivalent to the emotionality component of test anxiety as a situation-specific trait. High levels of S-Anxiety then stimulate test-anxious individuals to "plunge inward," thus activating worry cognitions stored in memory that distract the test-anxious student from effective performance.

From a state–trait perspective, both worry and emotionality contribute to the performance decrements that have been observed for high test-anxious individuals. Because test-anxious persons, especially those who are high on the worry component, have previously stored more self-derogatory worry cognitions in memory, high S-Anxiety experienced during an examination will activate a greater number of interfering worry responses. It is these self-centered, task-irrelevant worry cognitions that interfere most directly with task performance.

The conception of test anxiety as a situation-specific anxiety trait, with worry and emotionality as its major components, has stimulated considerable research on the relative impact of individual differences in worry and emotionality on test performance and academic achievement. In most studies, the worry component has generally been found to be negatively related to achievement, whereas emotionality has essentially been unrelated to performance. Such evidence clearly demonstrates the critical importance of distinguishing conceptually and empirically between worry and emotionality as psychological constructs, and this has led to development of objective measures of both of these major components of test anxiety.

MEASUREMENT OF TEST ANXIETY

The evolving conceptions of test anxiety have stimulated a variety of approaches to the measurement of this construct. In the early studies of examination stress, test anxiety referred primarily to the physiological and behavioral reactions that students experienced in test situations. Early conceptions of individual differences in test anxiety were also global in nature, which resulted in the inclusion of items in test anxiety scales that assessed a wide range of content, including physiological reactions and attitudes toward school, courses, and instructors. More recent conceptions of test anxiety as a situation-specific anxiety trait have focused on the frequency and intensity of the emotional reactions and worry cognitions that students experience during examinations. Later, in Part II, the antecedents, correlates, and consequences of test anxiety are examined in more detail.

The Test Anxiety Questionnaire (TAQ), the first widely used scale for evaluating individual differences in test anxiety, was developed by Mandler and Sarason (1952) to assess self-oriented cognitions and physiological reactions before, during, and after intelligence tests and course examinations. In responding to the TAQ, subjects were instructed to report the extent to which they experienced specific symptoms of anxiety in test situations by rating themselves on a graphic scale with specified anchor points.

The Test Anxiety Scale (TAS) developed by I. G. Sarason (1958b) proved easy to administer and score and soon replaced the TAQ as the most widely used measure of test anxiety. The TAS was based on the TAQ, consisting initially of 16 TAQ items that were rewritten in a true–false format. To increase the sensitivity and reliability of this scale, additional items were subsequently added to form the 37-item version of the TAS (I. G. Sarason, 1978).

Liebert and Morris (1967; Morris et al., 1981, 1975) developed the Worry–Emotionality Questionnaire (WEQ) to assess what they considered to be the two major components of test anxiety. In constructing the WEQ, they rationally selected 10 items from the TAQ on the basis of the content validity of these items for assessing students' emotional reactions (Emotionality scale) and cognitive concerns (Worry scale) about performance during examinations. The instructions for responding to the 5-item WEQ Worry and Emotionality scales require subjects to "indicate how you feel *right now;* that is, in relation to this examination" (Liebert & Morris, 1967, p. 976). Thus, the WEQ Worry and Emotionality scales assess the two major components of test anxiety as states rather than as traits.

The Test Anxiety Inventory (TAI), a 20-item self-report scale, was designed to measure individual differences in test anxiety as a situation-specific personality trait (Spielberger, 1980). Two major goals guided the development of the TAI: (a) to construct a relatively brief, objective, self-report scale with a total score that correlated highly with other widely used global measures of test anxiety and (b) to use factor analysis in deriving subscales for measuring worry and emotionality as the major components of test anxiety. In constructing the TAI, the 37 TAS items were revised so that these items could be given with the trait-rating instructions that are used to assess T-Anxiety with the State–Trait Anxiety Inventory (Spielberger, 1983). Items describing conditions or attributes that were not directly related to the anxiety experienced during examinations, such as study habits or attitudes about tests, were found to have low concurrent validity and were discarded. For the retained items, all references to intelligence tests or frequency of occurrence were deleted, and a number of new items with content validity as measures of worry and emotionality were constructed.

In responding to the TAI, subjects are instructed to indicate how they *generally* feel by reporting on a 4-point frequency rating scale how often they have experienced particular manifestations of test anxiety (Spielberger, 1980). The TAI yields a Total score based on all 20 items and factorially derived 8-item subscales for assessing worry and emotionality as the major components of test anxiety (Benson & Tippets, 1990). The TAI Total and subscale scores correlate highly with the TAS and other widely used test anxiety measures (Spielberger, 1980). Relatively high correlations of the TAI Worry (W) and Emotionality (E) subscales with the WEQ Worry and Emotionality scales provide strong evidence of concurrent and discriminant validity. For both men and women, the TAI W and E subscales were more highly correlated with their WEQ Worry and Emotionality counterparts.

Test anxiety is now conceptualized by I. G. Sarason (1984, 1988) as consisting of four components: worry, test-irrelevant thoughts, tension, and bodily symptoms. To measure these four postulated test anxiety components, Sarason developed the 40-item Reactions to Tests (RTT) scale, with 10-item subscales to assess each component. The RTT Worry subscale appears to be quite similar to the WEQ Worry and TAI W subscales. Emotionality is measured in the RTT by the Tension and Bodily Symptoms subscales. The RTT Test-Irrelevant Thinking subscale assesses distracting thoughts that are unrelated to the test situation (e.g., "I think about current events during a test"). Benson et al. (1992) have recently developed the Revised Test Anxiety (RTA) Scale to assess with only 20 items the four dimensions measured by the 40-item RTT.

Although information concerning the validity and usefulness of the RTT and RTA scales is as yet limited, the internal consistency of the RTT Bodily Symptoms subscale is relatively low, suggesting that there is a great deal of individual variability in the physiological reactions that are experienced in test situations. Benson and Bandalos (1992) reported moderate to high correlations among the RTA Worry, Tension, and Bodily Symptoms subscales and much lower correlations between these subscales and the Test-Irrelevant Thinking subscale. Given the content of the Test-Irrelevant Thinking items, the validity of this subscale as a component of test anxiety would seem questionable. Task-irrelevant thoughts that are unrelated to worry about test performance or consequences, like poor study habits and negative attitudes toward teachers and courses, would seem to be more meaningfully conceptualized as a correlate of test anxiety rather than a component.

Anderson and Sauser, in Chapter 2 of this volume, provide a comprehensive review and evaluation of the most widely used scales that have been developed to assess test anxiety. They also discuss facilitating and debilitating anxiety and the relation of "test wiseness" to test anxiety. In Chapter 3, Bedell and Marlowe examine evidence of the convergent, divergent, and predictive validity of selected test anxiety measures. The effects of test anxiety on academic aptitude are examined by Ball in Chapter 8, in which it is noted that test anxiety may actually be facilitative for some students, as is also suggested by Anderson and Sauser in Chapter 2.

The relation between test anxiety as a situation-specific trait and test performance is discussed by Hodapp, Laux, and Glanzman in Chapter 4. They present evidence of the superiority of situation-specific test anxiety measures in predicting test performance, as compared with measures of general trait anxiety. They also report research on the construction and validation of a German adaptation of the TAI, which includes additional subscales, Lack of Confidence and Interference, along with Worry and Emotionality subscales. From a causal (path) analysis, Hodapp et al. report strong evidence of the negative influence of the worry component of test anxiety on academic achievement.

Anton and Klisch, in Chapter 7, point out that definitions of math anxiety and test anxiety tend to overlap and offer suggestions for distinguishing between these correlated situation-specific anxiety traits. In general, measures of math anxiety are better predictors than test anxiety scales of the elevations in S-Anxiety that students experience in taking mathematics tests, and test anxiety measures are, in turn, better predictors of S-Anxiety during examinations than are general T-Anxiety measures. Thus, the greater the specificity of a situation-specific anxiety measure for a particular test situation, the better it will predict the intensity of the S-Anxiety and the worry cognitions experienced in that situation.

TRANSACTIONAL PROCESS MODEL FOR TEST ANXIETY

The conception of test anxiety as a situation-specific anxiety trait requires specification of the antecedent conditions that contribute to the development of this trait, the particular factors that evoke S-Anxiety and its worry and emotionality components during examinations, and the effects of worry and emotionality on behavior. In addition, a comprehensive theory of test anxiety must specify the nature of the intrapersonal perceptions and cognitions and of the information-processing and retrieval mechanisms that mediate the effects of worry and emotionality on performance, while also identifying important correlates of test anxiety, such as study habits and attitudes (study skills), test-taking skills (test wiseness), and task-irrelevant thoughts.

The Transactional Process Model presented in Figure 1.1 is intended as a heuristic framework for representing the antecedent conditions and dispositions that influence students' reactions to tests, the mediating emotional and cognitive processes involved in responding to evaluative situations, and the correlates and consequences of test anxiety. This model provides a cross-sectional analysis of test anxiety phenomena as a situation-specific dynamic *process* in which examinations and other evaluative situations evoke mediating affective states and task-irrelevant cognitions that have important behavioral consequences.

Relatively little is known about the developmental antecedents of test anxiety, which appear to be heterogeneous and diverse, as discussed by Anton and Lillibridge on the basis of their case studies of six college students (see Chapter 5). As may be noted in Figure 1.1, the immediate situational and dispositional factors that contribute to the perceptions of a test situation as more or less threatening include the particular domain of subject matter relating to the test questions and the study skills and attitudes that influence how much and how well a student has prepared for an examination. In addition,

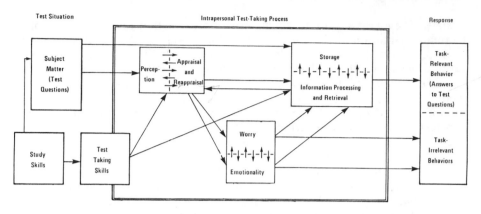

Figure 1.1   The transactional process model provides a conceptual framework for analyzing the effects of examination stress on the intrapersonal emotional and cognitive processes that are involved in responding to aptitude, ability, and intelligence tests. The model also encompasses important correlates of test anxiety such as study habits and attitudes (study skills), test-taking skills (test wiseness), and the effects of worry and emotionality on information processing and the retrieval of information from memory storage.

the test-taking skills that a student has acquired for coping with examinations will influence the perception and appraisal of the test situation.

When a student enters an examination, the test situation will initially be perceived as more or less personally threatening as a function of individual differences in test anxiety and the factors previously noted. This initial perception will be followed almost immediately by a continuing interpretive appraisal of the test situation. Depending on the degree to which an examination is perceived or appraised as threatening, the student will experience an increase in S-Anxiety, self-centered and self-derogatory worry cognitions, and other test-irrelevant thoughts. This emotional reaction and the associated test-related worry cognitions may provide additional negative feedback that further alters the appraisal of a test situation as more or less threatening.

Students with good test-taking skills generally perceive examinations as less threatening than students who are less "test-wise," as is noted by Anderson and Sauser in Chapter 2. If a student finds that he or she knows the answer to a particular test question, especially early in the test, this will likely lead to a reduction in S-Anxiety, with a corresponding decrease in worry cognitions. For students with good test-taking skills who can come up with correct answers to several questions, the perception of the testing situation will likely be reappraised as less stressful. Correctly answering several test questions might also result in feelings that evoke positive cognitions ("I am well prepared for this test"), which serve to further reduce anxiety and facilitate performance.

Inability to answer an initial test question is likely to result in more intense feelings of tension and apprehension and in physiological arousal such as an increase in heart rate. Feedback from increased S-Anxiety is also likely to lead test-anxious students to appraise an examination as more threatening. Such appraisals would then result in a further elevation in S-Anxiety, with additional worry cognitions and increased heart rate. Papsdorf, Ghannam, and Jamieson, in Chapter 6, examine other physiological manifestations of S-Anxiety in test situations that they interpret as suggesting that interhemispheric interference, resulting from simultaneous arousal of the right and left cerebral hemispheres, contributes to the difficulty of high test-anxious students in maintaining attention and to their poor test performance.

Processing the questions that are presented to students in a test situation will stimulate the initiation of a search for information that will enable them to formulate appropriate answers. This involves using cues to locate and retrieve information from memory storage that is needed to respond to the test questions. Feedback from this complex process may also stimulate thoughts and feelings that differ from those occurring earlier in the response chain, which may then contribute to reappraising the test situation as more or less threatening. If the information needed to respond to a test question is not available or cannot successfully be retrieved, the examination will be appraised as more stressful, especially for individuals who are high in test anxiety.

In the context of the Transactional Process Model presented in Figure 1.1, the final stage or outcome—that is, formulating the response to test questions—will require the individual to transform and synthesize the information recovered from memory so that it can be reported in the manner required by the questions. This will usually involve choosing the correct response to a multiple-choice question or organizing the information required to respond to an essay. Poor performance at this or any of the previous stages of responding to a test question can lead to emotional reactions and worry cognitions that interfere with attention and concentration and contribute to poor performance.

Given the complexity of the impact of test anxiety on emotional and cognitive processes and the influence of correlates of test anxiety such as ineffective study habits and poor test-taking skills, it is important to evaluate the particular strengths and weaknesses of each student in order to direct treatment interventions to those aspects of the test anxiety process that are most detrimental for a particular student. Studies of different approaches to the treatment of test anxiety are described in the five chapters that make up Part III of this volume. The locus of impact of each of the treatment components in these studies is examined in the final chapter, in which applications of the Transactional Process Model to the treatment of test-anxious students are considered.

SUMMARY

Research on examination stress and test anxiety was reviewed in this chapter. Approaches to the measurement of test anxiety and its worry and emotionality components were also described. In the context of the state–trait distinction in anxiety research, test anxiety was conceptualized as a situation-specific personality trait, with worry and emotionality as its major components. During examinations, it was noted that individuals high in test anxiety experience more frequent and more intense elevations in S-Anxiety and self-centered worry cognitions and test-irrelevant thoughts that interfere with attention, concentration, and test performance. A Transactional Process Model was then proposed as a conceptual framework for analyzing and evaluating the effects of examination stress on test anxiety and the adverse effects of worry and emotionality on information processing and academic achievement.

2

Measurement of Test Anxiety: An Overview

Scarvia B. Anderson and William I. Sauser, Jr.
Educational Testing Service, Atlanta, Georgia, USA

Anxiety competes only with bias for top billing as the villain in the melodrama of standardized testing. On the basis of a comprehensive review of the literature, Hembree (1988) concluded that test anxiety (a) causes poor performance; (b) is inversely related to students' self-esteem; (c) is directly related to students' fears of negative evaluation, defensiveness, and other forms of anxiety; (d) is influenced by ability, gender, and school grade level; and (e) can be reduced effectively by a variety of treatments. Clearly, test anxiety is a construct worthy of careful evaluation.

It is not surprising that researchers endeavor to understand test anxiety through measurement. This derives not just from an idiosyncrasy associated with their own general interests, but from the strong conviction that "science *is* measurement":

> The basic task of measurement is the generic task of all science: the marshalling of evidence to support an inferential leap from an observed consistency in the empirical world to a construct that will explain that consistency. In psychometric parlance, this is the problem of construct validity. In judging the adequacy of measurement, there are important statistical and methodological criteria (such as validity and reliability) that must be satisfied, but these are simply part of the central requirement of a theoretical rationale. (Anderson et al., 1972, p. 1)

Paul Diederich, a longtime friend and colleague, was once asked if he understood T. S. Eliot's "Four Quartets." He said he did not know; he had not tried to write a test on it. Attempting to measure a construct provides a meaningful and productive way to explore the adequacy and defensibility of theoretical concepts. If one's understanding is less certain, studying the measures developed by others is a useful way of entering a field of scientific inquiry. For this chapter we took the latter route.

Measures that have been developed, adapted, or borrowed to assess test anxiety, or anxiety in situations having some test-like qualities, are listed in

Most of the work on this chapter was carried out while the authors were associated with the Educational Testing Service. Scarvia B. Anderson is now a consultant in private practice in Atlanta, Georgia, and William I. Sauser, Jr., is now affiliated with the Department of Educational Foundations, Leadership, and Technology at Auburn University, Auburn, Alabama.

the Appendix at the end of this chapter. Spielberger (1966b) has made a clear and helpful distinction between anxiety as a relatively enduring personality trait (T-Anxiety), that is, individual differences in the disposition to exhibit anxiety responses in a wide variety of situations, and anxiety as an emotional state (S-Anxiety), triggered by particular environmental conditions and fluctuating over time. Although most of the measures listed in the Appendix were intended to assess S-Anxiety, several of these measures assess test anxiety as a situation-specific trait (see Hodapp et al., Chapter 4).

Morris and Liebert (1969, 1970, 1973) and Spielberger (1980) have urged separate consideration of worry and emotionality as components of test anxiety, and I. G. Sarason (1983, 1984) has suggested adding two additional dimensions to the test anxiety construct: bodily symptoms and test-irrelevant thinking. However, these more differentiated conceptions (definitions) of test anxiety are not universally accepted or used. In this chapter, we do not propose to provide critiques of particular test anxiety and related measures, such as those in Buros's *Mental Measurements Yearbooks*. Rather, from a review of selected measures, along with the studies in which they were embedded, we attempt to draw some generalizations about the status of the field and the theoretical views of workers who are tilling it. Our comments are grouped under eight headings; after we have presented those comments, we consider what is really a prior question: Why measure test anxiety at all?

WAYS OF MEASURING TEST ANXIETY

Ebel (1972) once commented that "the measurement of anxiety is no simple problem" (p. 237), and few researchers would disagree. Some attempts have been made to assess anxiety, along with other personality characteristics, through projective techniques such as the Rorschach (Levitt, 1967, p. 57; S. B. Sarason et al., 1958) and Human Figure Drawing tasks (Engle & Sieber, 1969; Fox et al., 1958). However, the most common method is through self-report inventories. On the surface, physiological measures of S-Anxiety would seem to be more attractive than self-report scales. Autonomic nervous system response can seldom be controlled voluntarily, and thus should be immune to effects of faking, defensiveness, and social desirability. However, as Levitt (1967, p. 56) has observed, "the results, viewed as a whole, are disappointing."

In a laboriously detailed report to the U.S. Department of Health, Education, and Welfare, Hopkins and Chambers (1966) described the use of five kinds of physiological measurements of anxiety, recorded continuously or at intervals while students took general ability tests under neutral conditions and conditions designed to evoke or reduce anxiety. The measures were (a) respiration measured in respiratory cycles per minute, (b) heart rate as determined by electrocardiogram, (c) galvanic skin response, (d) systolic and diastolic blood pressure and pulse pressures, and (c) oral and skin temperatures. Difficulties in the accuracy of measurement, especially of respiration rate and depth and galvanic skin response, led Hopkins and Chambers to conclude "that the physiological measures are essentially unrelated, and do not provide the basis for the identification of a preferred measure of anxiety" (p. 189). They also noted that the "uniqueness of the individual examinee's response pattern was expected, but not to the extent observed" (p. 189). Furthermore, the physiological measures were not related to test scores obtained under the different treatments, which may say more about the treatments' lack of definitiveness than about the physiological measures, and they were "not correlated to a significant degree" with the psychological measures of anxiety used in the study, whereas the psychological measures were "moderately and positively related" (p. 224) to each other and to performance on the ability test. As Papsdorf and his colleagues report in Chapter 6, using finger temperature and eye gaze as physiological (autonomic) measures of test anxiety shows somewhat more promise.

Morris and Liebert (1970) suggested that investigators may have expected physiological measures of anxiety to behave in inappropriate ways. They raised the possibility that autonomic indexes and self-report devices tap separate components of anxiety, both of which should be taken into account in attempting to understand the nature of the phenomenon. Nevertheless, the widespread dependence on self-report measures suggests that more investigators than not continue to be persuaded by Levitt's (1967) summary of the state of the art with respect to physiological measures of anxiety:

> *The best that we can surmise is that patterns of physiological reactivity to anxiety are idiosyncratic, a circumstance which renders them unsuitable for use at the current stage of research on anxiety as a construct. Furthermore, physiological measures are administratively disadvantageous. (pp. 56–57)*

Reliance on self-report inventories of anxiety implies not only a disillusionment with other types of measures, but also acceptance of the awareness of test anxiety as a *conscious* process (S. B. Sarason et al., 1960, p. 89). Thus, S. B. Sarason and other researchers who use the Test Anxiety Scale for Children (TASC) are willing to accept even young children's reports that when they are taking a test "the hand you write with" shakes "a little" or that the child does not "worry when the teacher says that she is going to ask you questions to find out how much you know." In taking the TASC, children listen to such statements read by an administrator and then simply circle *yes* or *no* on an answer sheet. N. J. King et al. (1991) have expressed concern regarding the reliability and validity of such diagnostic practices.

The TAQ, developed by Mandler and Sarason (1952) for use with older students, requires somewhat more sophisticated judgments; respondents indicate their level of anxiety on graphic rating scales anchored by such phrases as *worry a lot* to *worry not at all* or *perspire not at all* to *perspire a lot*. Although investigators may be disenchanted with physiological measures of test anxiety, they are frequently willing to accept subjects' reports of such physiological reactions as evidence of test anxiety. Only Morris and Liebert (1970) appear to have made a systematic comparison of self-reports of autonomic reactions to stress and actual measures of pulse rate under controlled conditions.

Other self-report formats that have been used to assess anxiety include Likert-type scales and adjective checklists. For example, a scale developed by Emery and Krumboltz (1967) asks students to rate the frequency with which statements such as "I get depressed after taking a test" apply to them. Responses are *rarely or never, infrequently, occasionally, frequently, almost always,* or *always.* Zuckerman's (1960) Affect Adjective Check List (AACL) requires respondents to describe their feelings in reaction to anxiety-provoking situations by checking such adjectives as *afraid, calm, cheerful,* and *desperate.*

ANXIETY AS FACILITATOR OR DEBILITATOR

The inverted-U relation between anxiety or arousal level and performance, which has been hypothesized for many years, has its roots in the old Yerkes–Dodson (1908) theory about motivation and performance (see Atkinson & O'Connor, 1966; Ebel, 1972, p. 237; Landy & Trumbo, 1976, p. 562; Lens, 1983). In 1960, Alpert and Haber made a small splash in the anxiety research waters by positing two kinds of anxiety—facilitating and debilitating—and providing separate measures for them. It was debated at the time whether these were truly separate dimensions or simply an artifact of the item development procedures, or whether amount of anxiety was the crucial variable, as suggested by the inverted-U hypothesis.

Research on anxiety as facilitator or debilitator has centered mainly on task differentiation. For example, anxiety might facilitate coping with relatively simple or routine tasks, but play havoc when the subject is confronted with more complex problems. With respect to the latter, S. B. Sarason and his associates (S. B. Sarason et al., 1960, p. 20) suggested that a high level of anxiety narrows the subject's perception of the external field and prevents dispassionate assessment of the nature of the problem-solving task. Although it is important to delineate the kinds of tasks in which anxiety tends to act as a facilitating or debilitating mechanism, investigators have not given equal attention to two other classes of variables that would seem to relate to the facilitating–debilitating role of anxiety, namely, the absolute amount of anxiety and the characteristics of the person. How much anxiety is facilitating for whom? Lazarus and Eriksen (1952), for example, hypothesized that "failure stress" increased group variability by increasing the test scores of good students and decreasing the scores of students with less ability, but this hypothesis was not confirmed by French (1962).

Actors, students, and others whose performances are subject to evaluation by critics, audiences, and professors frequently say that unless they experience a certain amount of nervousness, apprehension, palm sweating, and so forth (stage fright), they are not likely to give a good performance. How real is the phenomenon and how widespread? When does one need to try to increase rather than reduce anxiety? How does anxiety interact with other motivational mechanisms?

Ebel (1972) suggested that test anxiety can be useful educationally if it is distributed at a low level and occurs throughout the course. He has even advised that "skillful teaching involves the controlled release of the energy stimulated by test anxiety" (p. 237). As noted by Pekrun (1992), performance on examinations is influenced by a complex interplay of anxiety and other emotions.

It is disappointing that the ripples from the Alpert–Haber (1960) splash have all but disappeared. Whatever the controversies, the facilitating–debilitating properties of anxiety deserve more research and measurement attention. We wrote Ralph Haber to see if we could get more information about the Achievement Anxiety Test, first published in 1960. He responded that "it has never been copyrighted or formally sold as a test" and that he himself had not "used it much in recent years" (R. N. Haber, personal communication, March 1977).

ANXIETY AND PERFORMANCE ON ABILITY–ACHIEVEMENT TESTS

Scores on tests and other anxiety measures usually show negative correlations with performance on ability and achievement tests, at least when there is sufficient variation in the ability and achievement test scores (Hembree, 1988). As Anastasi (1976, pp. 37–38), I. G. Sarason (1972, p. 382), and others have pointed out, these correlations do not, in themselves, provide evidence for causality or direction of influence—the relative extent to which people develop test anxiety because they have a history of performing poorly on tests versus the extent to which poor test performance can be attributed to anxiety. S. B. Sarason and his colleagues (1960) concluded from their research that the explanation of negative correlations between test anxiety and IQ that conceives "of test anxiety primarily as an effect of rather than a source of . . . educational experience . . . is probably too simple, *although we do not doubt that in some cases there is an element of truth to it*" (p. 268, italics added). Hansen (1977), on the basis of his review of the evidence, tended to agree that "anxiety is the more probable cause of poor performance on an intelligence test" (p. 96) rather than vice versa.

There are, however, those who would disagree. Mounting evidence of a negative correlation between actual level of ability and level of test anxiety (I. G. Sarason, 1960) prompted one educational researcher (Ebel, 1972) to offer the following commentary:

> *Evidence to support the belief that some students of good or superior achievement characteristically go to pieces and do poorly on every examination is hard to find. . . . On the other hand, it is conceivable that apparent instances of underachievement on tests may actually be instances of overindication of ability in other situations. . . . All things considered, a teacher is well advised to take with several grains of salt a student's claim that his test performances never do justice to his real achievements. (pp. 237–238)*

Further insights into the cause–effect relation between test anxiety and scores on ability and achievement tests would seem to require experimental studies in which test anxiety serves as a dependent variable. The research literature is quite one-sided in this respect, with test anxiety almost always in the position of independent or moderator variable vis-à-vis test performance. Feedback on test performance over time is also important in the kind of research suggested. With a hypothesis that test anxiety may result from unsuccessful test performance, researchers must make sure that the student knows when his or her test performance is inadequate and not count entirely on internal feelings of failure and frustration to provide the "treatment." Furthermore, researchers should not seek evidence on this hypothesis from a single unsuccessful test experience; they would have to design the research to include a series of successful and unsuccessful test experiences.

The 6-year study of S. B. Sarason et al. (1964) and Hill and Sarason (1966) appears to stand alone in documenting changes in both test scores and anxiety scores over a significant span of years. Even though their longitudinal study is correlational in nature, with test anxiety described as an independent variable, the results do suggest some interactions between anxiety and test performance rather than a simple one-way relation.

Interpretations of relation between anxiety scores and scores on ability–achievement tests may also be clouded by the nature of the anxiety measures. To what extent do the anxiety measures tap some of the same skills as the ability–achievement measures: vocabulary, reading comprehension, test taking strategies, and so forth? The situation is further confounded when items are selected for inclusion in the anxiety measure on the basis of ability to predict academic performance. This was the case with the Achievement Anxiety Test developed by Alpert and Haber (1960). Such a measure cannot be used to investigate hypotheses about the effects of anxiety on achievement (Levitt, 1967, pp. 75–76).

Finally—and, we expect, reluctantly for some—researchers must at least entertain the thought that the game of relating anxiety and achievement scores may not be worth the candle. French (1962) showed that any differences in Scholastic Aptitude Test (SAT) Math and Verbal scores that might be associated with candidates' self-reports of test anxiety were much lower than the standard errors of measurement for the test. (It is regrettable that French's elegant study, conducted in connection with 1960 administrations of the SAT, has had no replication and so little follow-up.)

TEST ANXIETY AND GENERAL ANXIETY MEASURES

As we have indicated, the distinction between general anxiety and anxiety associated with specific situations that may be perceived as threatening by some people (e.g., test situations) is not universally made in either measurement or research. Thus some researchers use such general measures as the Manifest Anxiety Scale (MAS, Taylor, 1953) or the Institute for Personality and Ability Testing Anxiety Scale (Cattell & Scheier, 1961) interchangeably with the TAQ (Mandler & Sarason, 1952). Second, some investigators use measures that include a combination of both general and specific items. For example, the measures used by Phillips (1966) in *An Analysis of Causes of Anxiety Among Children in School* include both kinds of items, such as "do you sometimes worry about being different from many of the children in your class?" and "do other children in class seem to like you?" as well as items from the TASC, such as "when the teacher says that she is going to give the class a test, do you become afraid that you will do poorly?" and "do you worry a lot *while* you are taking a test?" (In fairness to Phillips, we should mention that he analyzed such items as falling on different scales.)

Third, there are some suggestions in the literature that test anxiety may be studied as a surrogate for school anxiety or even for general anxiety. S. B. Sarason and his colleagues (1960) explained that their focus on test anxiety was "in part . . . a convenient way of studying some of the properties of anxiety in general" (p. 84). Tobias and Hedl (1972) have suggested that test anxiety may be "considerably more general" than presently thought and its conception may have to be "significantly widened" (pp. 13–14).

We are calling attention to these ambiguities not because we feel that Spielberger's trait–state distinction or the interaction models (e.g., Endler & Hunt, 1969; Shedletsky & Endler, 1974) are the only positions deserving a hearing, but because the lack of clear statements of the theoretical rationales influencing the selection, adaptation, or development of many of the measures used in anxiety research makes interpretations, as well as generalizations across findings, next to impossible. We suspect, with I. G. Sarason (1972), that at least some of the investigations "have been of the 'shotgun' variety: 'Do you suppose test anxiety is related to scores students get on tests X, Y, and Z?' " (p. 382) and that the choice of measures has been dictated more by expediency than by ratiocination.

Here is as good a time as any to raise the question, Why do so many investigators feel it is incumbent on them to develop new measures or tinker around "just a little bit" with old measures rather than use existing measures of test or other state anxieties? These tendencies also interfere seriously with the ability to compare research results and to build a more comprehensive body of knowledge in the area.

WORRY AND EMOTIONALITY

As we have shown, one can look to investigators' measures to obtain some clues about their conceptions of anxiety as autonomic or conscious, facilitating or debilitating, predictor or effect, and general or situation specific. It is clear from examining a number of studies that some investigators are not committed to any particular theoretical position, and it is clear from examining others that many investigators view anxiety as a complex phenomenon with several components.

Two of those components that have been elucidated by Spielberger (1980) and by Morris and Liebert (1970) are *worry* (cognitive concern about the outcome of an event) and *emotionality* (physiological and affective arousal). For example, Spielberger (1980) exemplified worry by "agree" responses to such items as these from the Test Anxiety Inventory (TAI): "During exams I find myself thinking about whether I'll ever get through school" and "The harder I work at taking a test, the more confused I get." These are contrasted with items intended primarily to define an emotionality component, for example, "I feel very jittery when taking an important test" and "I start feeling very uneasy just before getting a test paper back."

This is not to suggest that these investigators view cognitive and emotional responses to stressful situations as independent. In fact, the correlations between subtests purporting to measure the two dimensions are frequently quite high. For example, Ware et al. (1990) found evidence to support an oblique, rather than an orthogonal, factorial relation between measures of worry and emotionality. Moreover, as several studies by Morris and Liebert (cited and discussed below) have shown, the two dimensions show different patterns of relation to other variables.

In an early study, Liebert and Morris (1967) found that students who reported low expectations for their performance on an examination had higher worry scores than students with medium or high expectations; emotionality scores, however, were unrelated to expectations. In subsequent studies, emotionality was not found to interact with test timing conditions, whereas worry did (Morris & Liebert, 1969). Worry was found to be more highly negatively related to examination grades than was emotionality (Morris & Liebert, 1970), and worry scores tended to increase under a failure-threat situation, whereas emotionality scores tended to be elevated only under a shock-threat condition (Morris & Liebert, 1973). Morris and Liebert used measures of worry and emotionality derived from the Mandler–Sarason (1952) TAQ or the Taylor (1953) MAS.

I. G. Sarason (1984) expanded on Spielberger's (1980) two-dimensional concept of test anxiety (worry and emotionality) by adding two new dimensions: *bodily symptoms* and *test-irrelevant thinking*. He measured these four dimensions using a 40-item self-report questionnaire, the Reactions to Tests (RTT). Zimmer et al. (1992) found evidence in support of the psychometric quality of the RTT, although worry and emotionality (tension) did not appear to be clearly distinct dimensions.

As noted above, Ware et al. (1990) also found a correlation between the two dimensions (worry and emotionality). They proposed a modification of the TAI to "fine tune" the instrument and enhance its discriminant validity. Benson et al. (1992) sought to resolve the dimensionality issue by creating a Revised Test Anxiety Scale, which combined items from Spielberger's (1980) TAI and I. G. Sarason's (1984) RTT. Benson et al. (1992) used extensive multinational factor analysis and cross-validation procedures to create their Revised Test Anxiety Scale, which appears to represent the state of the art as of this writing.

Wine's (1971) attentional interpretation of test anxiety is consistent with the work of Liebert and Morris (1967; Morris & Liebert, 1970, 1973). Specifically, she suggested that worry, an attentionally demanding cognitive activity, is more debilitating to task performance than is autonomic arousal. Tobias (1985) also suggested that test anxiety debilitates performance by reducing the cognitive capacity for task solution. Schwarzer and Jerusalem (1992) have weighed in with their own cognitive processing theory of anxiety.

The worry–emotionality relation now appears to be as well established as the state–trait relationship, and Liebert and Morris (1967) predicted that concerted attention to these components would enable better specification of the effects of anxiety on performance tasks and of clinical treatments that might be effective in reducing anxiety. Thus, there may be implications for both research and application. For example, Naveh-Benjamin (1991) found that test-anxious students could be differentiated on the basis of their information-processing skills and that effectiveness of various treatment techniques varied with the level of the client's information-processing skill. In Chapter 14, Vagg and Spielberger provide a framework, the Transactional Process Model, for analyzing and evaluating diverse treatment approaches along a cognitive–emotionality continuum.

TEST ANXIETY AND TEST WISENESS

When test anxiety and test wiseness are discussed in the same context, it is usually the emotional component of the former and the cognitive nature of the latter that are stressed. Furthermore, test anxiety is typically offered as an explanatory concept when a student performs more poorly on an examination than other indicators of ability level would predict, and test wiseness is more likely to be used to explain better-than-predicted performance.

Millman et al. (1965) have defined test wiseness as "a subject's capacity to utilize the characteristics and formats of the test and/or the test-taking situation to receive a high score" (p. 707). Their outline of test-wiseness principles includes such practical suggestions as "pay careful attention to directions, determining clearly the nature of the task and the intended basis for response" and "always guess if right answers only are scored" (p. 711). The test-wise individual will certainly capitalize on the advice of Millman et al. to "recognize and make use of resemblances between the options and an aspect of the stem" to respond easily and correctly to a test item such as the following:

The aeronautics board which has jurisdiction over civil aircraft is called:

*a) Civil Aeronautics Board

 b) Committee to Investigate Airlines

 c) Division of Passenger Airways (p. 723)*

Although the concept of test wiseness may have been invoked originally in response to a concern over an excess of test-taking skill, Ebel (1972) has concluded that for well-constructed tests, "error in measurement is likely to be due to too little, rather than too much, test wiseness" (p. 237). Words to the wise, similar to the advice presented above, may be found in popular guidebooks and practice materials intended to better prepare individuals for taking tests (e.g., Anderson et al., 1965).

Pike (1978), in a review of the literature in the area as it relates to the SAT, defined test wiseness somewhat more generally as "that set of skills and knowledge about test-taking itself that allows individuals to display their abilities . . . to their best advantage" (p. 6). He also emphasized that "the TW component is by no means unique to standardized tests," but "is also present in other modes of assessment, such as classroom recitation and essay writing" (p. 6). Pike (pp. 4–5) was also careful to distinguish among several different approaches to increasing test wiseness: (a) short-term instruction (efforts to improve test scores by relatively short periods of instruction); (b) coaching (in which instruction is essentially limited to very brief instruction on general test wiseness and practice in answering questions similar to those appearing in an examination); and (c) intermediate-term instruction (in which test scores are improved by special instruction, but accelerated when compared with the time generally considered necessary to improve the ability in question).

Experimental evidence indicates that, for at least some areas and test types, both short- and intermediate-term approaches can be effective in increasing students' test wiseness (Moore, 1968; Moore et al., 1966; Pallone, 1961; Pike & Evans, 1972; Slatker et al., 1970), and at least one study (Wahlstrom & Boersma, 1968) has presented direct evidence that instruction in test-wiseness principles can lead to improved achievement test performance. However, in general the intermediate-term approaches seem to hold more promise than crash efforts.

Test anxiety should not be considered the opposite of test wiseness (Anderson et al., 1975, p. 435). However, the two are probably related. Increasing test wiseness (presumably a cognitive variable) results in improvement in test scores; behavioral treatments that reduce test anxiety (which has a large emotional component) appear to have similar effects (Allen, 1972). Findings that both facilitating and debilitating anxiety measures are affected by an interaction between systematic desensitization treatments and a test-wiseness instructional program, but not by either treatment taken alone (e.g., Bajtelsmit, 1977), have blurred the distinction between test wiseness and test anxiety to an even greater degree.

INTERACTIONS AND NONLINEARITY

At least five classes of individual characteristics are known to influence test anxiety: (a) cognitive styles (including attention processes), (b) generalized personality traits (such as susceptibility to personal threat and fear of failure), (c) real and perceived ability–achievement levels, (d) perceived importance of the testing event and feelings of "preparedness," and (e) background characteristics (such as gender and family press) that are probably related to opportunities for acquisition or extinction of test anxiety. Furthermore, manifestations of test anxiety—or, if you will, scores on self-report inventories—are probably influenced by complicated interactions of such factors (Birenbaum & Gutvirtz, 1993). Add to these the knowledge that people with different levels and patterns of anxiety scores respond differently to different instructions and treatments in testing situations, classrooms, and laboratories, and one has a very complex situation indeed.

Anastasi (1976), after reviewing the work of Mandler and Sarason (1952), Lawrence (1962), Paul and Eriksen (1964), and others, offered the modest observation that

> *It thus appears likely that the relationship between anxiety and test performance is nonlinear, a slight amount of anxiety being beneficial while a large amount is detrimental. Individuals who are customarily low-anxious benefit from test conditions that arouse some anxiety, while those who are customarily high-anxious perform better under more relaxed conditions. (p. 38)*

The consistency of curvilinear relations between anxiety and performance on the kinds of convergent tasks typical of most ability and achievement tests has also been demonstrated by Klein et al. (1968), whereas with divergent tasks, poor performance is associated with an intermediate level of anxiety. In a domain in which U-shaped distribution and significant interaction terms are the rule rather than the exception, all but the most naive investigators have long since abandoned hope that simple linear models will suffice.

SPECIAL VALIDITY CONCERNS

At the simplest level, a measure is valid if it adequately reflects and represents the domain of interest and is not equally or more likely to be a measure of something else. Furthermore, higher scores should reflect more of the characteristic being measured than should lower scores.

Self-report measures are particularly susceptible to accusations that they may be measuring something other than, or in addition to, what was intended. The usual self-report measures of test anxiety have been variously examined with respect to the extent to which scores might reflect (a) response set (tendencies to mark responses in stereotypic ways), (b) social desirability (responding in ways judged socially acceptable to the self, examiner, or others expected to see the results), or (c) defensiveness ("allowing the subjects to 'cop out,' i.e., say they performed badly because they were anxious, not because they didn't know the answers on the test"; Bloxom, 1968, p. 12).

With few exceptions (e.g., S. B. Sarason et al., 1960, with their lie scale on the TASC), it has not been the original authors of the test anxiety measures who have raised these questions about rival explanations for the meaning of the scores, but rather independent investigators. However, a number of authors as well as users of test anxiety measures have shown an active concern for the vocabulary or reading comprehension levels required to complete the measures, lest scores be more descriptive of verbal skills than of test anxiety (e.g.,

Hopkins & Chambers, 1966, p. 31; see also Levitt, 1967, p. 68, for a discussion of the effects of vocabulary level and verbal fluency on AACL scores).

The development of homogeneous scales with meaningful (even if not equal) intervals is a challenge in any area of psychological measurement, but it seems to be especially troublesome in the test anxiety area. S. B. Sarason and his colleagues (1960, p. 90) placed considerably less credence in low scores than in high scores on test anxiety measures. I. G. Sarason (1972) addressed the middle-score problem as follows:

> One of the lacunae in the body of knowledge about test anxiety concerns the person who scores in the midrange of the score distribution. . . . Should scores along the test anxiety distribution be viewed as reflecting gradual increments in the habits that are part of the test anxiety syndrome? (p. 399)

I. G. Sarason suggested that higher scorers make up a separate and distinct group from persons with low to moderate scores in the score distribution.

Then I. G. Sarason made a point especially dear to our hearts: "Advances in the assessment of test anxiety are required to support advances in experimentation" (p. 399).

Validity begins at the item construction level, of course, and too many of the anxiety measures (apparently put together hurriedly for particular projects) contain items with the kinds of flaws we try to stamp out in the first course in tests and measurements. A couple of examples suffice to illustrate the point:

1. "Do some of your friends think you are a sissy because you make good grades?" Elementary school children are supposed to answer that question *yes* or *no*. What if the child does not make good grades? What if the child feels that he or she is labeled a sissy but does not know why? Is there sex bias in this item?
2. "Are most children sometimes unkind; or are most children kind to you?" Indeed, most children are sometimes unkind, but the opposite of that is not that most children are kind to you.

Because the literature on test anxiety seems to be based, to a large degree, on measurement of elementary school children and captive undergraduates, we would like to remind investigators of aspects of construct validity that deserve more attention, especially if the results of test anxiety research are to be generalized to real-life situations. We are referring to such questions as these: Do test anxiety measures have the same meaning—measure the same processes or traits—in different demographic groups (as defined by age, sex, socioeconomic status, cultural background, etc.)? Do these measures have the same meaning in different environmental settings (Anderson et al., 1975, p. 459) and when translated from one language to another (O'Neil et al., 1992)?

Thus far, we have discussed the validity, and threats to validity, of test anxiety measures. A related point also deserves more than the cursory consideration we can give to it here: Is anxiety a legitimate part of the test-taking experience? When a test is designed as a predictor of achievement in a particular situation (college studies, job performance, etc.), the test should reflect the key elements of that situation (and not just because the Equal Employment Opportunity Commission and courts require that one proceed this way). If anxiety is expected to be evoked in the criterion performance, then attempts to minimize anxiety in the selection instrument may in fact reduce its validity as a predictor. The burden on those attempting to assess criterion-related anxiety in the predictor is, of course, to demonstrate that the same kinds of anxiety are also triggered in the performance criterion situation.

WHY MEASURE TEST ANXIETY?

I. G. Sarason (1972) remarked in 1970 at a conference at Florida State University that test anxiety had "achieved a notable milestone—its 20th anniversary" and questioned, "Should the occasion be observed as a propitious time for a loyal service pin, disengagement, and retirement?" (p. 381). He went on, however, to label the question unrealistic. "Only in fantasy," he said, "can the faucet of a particular line of inquiry be turned off abruptly—the washer inevitably cracks and annoying, slow drips persist" (p. 381).

Thus we return to the question we promised to deal with at the beginning of this chapter: Why measure test anxiety? There seem to be both philosophical and practical answers. We measure test anxiety to confirm its existence—and to determine whether it deserves construct status in our discipline. This implies exploring not only the variables to which it bears a hypothesized relation, but also the variables with which, theoretically, it should be unrelated. It also implies a commitment to (a) developing measures that are psychometrically sound; (b) reexamining the hypothesis that test anxiety is necessarily a conscious process; (c) concerning ourselves again with debilitating versus facilitating functions of anxiety; (d) abandoning any unexplained admixtures of general and test anxiety concepts and measures; (e) delineating the components of test anxiety if, as we suspect, it is not a global characteristic; (f) documenting more systematically than we have in the past individual differences in absolute amounts of anxiety as well as personal–situational interactions that are important; and (g) trying to encourage a greater variety of investigations in the field.

In practical terms, many researchers measure test anxiety in the interest of doing something about it. They want to identify those persons whose performance and emotional well-being may be significantly affected by it. Researchers want to use the two means available, environmental design and personal treatment, to reduce test anxiety in those situations in which research has shown it to be deleterious and to harness it to achieve greater effectiveness and satisfaction if that is indicated.

SUMMARY

Test anxiety is a construct worthy of careful evaluation because of its important theoretical and practical implications. In this chapter we endeavored to understand the construct of test anxiety by examining the instruments used to measure it. Although a variety of approaches (e.g., projective techniques and physiological measures) have been used to operationalize test anxiety, the most common method of measurement is through self-report inventories. Many such inventories are listed and annotated in the Appendix at the end of this chapter.

Our exploration has uncovered eight themes that are currently reflected in the research literature. These themes, which are also addressed in several other chapters of this volume (e.g., Chapter 4, Chapters 8–13), are stated here in the form of the following questions: (a) Is anxiety a facilitator or debilitator of performance? (b) How does anxiety affect performance on ability–achievement tests? (c) How does test anxiety relate to general anxiety? (d) Are worry and emotionality basic components of test anxiety? (e) How does test anxiety relate to test wiseness? (f) What variables interact with test anxiety to affect performance, and what is the nature of their complex interrelation? (g) Do measures of test anxiety possess construct validity?

Appendix

Annotated List of Objective Self-Report Measures of Test Anxiety and Related Constructs

Achievement Anxiety Scale (Stanford et al., 1963)
    Consists of 18 items from the Achievement Anxiety Test, translated into language meaningful to elementary school children and requiring *yes–no* responses. Treats the facilitating–debilitating dichotomy of the Achievement Anxiety Test as one dimension, thus results in one overall test anxiety score.

Achievement Anxiety Test (Alpert & Haber, 1960)
    Consists of two independent rating scales, a 9-item facilitating anxiety scale and a 10-item debilitating anxiety scale. Designed for use with college students as a measure of test anxiety.

Affect Adjective Check List (Zuckerman, 1960; available from the Educational and Industrial Testing Service)
    Consists of 11 anxiety-positive and 10 anxiety-negative adjectives. Instructions can be varied so that the check list can be used to describe feelings in a variety of situations, including the testing situation. Most appropriate for use with college students.

Anxiety Differential (Alexander & Husek, 1962)
    Consists of 18 semantic differential items claimed to be sensitive to an individual's changes in anxiety. Originally developed to measure anxiety with respect to bodily harm; has been used to measure test anxiety of college students.

Anxiety Questionnaire ("Experiences Questionnaire") (Morris & Liebert, 1969)
    Consists of 30 items selected from the Manifest Anxiety Scale and modified into a 5-point rating format. Two subscale scores, each based on 15 items, are obtained: Worry and Emotionality. Originally developed for use with college students.

Audience Sensitivity Inventory (Paivio & Lambert, 1959)
    Consists of 21 items referring to reactions to various audience situations. Two-category and five-category response versions are available. Some items were adapted from the Minnesota Multiphasic Personality Inventory (MMPI) and the Bernreuter Personality Inventory; others are original. Intended for use with adults.

Children's Audience Sensitivity Inventory (Paivio et al., 1961)
    Consists of 35 *yes–no* items measuring reactions to various audience situations, including reciting in class. Modification of the Audience Sensitivity Inventory; designed for oral administration to groups of elementary school children.

Children's Manifest Anxiety Scale (Castaneda et al., 1956)
    Consists of 42 *yes–no* items selected from the Taylor (1953) Manifest Anxiety Scale and modified to measure general anxiety in children plus an 11-item *yes–no* lie scale. Designed for use with elementary school children.

Children's Manifest Anxiety Scale (Short Form; Levy, 1958)
    Consists of 10 items taken directly from the Children's Manifest Anxiety Scale.

Children's School Questionnaire (Phillips, 1966)
>   Consists of 198 objective questions derived from the Test Anxiety Scale for
>   Children, the Achievement Anxiety Scale, the Audience Anxiety Scale, a
>   defensiveness scale, and a personality questionnaire. Designed to be administered
>   orally to elementary school children.

College Entrance Examination Board Questionnaire on Anxiety About the SAT
(French, 1961, 1962)
>   Consists of 55 objective questions, some of which were taken from the
>   Educational Testing Service (ETS) Personality Research Inventory—Anxiety Scale
>   and the Manifest Anxiety Scale (Short Forced-Choice Form). Designed specifically
>   for use with students taking the Scholastic Aptitude Test.

Concept-Specific Anxiety Scale (Cole et al., 1969)
>   Consists of a set of 15 bipolar adjective pairs presented in a seven-interval
>   semantic differential format. Can be used to measure reactions to any clearly
>   defined stimulus situation, including test taking. Developed originally for use with
>   college students.

ETS Personality Research Inventory—Anxiety Scale (Saunders, 1955)
>   Consists of 10 *yes–no* items measuring general anxiety included in a multipurpose
>   personality inventory.

Expanded Test Anxiety Scale for Children (Feld & Lewis, 1969)
>   Consists of the Test Anxiety Scale for Children plus additional items designed to
>   control for response-set bias in the original scale. Two experimental versions are
>   available.

Fear Survey Schedule (Geer, 1965; Wolpe & Lang, 1964; available from the
Education and Industrial Testing Service)
>   Consists of 7-point rating scales on which the subject indicates the extent to which
>   he or she fears each of 51 (FSS–II) or 72 (FSS–III) stimulus situations–objects.
>   Originally designed for use with college students. Several versions are available;
>   "failing a test" is included in FSS–II.

Fear Survey Schedule for Children (Scherer & Nakamura, 1968)
>   Consists of 80 5-point rating items measuring fear of situations relevant to
>   elementary school children, including testing situations. Patterned after the Fear
>   Survey Schedule.

Fear Thermometer (Wolpe et al., 1964)
>   Consists of a 100-point rating scale, with 0 representing the most relaxed a person
>   has ever been and 100 representing the most anxious. Can be used to rate any
>   situation, including test taking.

Final Exam Anxiety Index (Prochaska, 1971)
>   Consists of a 100-point rating scale modeled after the Fear Thermometer. Used to
>   compare pre- and posttherapy test anxiety. Originally designed for use with college
>   students.

General Anxiety Scale for Children (S. B. Sarason et al., 1960)
>   Consists of 45 *yes–no* items dealing with anxiety in a variety of situations within
>   the realm of childhood experience. Designed to be administered orally to
>   elementary school children. Eleven of the scale items compose a lie scale.

Inventory of Test Anxiety (Osterhouse, 1972; Osipow & Kreinbring, 1971)
Includes scales to measure two factors of test anxiety: worry and emotionality. Each scale consists of 10 items; some are original, others are taken from the Achievement Anxiety Test, Pre-examination Questionnaire, and Test Anxiety Scale. Originally developed to evaluate effects of desensitization and study-skills training on test anxiety.
IPAT Anxiety Scale (Cattell & Scheier, 1961; available from the Institute for Personality and Ability Testing)
Consists of 40 3-point rating items designed to measure "free-floating, manifest" anxiety (anxiety proneness). Designed for use as a general anxiety evaluation scale.

Manifest Anxiety Scale (Taylor, 1953)
Consists of 50 true–false items selected from the Minnesota Multiphasic Personality Inventory. Items were selected on the basis of their ability to detect clinical anxiety.
Manifest Anxiety Scale (Short Form) (Bendig, 1956)
Consists of 20 items taken directly from the Manifest Anxiety Scale.
Manifest Anxiety Scale (Forced-Choice Form) (Heineman, 1953)
Consists of the 50 items of the Manifest Anxiety Scale, each paired with a Minnesota Multiphasic Personality Inventory item of equal favorability but no relevance to anxiety, to form a forced-choice item format.
Manifest Anxiety Scale (Short Forced-Choice Form) (Christie & Budnitzky, 1957)
Consists of 20 items from the Forced-Choice Form of the Manifest Anxiety Scale corresponding to the 20 items on the Short Form.
Modified Test-Anxiety Scale (Harleston, 1962)
Consists of 20 items from the Test Anxiety Questionnaire. The response format was changed from a graphic scale to a 6-point rating scale. Originally designed for use with college students.
Multiple Affect Adjective Check List (Zuckerman & Lubin, 1965)
Affect Adjective Check List combined with similar measures of two related constructs: depression and hostility.

Perceived Stress Index (P. D. Jacobs & Munz, 1968)
Consists of 15 adjectives ordered on a pleasantness–unpleasantness continuum ranging from *thrilled* to *extremely terrified*. Respondents check the one adjective describing how they "normally feel" (Scale I) or how they feel "at this moment" (Scale II). Designed to measure college students' anxiety levels in a variety of situations, including test taking.
Pre-Examination Questionnaire (Liebert & Morris, 1967)
Consists of 10 items selected from the Test Anxiety Questionnaire and modified so that responses refer only to immediate feelings or experience ("How do you feel *right now*?"). Two subscale scores, each based on 5 items, are obtained to measure worry and emotionality. Originally developed for use with college students.

Reactions to Tests (I. G. Sarason, 1984; see also Benson & Bandalos, 1992; Zimmer et al., 1992)
Consists of 40 items designed to measure I. G. Sarason's four theoretical dimensions of test anxiety. Produces four subscale scores: Worry, Test-Irrelevant Thinking, Tension, and Bodily Symptoms. Designed for use with college students.

Refined Test Anxiety Scale (Emery & Krumboltz, 1967)
    Consists of 19 5-point rating items designed to measure test anxiety of college
    students. Refinement of an earlier experimental scale used in Emery's research.
Revised Test Anxiety Scale (Benson et al., 1992; Benson & El-Zahhar, 1994)
    Consists of 18 items, rated on 4-point scales, which produce four subscale scores:
    Tension, Worry, Bodily Symptoms, and Test-Irrelevant Thinking. Developed by
    subjecting the nonredundant items from the original Reactions to Tests and the
    Test Anxiety Inventory to extensive multinational factor analysis and cross-
    validation procedures. Appears to be the state of the art at this writing.

School Anxiety Questionnaire (Dunn, 1968, 1970)
    A five-scale, 105-item multiple-choice questionnaire that measures anxiety
    concerning evaluation, failure, achievement, tests, and recitation. The School
    Anxiety Questionnaire Test Anxiety subscale contains 13 5-point Likert-type
    items. Designed to be administered to groups of fourth- or fifth-grade children;
    includes tape-recorded standardized instructions.
S–R Inventory of Anxiousness (Endler et al., 1962)
    Consists of 14 5-point rating scales used to evaluate response tendencies
    (behavioral and physiological) to 11 anxiety-provoking situations, one of which is
    "entering a final examination in an important course." Designed to measure
    anxiety proneness of college students.
State–Trait Anxiety Inventory (Spielberger et al., 1970; Revised, Spielberger, 1983;
available from Consulting Psychologists Press)
    Consists of two 20-item 4-point rating scales. One scale measures state anxiety
    (specific to some situation, such as taking a test); the other measures trait anxiety
    (anxiety-proneness). Designed for use with high school and college students.
State–Trait Anxiety Inventory for Children (Spielberger et al., 1973; available from
Consulting Psychologists Press)
    Consists of two 20-item 3-point rating scales, one for state and one for trait
    anxiety. Designed for use with elementary school children; patterned after the
    State–Trait Anxiety Inventory.
Stressful Situations Questionnaire (Hodges & Felling, 1970)
    Consists of 5-point rating scale items to measure degree of apprehensiveness or
    concern for 40 stressful situations that college students might face. Five items deal
    with failure in classroom participation situations; five with academic failure.
Subjective Stress Scale (Berkun et al., 1962; Kerle & Bialek, 1958)
    Consists of a 14-point rating scale anchored by weighted adjectives ranging from
    wonderful to *scared stiff*. Subject checks the one adjective that most adequately
    describes his or her strongest feeling. Originally developed for evaluating anxiety
    of soldiers in simulated combat conditions. Can be adapted to measure test
    anxiety.
Suinn Test Anxiety Behavior Scale (Suinn, 1969)
    Consists of 50 items describing behavioral situations related to test anxiety.
    Respondents rate, on a 5-point scale, how frightened they are of each situation.
    Developed for use with college students.

Test Anxiety Questionnaire (Mandler & Sarason, 1952)
    Consists of 35 graphic rating items dealing with reactions to facing or taking a
    course examination or intelligence test. First inventory designed specifically for
    measuring test anxiety. Originally developed for use with college students.

Test Anxiety Inventory ("Test Attitude Inventory") (Spielberger et al., 1978; Spielberger, 1980, available from Consulting Psychologists Press)
> Consists of 20 items, rated on 4-point Likert-type frequency scales, regarding general feelings about taking tests. In addition to a total score, two subscale scores, "worry" and "emotionality," each based on eight items, are obtained. Developed for use with high school and college students.

Test Anxiety Scale (I. G. Sarason, 1958a; I. G. Sarason & Ganzer, 1962)
> Consists of 16 true–false items dealing with physiological, emotional, cognitive, and behavioral reactions during test-taking situations. Items taken from the Test Anxiety Questionnaire were modified to true–false format. Originally developed for use with college students. A later revision (I. G. Sarason, 1968) includes 37 true–false items.

Test Anxiety Scale for Children (S. B. Sarason et al., 1960)
> Consists of 30 *yes–no* items dealing with anxiety in evaluative situations at school. Designed to be administered orally to elementary school children.

Test Reaction Questionnaire (Sperber, 1961)
> Consists of 22 graphic-rating items designed to measure reactions to various aspects of the testing situation. Patterned after the Test Anxiety Questionnaire; designed for use with Air Force recruits.

Worry–Emotionality Questionnaire (Liebert & Morris, 1967; Morris et al., 1981)
> Consists of 10 items designed to measure worry and emotionality. Refinement of the Pre-Examination Questionnaire. Designed for use with college students.

3

An Evaluation of Test Anxiety Scales: Convergent, Divergent, and Predictive Validity

Jeffrey R. Bedell and Herbert A. Marlowe
Florida Mental Health Institute, Tampa, Florida, USA

The detrimental effects of test anxiety on learning and academic performance are well documented (e.g., Hembree, 1988; Grooms & Endler, 1960;
Lam & Hong, 1992; S. B. Sarason, Hill, & Zimbardo, 1964; see Anderson &
Sauser, Chapter 2). Appropriately, psychologists have attempted to help test-
anxious students by developing a variety of treatment programs designed to
reduce the adverse effects of test anxiety during examinations (e.g., Allen,
1971; Dykeman, 1989; Hembree, 1988; Spielberger et al., 1976; Suinn, 1968;
see also Chapters 9–14). To understand and assess the construct of test anxiety,
and to evaluate the effectiveness of treatment programs, valid and sensitive
measures of test anxiety are needed. There is, however, considerable controversy with regard to the measurement of test anxiety that impedes progress in
this field.

Historical issues relating to the measurement of test anxiety have been
carefully and extensively reviewed in Chapters 1 and 2 (also see Hembree,
1988; Spielberger et al., 1978). Therefore, it is not necessary to delve deeply
into this topic here. It is instructive, however, to note briefly those developments most relevant to the goal of this chapter, which is to clarify important
issues in the measurement of test anxiety.

EVOLUTION OF THE MEASUREMENT OF TEST ANXIETY

In one of the earliest test anxiety studies (cited by Cannon, 1929), the
measure of test anxiety was physiological—the level of blood sugar found in
students' urine. As sophistication in psychological assessment developed, researchers developed rating scales to be used as assessment techniques. These
psychological measures initially emphasized the role of global personality factors such as Stability, Emotional Arousal, and Neuroticism as determined on
the basis of clinical judgments. Eventually, self-report paper-and-pencil tests
were developed to measure test anxiety.

The roots of the early test anxiety measures were firmly grounded in the
macro theories of personality popular at the time. Subsequently, the use of

self-report personality tests for the assessment of micro personality factors became an accepted practice, and self-report assessment techniques currently dominate research on test anxiety. The current level of interest in test anxiety is partially due to the availability of self-report questionnaires that are easily administered and scored.

Most recently, the assessment of test anxiety has been influenced by the general controversy in personality research that centers on the relative role of situational versus personal factors in the determination of behavior. Consequently, there is now an emphasis on the situational aspects of test anxiety among some researchers, while others emphasize its stable "trait" aspects. Contemporary test anxiety scales may be seen as adhering to one of three major positions with regard to this controversy: trait, situational, or interactionist.

The trait school of thought emphasizes the stable, cross-situational characteristics of the test anxiety construct. According to this conceptualization, the test-anxious individual has acquired a stable disposition to experience anxiety in nearly all types of evaluative situations. This theory suggests that the individual's perception that he or she is being evaluated triggers internal tensions and anxiety regardless of the specific situational characteristics of the environment. I. G. Sarason, a major proponent of this position, has developed the Test Anxiety Scale (TAS) to measure test anxiety from this theoretical viewpoint.

A viewpoint that contrasts strongly with the trait theory approach emphasizes the situational determinants of test anxiety. Assessments developed according to this view focus on the stimulus characteristics of evaluative situations that elicit anxiety reactions. According to these researchers, test anxiety is a stimulus-bound phenomenon with relatively little cross-situational generalization. Behavior therapists such as Suinn (1969), who developed the Suinn Test Anxiety Behavior Scale (STABS), advocate such a viewpoint.

A middle-of-the-road position is suggested by Endler (1974), whose interaction model considers both trait and situational factors to be equally important in the measurement of test anxiety. Endler contended that the trait characteristics of the individual, in interaction with specific situational stimuli, combine to produce test anxiety responses. The S–R Inventory of General Trait Anxiousness (Endler et al., 1962) is the primary example of a scale formulated to measure test anxiety from this point of view.

Because the trait, situational, and interactionist models represent competing theoretical positions, there is seldom any comparative research among these schools of thought. On the contrary, research programs generally operate exclusively within one theoretical orientation, and assessments are made using only one type of test anxiety scale. An unfortunate outcome of this trifurcation of research occurs when experimental results using one type of scale are contradictory to those using another scale. It is difficult to consolidate the information and resolve the contradictions because it is not possible to know how much of the variability in the research results is due to the different assessment devices. Until this situation is rectified, progress in the understanding of the construct of test anxiety and the evaluation of treatment programs will be impeded.

VALIDITY ISSUES IN THE MEASUREMENT OF TEST ANXIETY

The comparative validity of test anxiety scales has not been empirically determined due to the separateness of the three research groups. In this chapter, we address this problem by comparing the convergent, divergent, and predictive validity of test anxiety scales representing the trait, situational, and interactionist models of assessment.

A first issue regarding these test anxiety scales has to do with their *convergent* validity. In this case, interest is in the extent to which a variety of test anxiety questionnaires, each developed according to a different theoretical orientation, are highly correlated with each other. If they are highly correlated, then it may be assumed that they measure one basic construct and their individual theoretical underpinnings are of limited importance. If, however, they are poorly related, then they may assess a different construct or different parts of a global construct. Establishing convergent validity would determine whether test anxiety scales based on the trait, situational, and interactionist models are interchangeable or represent unique ways of measuring the construct.

The second validity issue has to do with the assessment of *divergent* validity. The logic underlying the need to establish divergent validity is that if two scales do not measure something different, then the utility of the more specific assessment device is not sufficient to represent a refinement in theory or techniques.

Finally, scores on a test anxiety scale should relate to performance on relevant measures of academic achievement. Unless a test anxiety scale is negatively related to test performance, it will not help in evaluating the efficacy of treatment programs. This type of information is established by using *predictive* or *criterion*-related validity procedures.

In summary, it is of interest to know the degree to which test anxiety assessments derived from theoretically different scales are related to each other. Also, a good test anxiety questionnaire will measure something different than general trait anxiety and will be predictive of test performance.

MEASURES OF TEST ANXIETY

To obtain information on scales representing different theoretical orientations toward the construct of test anxiety, three test anxiety scales and one trait anxiety scale were selected for evaluation. I. G. Sarason's (1978) TAS is the most widely used test anxiety measure and clearly represents a trait orientation. The STABS (Suinn, 1969) is strongly grounded in the situational orientation. Endler et al.'s (1962) S–R Inventory of Anxiousness, which is based on an interaction model, attempts to consider both the trait and situational aspects of anxiety. The fourth measure selected for this study, the Trait Anxiety (A-Trait) subscale of Spielberger et al.'s (1970) State–Trait Anxiety Inventory (STAI), is widely used for measuring trait anxiety, that is, the general tendency to experience anxiety reactions in a variety of situations. A brief review of the development and standardization of each of these four representative scales will provide information on the degree to which they represent different orientations to the assessment of test anxiety.

The TAS was developed from an older measure, the Test Anxiety Questionnaire (TAQ; Mandler & Sarason, 1952). The items from this scale were recast from a graphic rating scale to a true–false format. The TAQ yields a single score that is assumed to reflect the intensity of the internal anxiety responses associated with past evaluations. According to I. G. Sarason (1958a), the TAS measures a personality trait that causes decrements in performance that result from self-centered interfering responses that are experienced in response to evaluative threat. Test anxiety as measured by the TAS is similar to general trait anxiety, measured by the Taylor (1953) Manifest Anxiety Scale (MAS) and the A-Trait subscale of the STAI. The primary difference between the TAS and these general anxiety measures, according to Sarason, is that test anxiety is a more focalized trait (I. G. Sarason, 1959; I. G. Sarason & Ganzer, 1962; I. G. Sarason et al., 1968). Further indications of the trait nature of the TAS can be seen from inspection of the test items, which lack situational or environmental specificity.

The STABS is clearly grounded in the tradition of behavior therapy and emphasizes the assessment of the situational characteristics of test anxiety. This test consists of a series of statements that describe "behavioral situations that may arouse different levels of test anxiety in clients" (Suinn, 1969, p. 335). Examination of the STABS items reveals that they strongly emphasize temporal and situational variables. Several questions evaluate the role that time before an exam plays in eliciting test anxiety, and other questions involve situational specificity, for example, asking the individual to indicate the amount of apprehension experienced in "looking at the clock to see how much time remains during an exam."

The S–R Inventory is a more trait-oriented assessment than the STABS, but it is more situationally oriented than the TAS. This test was developed on the basis of an interaction model. It was designed to measure an individual's tendency to experience anxiety in a variety of settings, including testing situations. The S–R Inventory items require the individual to indicate the extent to which a variety of personal responses are experienced during an imagined testing situation.

The STAI has become the most widely used measure of both trait and state anxiety. The STAI A-Trait subscale measures individual differences in the disposition to experience anxiety states in response to a variety of situations. Scores on this scale provide an indication of the tension and apprehension experienced by the individual during everyday life. Conceptually, the STAI measures a global anxiety construct when compared with the more specific orientation of the test anxiety scales.

These four scales were selected because they differ in the degree to which they are situational or trait measures of test anxiety, or measures of general anxiety proneness. The TAS, STABS, and S–R Inventory seem to assess both trait and situational factors to some degree, but differ in their relative emphasis on traits and situations. Although the S–R Inventory appears to be more similar to the TAS as a measure of test anxiety, its theoretical underpinnings clearly emphasize the interactive role of personal and situational characteristics. The STAI A-Trait subscale is clearly more trait oriented than any of the other measures.

In this chapter, the convergent, divergent, and predictive validity scores on the four anxiety scales were examined for a sample of undergraduate college students in relation to their performance on course examinations.

1. Convergent validity was evaluated in terms of the degree to which the three test anxiety scales were correlated with one another.
2. Divergent validity was evaluated by the degree to which the test anxiety scales correlated with the STAI A-Trait subscale. This analysis examined the degree to which test anxiety scales measure a construct that was different from general trait anxiety.
3. Predictive validity was evaluated by determining the degree of correlation between each of the anxiety scales and classroom test performance. The basic question evaluated here was whether the test anxiety scales were better predictors of classroom performance than the general measure of trait anxiety.

PROCEDURES AND RESULTS

The subjects were 105 students enrolled in an undergraduate psychology class who volunteered to complete a questionnaire battery. They were told that the questionnaires were part of a research project and that participation would not affect their course grades. They were also informed that they would receive a class lecture later in the semester that would discuss the tests administered in the experiment. The single student who did not wish to participate in the experiment was excused.

Several days before a regularly scheduled class exam, the students were asked to complete a battery of psychological tests as part of an experiment. The students had no advance information that an experiment would be conducted with the class. The four anxiety measures were administered with standard instructions in the following order: STAI A-Trait subscale, TAS, S–R Inventory, and STABS.

All subjects who completed the test anxiety scales also took three class exams during the semester. The exams each contained 50 multiple-choice items, and the average of the three exams determined the students' course grades. Thus, subjects were administered three test anxiety scales and reported their general anxiety proneness, and their test performance data were available from the class exams.

Table 3.1 Intercorrelations among test anxiety scales, a general trait anxiety scale, and test performance

Measure	1	2	3	4	5
Test anxiety scales					
1. Test Anxiety Scale	—				
2. S–R Inventory of Anxiousness	.66*	—			
3. Suinn Test Anxiety Behavior Scale	.63*	.62*	—		
General trait anxiety					
4. State–Trait Anxiety Inventory A-Trait subscale	.45*	.46*	.59*	—	
Test performance					
5. Class grade (mean of three class exams)	.16	.33*	.27*	.33*	—

*$p < .01$.

Pearson product–moment correlations were calculated among the test anxiety, trait anxiety, and class grade scores; these correlations are presented in Table 3.1. Convergent validity was evaluated by determining the intercorrelations among the three test anxiety scales. These correlations ranged from .62 to .66, and assessment of these figures (according to Brunig & Kintz, 1968) indicated no significant differences in the degree to which the various test anxiety scales were correlated. Thus, the lowest degree of correlation observed between the S–R Inventory and the STABS (.62) was not significantly different from the highest correlation obtained between the S–R Inventory and TAS (.66).

The next section of Table 3.1 evaluates divergent validity and shows the degree of correlation between the three test anxiety scales and assessments of general anxiety proneness (STAI A-Trait Subscale). The degree of correlation among the various test anxiety scales and the STAI A-Trait subscale score ranged from .45 to .59. Comparisons of these correlations indicated that they were not significantly different. It may, therefore, be concluded that the test anxiety scales were equivalent in the degree to which they were correlated with general trait anxiety.

As may be observed in Table 3.1, the overall magnitude of the correlations among the test anxiety scales was greater (.64) than those observed between the test anxiety scales and the measure of trait anxiety (.50).

The next group of correlations presented in Table 3.1 represents the degree to which class grades were predicted by the test anxiety scales and the A-Trait subscale. All these predictions were significant with a probability of at least .01, with the exception of the correlation between the TAS and test performance, which was not significant. There were no significant differences among the other three correlations, and this finding indicated that these scales (S–R Inventory, STABS, and STAI A-Trait) were equally good predictors of test performance. As may be observed in Table 3.1, the magnitude of the correlations between the anxiety questionnaires and exam performance ($m = .17$)

were of a lesser magnitude than the correlations between the test anxiety scales and the A-Trait subscale and among the three test anxiety scales.

DISCUSSION

In light of the fact that the measurement of test anxiety is a major area of controversy in the psychological literature, our results provide important practical information regarding the relative merits of the major test anxiety scales. Also, as the questionnaires evaluated here represent distinct and divergent theoretical orientations toward the assessment of test anxiety, the relative strengths of these different theoretical viewpoints may be evaluated. Specifically, the convergent, divergent, and predictive validity of the S–R Inventory, STABS, and STAI A-Trait as related to trait anxiety and test performance were assessed.

Convergent Validity of the Test Anxiety Scales

The convergent validity of the test anxiety scales was assessed first, and the results indicated that there was a high degree of similarity among scores on the three scales. In fact, an evaluation of the correlation coefficients among the scales suggested that these test anxiety questionnaires were essentially equivalent in their assessments. This finding is particularly interesting in light of the fact that there has been much discussion in the literature about the differences among the theories underlying each of the scales. Because the three test anxiety questionnaires were independently developed according to these varying orientations and exhibit different formats and because their questionnaire statements have very different content, it is surprising that they would be so uniformly correlated.

On the basis of the finding that the scales measure essentially the same construct, it is obvious that the differences in their theoretical basis have little bearing on what is being measured. Clearly, the theoretical differences among the scales have not been translated into measurable differences in performance on the scales. This finding may be due to several factors. First, it is possible that the situation–trait dimension on which these scales vary is not a significant factor with regard to the measurement of test anxiety. In light of the work by many researchers and theoreticians (as reviewed by Hembree, 1988, and Cronbach, 1975), this explanation is not very satisfactory as the situation–trait variable has evolved to be a significant factor in predicting behavior. It is, however, possible that the construct of test anxiety is in an unique way relatively independent of situation–trait influence. This would be the case, for instance, if it could be assumed that individuals form a generalized set or "situation perception" (Ekehammar & Magnusson, 1972) toward nearly all testing or evaluative situations. If this were the case, it would be difficult to develop a questionnaire that could truly assess meaningful situational characteristics of testing situations. Because evaluation and testing is such a ubiquitous part of American life, it is possible that this long-term and frequent contact with a variety of tests causes individuals to ignore the situational component of each different testing situation.

Another possible explanation for the similarity of scores on the test anxiety scales is that, although the underlying theoretical differences may be important, these differences were inadequately translated into the questionnaire items. If this is the case, questionnaire developers would be well advised to pay closer attention to test and measurement issues when developing scales to ensure that they are assessing the desired phenomenon. This is clearly a problem in the present scales. For example, the large number of temporal questions on the STABS may overly assess this one situational factor at the expense of other important factors. Also, the S–R Inventory assesses the frequency of vomiting and urination during tests. It is likely that these responses are not relevant to most test-anxious students and cloud the assessment of more subtle personal and situational factors. Perhaps the developers of these test anxiety scales paid too much attention to the sophistication of their theories and insufficient attention to issues of test construction.

Other explanations for the homogeneity of the test anxiety scales are, of course, possible. It is clear that much work is needed on the development of test anxiety questionnaires if it is to be demonstrated that their theoretical underpinnings have any bearing on the measurement of test anxiety. As currently constructed, the present scales assess test anxiety very similarly and may be used interchangeably.

Divergent Validity of the Test Anxiety Scales

The next set of evaluations addresses the issue of divergent validity and assesses the degree to which the test anxiety scales measured a construct that was different from general trait anxiety. The results of this evaluation suggest that the test anxiety scales do, in fact, measure a slightly different construct from that measured by the STAI A-Trait subscale. The degree of divergence between the test anxiety scales and the A-Trait subscale was, however, not extremely large compared with the divergence among the test anxiety scales themselves. It might, therefore, be concluded that the test anxiety scales measure a construct that is similar to, but somewhat divergent from, the construct of general trait anxiety. Such a degree of divergence is appropriate as the constructs of test and trait anxiety are similar and overlapping. It is possible, however, that test anxiety scales could be improved to show a greater divergence from general trait anxiety assessments.

The comparisons of the test anxiety scales to the A-Trait subscale again emphasize the homogeneity of the test anxiety questionnaires. It was found that there was an equivalent degree of correlation among the three test anxiety scales and A-Trait measure. This finding is of interest as the highly trait-oriented TAS showed an equivalent degree of correlation to the A-Trait subscale as did the highly situational STABS. Clearly, the situation versus trait basis of the test anxiety scales does not seem to strongly affect the test anxiety questionnaire scores.

Predictive Validity of the Test Anxiety Scales

The third area of evaluation has to do with the predictive validity of the test anxiety and trait anxiety scales. This is an important area of validation for these scales. Predictive validity is of general interest first because it shows the degree of relation between responses on a self-report paper-and-pencil test and actual observable behavior. Second, it is important because it indicates the degree to which test anxiety questionnaire responses are related to test performance. Predictive validity of this sort is particularly critical if test anxiety scales are to be helpful in the evaluation of test anxiety treatment programs. The scale that is most predictive of actual test performance would be of the greatest utility in assessing treatment programs.

The results of the prediction evaluations were unexpected in two ways. First, the well-established "granddaddy" of all the test anxiety scales, the TAS, proved to be the only scale that did not significantly predict actual test performance. The other two scales (STABS and S–R Inventory) were able to account for about 10% of the variability in class examination scores. Considering the variety of identifiable factors that can influence test performance, such as mental ability, study skills, motivation to learn, and instructional variables, the fact that 10% of performance was associated with a personality characteristic indicated the importance of the test anxiety construct. It appears, however, that the TAS does not measure test anxiety in a way that is effective in predicting test performance.

The second unexpected finding was the indication that a measure of general trait anxiety was as effective as the STABS and the S–R Inventory in predicting test performance. Also, the STAI A-Trait subscale was a better predictor than the TAS. It would be expected that the specific measures of test anxiety would be better predictors of test performance than the general A-Trait subscale. The finding that this was not the case can give rise to both pessimism and optimism regarding test anxiety assessment. Pessimism may arise due to the failure of the test anxiety scales to perform as well as they should, indicating their relative lack of utility. As indicated earlier in this chapter, there is an obvious need for the development of better test anxiety questionnaires. Optimism, however, is also in order. The present results indicate that two questionable test anxiety scales and an A-Trait subscale can predict 10% of the variance associated with test performance. It is, therefore, reasonable to expect that a carefully conceived and well-constructed test anxiety questionnaire might predict test performance to a much greater degree. The optimal use of contemporary test construction techniques along with careful theorizing should result in the development of a test anxiety scale of great merit and utility.

Implications for Future Research

Given the findings of this study, several suggestions can be offered to guide future research on the assessment of test anxiety. First, scale development needs to move beyond emphasizing the trait versus situation distinction in test anxiety assessment, which did not result in divergent validity among the scales used in this study, nor did it increase the predictive power of test anxiety scales over trait anxiety measures. This is not to say that the situational specificity of test anxiety measures is irrelevant; rather, it is suggested that other factors appear to play a stronger role in the prediction of test performance.

Examination of the cognitive processes that are involved in how test anxiety is perceived and experienced provides a critically important element in the assessment of test anxiety, as was noted by Bem and Allen (1975) and more recently by Schwarzer and Jerusalem (1992). Liebert and Morris (1967) and Spielberger et al. (1976) have identified worry and emotionality as major components of test anxiety; and worry, the cognitive component, appears to be responsible for most of the observed decrements in test performance. The Test Anxiety Inventory (TAI), developed by Spielberger (1980) and his colleagues (Spielberger et al., 1976) to assess test anxiety as a situation-specific trait, incorporates factorially derived Worry and Emotionality subscales. Findings with the TAI demonstrate that worry is negatively correlated with test performance, whereas emotionality is essentially uncorrelated with performance (Spielberger, 1980). As progress has been made in the measurement of test anxiety, scales such as the TAS are being replaced by more valid and psychometrically sound measurement instruments (see Anderson & Sauser, Chapter 2). Further refinements in test anxiety scales will undoubtedly make them more sensitive and ensure a divergence in their predictive power as compared with general trait anxiety measures.

Two general conclusions may be drawn from the research reported in this chapter. First, the three major theoretical orientations that have guided research on the assessment of test anxiety—trait, situation specific, and interactionist—either are not important facets of test anxiety or their nuances are not adequately incorporated in the questionnaire items. Because the test anxiety scales used in this study accounted for only 10% of the variance associated with test performance, a second conclusion is that well-constructed scales that include worry and emotionality as components of test anxiety should predict test performance to a much greater degree.

SUMMARY

This chapter evaluated three types of test anxiety scales in terms of their convergent, divergent, and predictive validity. These scales represent three major theoretical positions in test anxiety research with regard to the relative role of situational versus personality or trait factors in the determination of behavior and test performance. The trait model for assessing test anxiety was represented in this study by the TAS (I. G. Sarason, 1978), the situational model was represented by the STABS (Suinn, 1969), and the integrationist position was represented by the S–R Inventory of Anxiousness (Endler et al., 1962). A major goal of this study was to determine the degree to which test anxiety assessments based on these theoretically different models were related to each other and divergent from a general trait anxiety measure, the STAI (Spielberger, et al., 1970), in their power to predict classroom test performance.

A study was conducted with 105 undergraduate volunteers who completed the four anxiety questionnaires and whose performance in three class examinations was evaluated. Results indicated moderately high correlations among the three test anxiety scales, suggesting that they were essentially equivalent. Some evidence of divergent validity was also found, as determined by the finding that the construct measured by the test anxiety scales was somewhat different from general trait anxiety. In terms of predictive validity, the general measure of trait anxiety (the STAI) was equally or more effective than the three test anxiety measures in predicting test performance. Moreover, the TAS was the only questionnaire that did not significantly predict actual test performance.

4

Theory and Measurement of Test Anxiety as a Situation-Specific Trait

Volker Hodapp
Heinrich-Heine-Universität, Düsseldorf, Germany

Peter G. Glanzmann
Johannes-Gutenberg Universität, Mainz, Germany

Lothar Laux
University of Bamberg, Bamberg, Germany

Attacked by proponents of situationism and interactionism, the trait model of personality has begun to change in its appearance. Specific reference to situational variables in the design of trait tests provides a useful step in the refinement of trait theory. In anxiety research, such tests have been classified as situation-specific trait anxiety measures (Spielberger et al., 1976; Spielberger & Vagg, 1987). They assess individual differences in the disposition to react with anxiety to selected stressful situations, such as examinations or giving speeches.

Situation-specific traits such as test anxiety may be conceptualized as refinements of the trait concept that take into account a particular anxiety-provoking situation, as well as Person × Situation interactions. The advantage of measures of situation-specific traits, as compared with "general" trait scales, is reflected in their greater predictive validity in criterion-related situations (Laux et al., 1985). This advantage is relevant not only to the actual anxiety reaction, but also to the relation between the situation-specific trait and achievement.

In this chapter, the relation between anxiety and achievement is discussed in two different contexts. First, the joint influence on achievement of general trait anxiety (T-Anxiety) and test anxiety as a situation-specific trait is demonstrated. Second, a model of the complex reciprocal relation between anxiety and achievement is proposed that avoids a major shortcoming of the unidirec-

This chapter was revised while Volker Hodapp was a visiting professor in the Department of Educational Psychology of the University of Georgia. He would like to thank Professor Jeri Benson for her assistance during this visit, which was supported by a grant from the Deutcher Akademischer Auslandsdienst.

tional trait approach by explicitly taking into account interactions of persons with situation-specific determinants of behavior. After first examining the measurement of situation-specific traits, the development of a German adaptation of the Test Anxiety Inventory (TAI, Spielberger, 1980) is then briefly described.

ANXIETY–ACHIEVEMENT RELATION

Depending on one's theoretical frame of reference, the relation between anxiety and achievement may be conceived quite differently. The suggestion by Liebert and Morris (1967) that test anxiety should be regarded as consisting of two separate components, worry and emotionality, has received special attention. The worry component is related to cognitions primarily concerning performance outcomes and their consequences. Emotionality, however, is related to the perception of feelings and reactions of the autonomic nervous system.

Trait–state anxiety theory (Spielberger, 1972a) conceptualizes test anxiety as a situation-specific anxiety trait (Spielberger et al., 1976). Persons high in test anxiety are expected to respond with excessive worry, self-deprecatory thoughts, and intense affective and physiological arousal when exposed to examination situations. Emotional reactions as well as worry responses are assumed to contribute to the performance decrements of high test-anxious persons. Whereas cognitive theory emphasizes the adverse effects of the worry component, Trait–state anxiety theory predicts that both worry and emotionality affect achievement. Emotionality elicits task-irrelevant affective responses that are activated by high drive levels associated with elevations in state anxiety.

The concept of test anxiety as a situation-specific anxiety trait has led to the identification of a number of basic processes related to anxiety in evaluative situations. The superiority of situation-specific traits as compared with general traits in the prediction of achievement is demonstrated by a reanalysis of correlational data reported by Spielberger et al. (1978). These data were analyzed by means of covariance selection and path analysis to permit the formulation of hypotheses that specify the causal direction of influence rather than only the correlational pattern of relation of the involved variables (Hodapp, 1982). The findings of these analyses, reported in Figure 4.1, show that the situation-specific anxiety components, worry and emotionality, exert a direct influence on achievement, whereas general anxiety measures do not have a direct effect on achievement.

Although there is a close relation between test anxiety and general trait anxiety (T-Anxiety), the results reported in Figure 4.1 support the hypothesis that only test anxiety has a direct impact on achievement. Nevertheless, the relation between measures of general and test anxiety is quite strong because both assess relatively stable individual differences in the disposition to respond to situations perceived as threatening with elevations in state anxiety. Any "ego-involving" situation that poses a direct or implied threat to self-esteem will be perceived as threatening, including examination situations in school

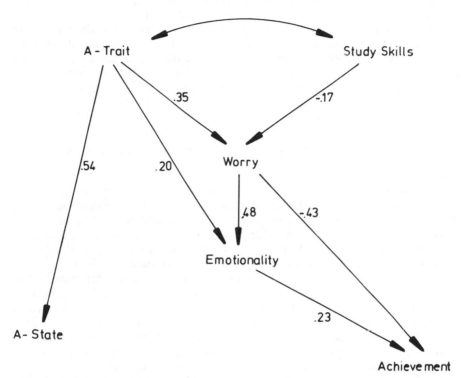

Figure 4.1 Path diagram for the reanalyzed data of Spielberger et al. (1978). From "Causal inference from non-experimental research on anxiety and educational achievement" by V. Hodapp, in H. W. Krohne & L. Laux (Eds.), *Achievement, stress, and anxiety* (1982, p. 362). Washington, DC: Hemisphere. Reprinted by permission.

or university. Because examination situations are characterized by a particular type of evaluative stress, they form a special category of ego-involving situations.

In Figure 4.1, the most obvious relation between test anxiety and academic performance is the negative influence of worry on achievement, which provides strong evidence that cognitive worry responses adversely affect performance during examination situations. Furthermore, the path coefficients indicate, in agreement with the vast majority of pertinent findings, that worry is the prime source of interference (Deffenbacher, 1980; Morris & Liebert, 1970; Mueller, 1992; I. G. Sarason et al., 1986; Seipp, 1991; Tobias, 1992). Consistent with the cognitive–attentional approach (I. G. Sarason, 1975a; Wine, 1982), the high test-anxious person's self-preoccupation interferes with the efficient processing of information in achievement situations by distracting the individual's attention from task-relevant cues.

With regard to the emotionality component, which is usually either not related to achievement or related only in connection with high worry scores, the model presented in Figure 4.1 reveals a positive relation to achievement. This finding might be due to activating task characteristics, or to the energizing influence of heightened activation. Given the observed positive influence of emotionality on achievement and, at the same time, a negative influence of worry (Glanzmann, 1985), it would seem that worry and emotionality not only are different facets of test anxiety, but also appear to differ in their functional properties. Furthermore, causal modeling tends to support the hypothesis that emotionality is influenced by cognitive factors (Hodapp, 1982, 1989).

FEEDBACK LOOPS FROM ACHIEVEMENT TO TEST ANXIETY

Evaluations of the causal relation between anxiety and achievement in educational settings have used time series analyses based on cross-lagged panel designs or structural equation modeling of longitudinal data (Fincham et al., 1989; Hodapp, 1982, 1989; Jerusalem, 1985; F. J. King et al., 1976; Meece et al., 1990; Pekrun, 1991). Test anxiety is generally conceptualized in these studies as a predictor of educational achievement (Hembree, 1988).

Although the influence of anxiety on achievement seems empirically well established, less interest has been focused on possible feedback effects from performance outcome to test anxiety. An exception is a model by B. Jacobs and Strittmatter (1979) that describes the effects of achievement on anxiety. According to this model, the relation between anxiety and achievement is characterized by mutual causality; anxiety has a negative influence on achievement, and increases in anxiety follow negative feedback. These mutual effects not only correspond to common experience, but can also be inferred from experimental data (e.g., Auerbach, 1973; Gaudry, 1977).

Evidence of the reciprocal effects of anxiety and achievement may be found in research on achievement motivation theory (e.g., Dusek, 1980; Hill, 1972). Hill (1972) and Hill and Eaton (1977) stressed the importance of children's success and failure experiences in the development of test anxiety. Experiences of low-anxious children are generally characterized by success in school or other evaluative situations. Positive experiences of interactions with adults in evaluative settings contribute to the development of a relatively higher motive to succeed than a motive to avoid failure. In contrast, the life history of high-anxious children is dominated by failure experiences, which lead to the development of a strong fear-of-failure motive (Krohne, 1992). Because these children's evaluations of their own performance have been strongly influenced by parental disapproval (Dusek, 1980, p. 91), they tend to avoid evaluative situations.

The fear-of-failure motive is a habitual disposition that is invoked to explain individual differences in achievement situations. In the past, fear of failure was often assessed by means of test anxiety questionnaires (Atkinson & Litwin, 1960; Feather, 1965). In his model for achievement motivation, Heckhausen (1991) has described the motivational aspects of achievement-related affective and cognitive processes. Within the context of this model, findings from re-search on the fear-of-failure motive and test anxiety can be integrated (Heckhausen, 1982; see also Covington, 1992; Hagtvet, 1984; Hagtvet & Min, 1992).

Following Heckhausen's (1991) model, success and failure experiences are the consequences of appraisal processes. Another important feature of the model is self-evaluation, which is determined in two ways: first, by a comparison process in which performance outcome is compared with the goal set by an individual's aspiration level, and second, by an attribution process whereby performance outcome is ascribed to a subjectively perceived "naive" cause. The causal ascription of performance outcome to ability is of prime importance because, both in achievement motivation (Kukla, 1972; Meyer, 1973) and in cognitive interpretations of test anxiety (Nicholls, 1976), self-evaluation of one's own ability markedly influences differences in success and failure orientations and individual differences in low and high test anxiety.

The relation between the fear-of-failure motive and test anxiety was investigated by Hodapp (1989) with a group of 91 students attending the seventh grade of a comprehensive school in Germany. These students were administered questionnaires designed to assess several components of the fear-of-failure motive and a trait test anxiety measure (an earlier German adaptation of the TAI); academic achievement scores were also obtained. Path-analytical statistical techniques were used to test the general hypothesis that test anxiety exerts a causal influence on academic achievement. It was further hypothesized that achievement influences the following four motivational variables: aspiration level, achievement-related self-evaluation, self-concept of academic achievement, and causal attributions. The motivational variables were expected to mediate the relation between achievement and test anxiety.

Figure 4.2 presents the model for the anxiety–achievement relation, which was computed by means of the LISREL approach (Jöreskog & Sörbom, 1988). The most prominent feature of this model is the conceptualization of the anxiety–achievement relation in terms of a regulated system. Negative influences on achievement are mediated by worry, which is in turn influenced by a chain system consisting of negative self-evaluation of one's own performance, an unfavorable self-concept with regard to achievement, and a general disposition to attribute poor performance outcome to low ability and bad luck. Worry responses obstruct efficient task performance, and poor performance elicits further negative self-evaluation through a feedback loop.

Another self-sustaining process identified in the LISREL model presented in Figure 4.2 concerns the relation between achievement, aspiration level, the ascription of success to task difficulty (S+), and the emotionality and worry components of test anxiety. Here again, an attributional variable appears to be the prime mediator between achievement and its effects on level of aspiration, emotionality, and worry. Furthermore, feedback loops appear to form a stable system of attribution tendencies, performance standards, and worry and emotional test anxiety responses, which may be regarded as consequences of the appraisal of performance outcome.

Self-evaluation processes seem to be at the core of the model system presented in Figure 4.2. On the one hand, they are immediate consequences of

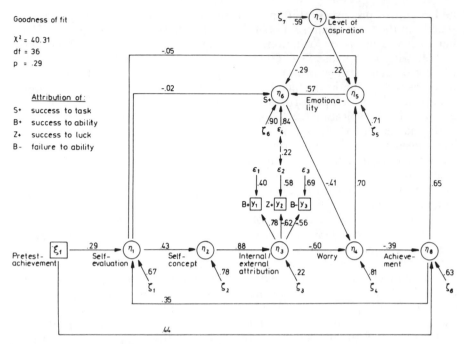

Figure 4.2   LISREL model of anxiety–achievement relation. From "Anxiety, fear of failure, and achievement: Two path analytical models" by V. Hodapp, in *Anxiety Research* (1989, Vol. 1, p. 303). Reprinted by permission of Harwood Academic Publishers GmbH.

performance outcome; on the other hand, they seem to be of importance in the formation of relatively stable self-concepts and preferred attributional patterns. The latter largely determine the worry component of test anxiety, which in turn exerts a direct influence on achievement. In general, high test-anxious persons are characterized by unfavorable self-evaluation: Test anxiety not only leads to negative self-evaluation, but is also indirectly determined by negative self-evaluation. Thus, attributional processes stabilize an asymmetrical balance of self-evaluation as either more favorable or more unfavorable.

In contrast to the classical trait approach, in which situational factors are largely neglected, a situation-specific trait such as test anxiety seems to be markedly affected by the feedback of situation-specific behavior. The fear-of-failure motive and its components (self-evaluation, causal attribution, self-concept of academic achievement, and aspiration level) mediate this feedback of performance outcome. Moreover, the asymmetry of the attributional processes is of prime importance in maintaining this self-sustaining system, as well as in explaining the relative consistency of the achievement behavior of persons characterized by fear of failure or high test anxiety (cf. Heckhausen, 1975).

The foregoing analysis of the test anxiety–achievement relation suggests that much more attention should be paid to situation-specific trait theories. This is especially true in the area of test anxiety, which has been criticized because of a lack of correspondence between theoretical conceptions and the characteristics of the scales used (Hodapp, Laux, & Spielberger, 1982; Nicholls, 1976; Spielberger et al., 1978). Therefore, important problems related to the measurement of test anxiety are discussed, including the development of a new questionnaire, the German adaptation of Spielberger's (1980) TAI.

DEVELOPMENT OF THE GERMAN ADAPTATION OF THE TAI

In developing a German inventory for measuring test anxiety as a situation-specific anxiety trait, a primary goal was to construct Worry and Emotionality subscales that were as independent as possible. The guidelines for the test construction procedures were derived from a critical evaluation of traditional test anxiety measures.

Most items in test anxiety scales contain specific situation–response statements. A rather general description of an examination situation is linked with a particular anxiety response, representing either the worry component ("During tests I find myself thinking of the consequences of failing") or the emotionality component ("While taking an important exam I perspire a great deal") of test anxiety.

Some test anxiety items also specify whether the subjective experience occurs before, during, or after the examination in question. Thus, each item describes a specific situation, a particular response, and a point in time. These situation–response–time patterns are arbitrarily fixed in a given item; that is, the various situational and response elements are not combined in any systematic way, as has been proposed in situation–response questionnaires (Endler et al., 1991; Endler & Okada, 1975).

Furthermore, several traditional test anxiety measures, for example, the Test Anxiety Questionnaire (Mandler & Sarason, 1952) and the Test Anxiety Scale (TAS; I. G. Sarason, 1958a, 1978), contain items that refer to study habits or attitudes toward tests. Because many facets and correlates of test anxiety are represented in these instruments, it is not surprising that factor-analytic studies have yielded inconsistent results in relation to the worry–emotionality distinction (see Spielberger et al., 1978).

As an alternative to the TAS, which is factorially complex and does not take the state–trait distinction into account, Spielberger (1980) introduced a new instrument for measuring test anxiety, the TAI. This 20-item questionnaire includes Worry (W) and Emotionality (E) subscales, each with 8 items. In developing the TAI, as discussed earlier in Chapter 1, the entire set of 37 TAS items (I. G. Sarason, 1978) was rephrased as trait items and included in the initial pool. Those items with relatively low correlations (below .40) with the preliminary TAI Total score were discarded. Most of the discarded items contained references to study habits or attitudes about taking exams.

The second step in constructing the TAI was to revise and simplify the surviving items and to add new items with content validity as measures of worry and emotionality (Spielberger, 1980). All 20 items in the final form of the TAI refer to subjects' experiences in examinations or tests. In contrast to

Table 4.1 Modified instruction for the TAI–G

Following you will find a set of statements with which you can describe yourself. These statements deal with your *feelings and thoughts in examination situations*. Please read every statement and choose among the four answers that answer which indicates how you generally feel during written classroom exercises, tests, or oral examinations, and what you think in such situations. Please check off the chosen answer for every statement.

There are no right or wrong answers. Please do not spend too much time on any statement but give the answer describing best how you *generally feel* and what you *generally think in examination situations* (written classroom exercises, tests, or oral examinations).

	Almost never	Some-times	Often	Almost always
1. I'm confident and relaxed	1	2	3	4
2. I have an uneasy, upset feeling	1	2	3	4
3. I'm thinking of doing poorly	1	2	3	4
4. I feel tense	1	2	3	4
5. I'm worrying about doing right	1	2	3	4
6. I'm thinking of the consequences of failing	1	2	3	4

Note. TAI–G = German adaptation of the Test Anxiety Inventory.

the TAS, which provides only a total test anxiety score, the TAI yields a total score and scores on factorially derived 8-item subscales for measuring worry and emotionality as the major components of test anxiety.

In developing the German adaptation of the TAI, the TAI–G, special attention was given to problems that arise from situational descriptions containing time references. In several widely used test anxiety questionnaires, there are a number of items with time references such as "before," "during," or "after" an examination. The problem with such time references is that the validity of a test anxiety item that inquires about worry or emotionality may be different for different stages of the examination process. For example, Spielberger (1980) found that one of his worry items, "I worry a great deal before taking an important examination," actually had a higher loading on the TAI Emotionality factor than on the Worry factor. The same was true for another worry item, "After an exam is over I try to stop worrying about it, but I just can't." Alternatively, worry and emotionality items that describe experiences during the exam situation all had dominant and unique loadings only on the expected factors.

To avoid time-dependent differences in worry and emotionality items in constructing the TAI–G, only items that referred to subjects' experiences during an actual examination situation were considered. This restriction seemed reasonable as only worry and emotionality cognitions during an actual exam exert a direct influence on performance. In a further effort to avoid an arbitrary combination of situational and response characteristics, all situational references in the TAI–G items were eliminated; the instructions for responding to this scale emphasized the experience of anxiety in examination situations (see Table 4.1). Wording the instructions in this manner also avoided the unnecessary repetition of specific situational references to exams, tests, or courses.

The construction of the TAI–G began with the translation of the original 20 TAI items. Because the factor loadings for the translated items in several samples were not very stable, the item pool was expanded. The initial pool consisted of 78 items from various American and German test anxiety scales, including translations of all 20 of the original TAI items. In accordance with the guidelines described above, each item was rewritten and presented in the rating scale format described in Table 4.1, which is essentially the same as in the original TAI (Spielberger, 1980).

The 78-item preliminary version of the TAI–G was administered to 477 adolescents, 13 to 16 years old (253 boys and 224 girls), enrolled in different grades (8 through 10) and school types (Gymnasium, Realschule, and Haupt-schule). Factor analyses based on the principal-factor method with varimax and oblimin rotations yielded well-defined Worry and Emotionality factors. The factor structure remained stable when the data for boys and girls, and for the different school types, were analyzed separately (Hodapp et al., 1982).

Despite the psychometric adequacy and empirical support for the validity of the new adaptation (Hodapp, 1989; Hodapp & Henneberger, 1982; Kerres, 1988; Liepmann et al., 1992; Schwarzer, 1984), some remaining questions stimulated reconceptualizing and expanding the scope of the TAI–G (Hodapp, 1991). The main reasons for doing so were twofold. The initial adaptation of the TAI–G included several items relating to confidence about performance, which constituted a separate factor. A second issue resulted from recent re-search regarding the emotional and cognitive processes that are linked with test anxiety, especially recognition of test worry as a more heterogeneous and differentiated cognitive construct (Heckhausen, 1982; Jerusalem, 1985; Sal-amé, 1984; Schwarzer & Quast, 1985; Stephan et al., 1983; Wine, 1982). Thus, in the development of the TAI–G, several new test anxiety items were added to assess existential worry, self-concern, anticipation of failure, and several other categories (for more detail, see Hodapp, 1991, 1994).

The revised questionnaire was given to 387 students enrolled in technical colleges (202 men and 185 women) and 326 grammar school students (147 boys and 179 girls) in Grades 5 through 13. The mean age of students at the technical colleges was 19.9 years (*SD* = 2.2 years); the mean age of the grammar school students was 15.8 years (*SD* = 2.9 years).

The data were evaluated by means of factor analyses, item analyses, and Rasch analyses (Hodapp, 1991). Exploratory factor analyses and item analyses yielded four subscales: Worry, Emotionality, Lack of Confidence, and Interference. Scores on the four subscales are added to yield a Total score. The Total scores and all subscales showed satisfactory alpha coefficients.

The means, standard deviations, and alpha coefficients for the revised TAI–G for the normative sample are presented in Table 4.2. Three of the four subscales (Emotionality, Lack of Confidence, and Interference) fit the Rasch model, providing convincing evidence of the unidimensionality of these sub-scales. These results provide evidence of the psychometric adequacy of the newly developed TAI–G and its subscales. It is interesting to note, however,

Table 4.2 Means, standard deviations, and alpha coefficients for the TAI–G total and subscales scores for the normative sample and university students

			University students	
Scale	No. items	Normative sample (*n* = 637)	Men (*n* = 152)	Women (*n* = 127)
TAI-G total	30			
M		66.15	61.04	69.28
SD		15.19	13.81	16.71
Alpha		.93	.93	.94
Worry	10			
M		24.53	22.33	24.43
SD		6.29	6.35	7.16
Alpha		.87	.90	.91
Emotionality	8			
M		14.97	15.67	19.32
SD		5.11	5.05	6.38
Alpha		.88	.90	.92
Lack of confidence	6			
M		15.04	12.96	14.61
SD		4.14	3.53	4.33
Alpha		.90	.86	.92
Interference	6			
M		11.60	10.08	10.93
SD		3.72	3.04	3.42
Alpha		.85	.80	.79

Note. TAI–G = German adaptation of the Test Anxiety Inventory.

that the Worry subscale did not fit the Rasch model, which reflects the fact that the worry construct appears to be heterogeneous.

A slightly modified version of the TAI–G has been used to study test anxiety in university students. The only difference between this version and the standard form is that in the instructions for the university students, *classroom exercises* was replaced with *written exams,* which may be regarded as analogous to written classroom exercises in schools. The means, standard deviations, and alpha coefficients for the TAI–G Total and subscale scores for a sample of university students from different faculties at the Heinrich-Heine-University Düsseldorf are also reported in Table 4.2. The mean age of university students was 23 years; no students of psychology were included in this sample. Comparing the means for the normative sample and the university students, the Lack of Confidence and Interference subscale scores for university students were somewhat lower than those of the normative sample, whereas the Emotionality subscale scores for the university students were higher, especially for the women.

The results of a factor analysis of the TAI–G items, with oblique factor rotation, are presented in Table 4.3, in which it can be noted that the factorial

Table 4.3 Item loadings for university students on the TAI–G Worry (W), Emotionality (E), Lack of Confidence (LC), and Interference (I) subscales

Item	Subscale	Factor			
		I	II	III	IV
2	W	.71			
4	W	.55			
6	W	.40			
9	W	.85			
10	W	.61			
14	W	.69			
17	W	.78			
21	W	.64			
27	W	.84			
23	W	.40	.45		
3	E		.66		
7	E		.70		
12	E		.75		
16	E		.89		
18	E		.73		
22	E		.84		
25	E		.82		
28	E		.79		
1	LC			.74	
8	LC			.84	
13	LC			.77	
20	LC			.69	
26	LC			.82	
29	LC			.88	
5	I				.58
11	I				.86
15	I				.51
19	I				.47
24	I				.89
30	I			.35	

Note. Only salient loadings of .35 or higher are reported.

structure of the TAI–G is strongly supported. All four TAI–G subscales are clearly identified; one Interference item failed to load on this factor and only one item had double loadings.

There is a clear-cut differentiation in the TAI–G between the worry and the emotionality components of test anxiety, which was quite obvious in the orthogonal rotation and still more pronounced for the oblique rotation reported in Table 4.3. The Worry and Emotionality subscales were moderately correlated (r = .58 for males and r = .58 for females), but these correlations are substantially lower than the W and E subscale correlations reported for the TAI by Spielberger et al. (1978). Given the moderate magnitude of the Worry and Emotionality subscale correlation coefficients in the TAI–G, worry and emotionality may be considered separate components of test anxiety as a situation-specific anxiety trait.

The identification and measurement of the different components of test anxiety have far-reaching implications for formulations of more precise hypotheses about anxiety–achievement relation. In addition to improved predictions in achievement situations, the worry–emotionality distinction has inspired the development of differential intervention programs for the modification of these two components of test anxiety (see Part III of this volume).

Situation-specific trait theory and measurement have contributed to new conceptions of the anxiety–achievement relation. Causal models of this relation indicate that behavioral changes in high test-anxious students, such as improvement in grades, are difficult to establish. Reducing test anxiety does not generally lead to better grades because test anxiety is influenced by study habits and attitudes, test-taking skills, individual differences in the perception and interpretation of examination situations, and feedback processes from actual behavior when taking tests. Taking into account the new dimensions of test anxiety identified in the revised TAI–G, Lack of Confidence and Interference, may contribute to even better predictions of achievement.

SUMMARY

The relation between test anxiety as a situation-specific anxiety trait and academic achievement was examined and discussed. Causal analyses of test anxiety–achievement relation provided evidence of a strong negative influence of worry on achievement and demonstrated that this relation was mediated by variables associated with the fear-of-failure motive. Following a critical evaluation of widely used measures of test anxiety, the development of a German adaptation of the TAI, the TAI–G, was briefly described. The results of studies of the factor structure of this new measure and information about its psychometric properties were reported.

II

ANTECEDENTS, CORRELATES, AND CONSEQUENCES OF TEST ANXIETY

5

Case Studies of Test-Anxious Students

William D. Anton and E. Michael Lillibridge
University of South Florida, Tampa, Florida, USA

Some test anxiety researchers have been concerned with describing the behavior of test-anxious persons in examination situations (Alpert & Haber, 1960; Liebert & Morris, 1967; Mandler & Sarason, 1952, 1953; I. G. Sarason, 1972, 1975a; Wine, 1971). Others have investigated the types of situations that have differential effects on the performance of students who are high or low in test anxiety (e.g., I. G. Sarason, 1958a, 1960, 1965; I. G. Sarason & Ganzer, 1962, 1963; I. G. Sarason & Koenig, 1965). In general, as discussed earlier in Chapter 1, the research evidence has shown that high test-anxious individuals are more self-centered and self-critical and more likely to experience feelings of inadequacy, helplessness, autonomic reactivity, and cognitive responses of a personalized, self-centered, derogatory nature in testing situations than are individuals who are low in test anxiety (e.g., Schwarzer & Jerusalem, 1992). These behaviors are maladaptive because they interfere with test performance.

Irwin G. Sarason has described the behavior of test-anxious individuals in evaluative situations as follows:

> *The highly test-anxious individual is one who is prone to self-centered interfering responses when confronted with evaluative conditions. Two response components have been emphasized by writers who espouse this view. One is emotional and autonomic reactivity—sweating, accelerated heart rate, etc. The other concerns cognitive events— e.g., saying to oneself while taking a test, "I am stupid. Maybe I won't pass."* (1975a, p. 175)

According to I. G. Sarason, saying such things to oneself during a test might interfere considerably with the task at hand, especially if the task requires acquisition of a new skill such as learning to drive a car or figuring out how to answer specific questions, for example, responding to questions on an income tax form.

Spielberger (1972a) has conceptualized test anxiety within the context of his trait–state anxiety theory. He defined test anxiety as a situation-specific form of trait anxiety, that is, *trait test anxiety* refers to individual differences in anxiety proneness in evaluative situations. According to this view, persons high

The authors would like to express their appreciation to Ms. Madeline Ross for her assistance in test scoring and data analysis and for comments in the preparation of this chapter.

in test anxiety perceive evaluative situations as more threatening and are more likely to experience elevations in state anxiety and worry than are persons low in test anxiety (Spielberger et al., 1976).

Because test anxiety research has been directed toward understanding the effects of situational factors on the behavior of test-anxious persons in evaluative situations, only limited information is available on the etiology and personality characteristics of test-anxious persons themselves. The chapters in Part I reviewed test anxiety theory and measurement. Part II examines the antecedents, correlates, and consequences of test anxiety. In this chapter, the developmental history and personality characteristics of six college students who requested treatment for test anxiety in a university counseling center are described. In essence, we examine what is usually regarded as error variance in experimental studies of test anxiety, with the hope that describing individual cases will provide information about test-anxious college students that is not readily available in empirical research.

SETTING AND CASE STUDY PROCEDURES

The case studies were conducted in the context of a test anxiety treatment program offered by the counseling center of a large state university. Printed announcements describing this program were distributed to the student body, supplemented by student newspaper coverage to ensure that members of the target population were made aware of the program. Six students who sought help for their test anxiety problems were selected for the case studies, and these students were scheduled for interviews with a staff psychologist (E. Michael Lillibridge) before they were assigned to treatment groups.

The clinical procedures used in the case studies included structured interviews in conjunction with psychological testing. Each student was interviewed in at least two 1 hour sessions, and some were interviewed three or more times. The interviews were loosely structured and consisted of three parts: (a) developing rapport, (b) obtaining a brief developmental history, and (c) exploring the antecedents and concomitants of test anxiety.

In the first interview, students were asked to recall their earliest manifestations of anxiety while taking tests and in other evaluative situations. This was followed by an inquiry into the frequency and intensity that test anxiety was experienced and the extent to which academic performance was disrupted by anxiety. The interviewer also attempted to identify specific situational factors that seemed to influence the degree to which each student experienced test anxiety. During the second interview, a brief developmental history was obtained. The interviewer also evaluated the students' current problems and any stresses that disrupted their effectiveness in academic settings. These topics were pursued further in subsequent interviews with some of the students.

The battery of structured psychological tests that was given to each student consisted of the Minnesota Multiphasic Personality Inventory (MMPI), the State–Trait Anxiety Inventory (STAI), the Test Anxiety Inventory (TAI), the Fundamental Interpersonal Relationship Orientation—Behavior (FIRO–B), and the Inner Child Inventory (ICI). The MMPI, the STAI, and the FIRO–B are commonly used in clinical settings. Spielberger et al. (1978), as described in earlier chapters, developed the TAI as a measure of test anxiety as a situation-specific personality trait. This scale yields a total score and has subscales for measuring worry (*W* subscale) and emotionality (*E* subscale) as components of test anxiety. The ICI, an unpublished experimental test developed by Mathis and Lillibridge (Mathis, 1978), was designed to measure six pathogenic parental attitudes that are thought to reflect important dimensions of adult life. These six attitudes are overcoercion, oversubmission, perfectionism, overindulgence, punitiveness, and neglect.

GENERAL CHARACTERISTICS OF THE SAMPLE

The scores on the TAI for all six students were uniformly high, but there were wide variations in scores on the other psychological tests. Diverse developmental patterns and historical experiences were also observed in the interviews. The degree of psychological disturbance found in these students reflected the full range of emotional problems observed at the counseling center.

Test anxiety was a relatively isolated problem for two students whose psychological and interpersonal functioning in all other areas was otherwise effective. Given the circumscribed nature of their test anxiety problem, these students were labeled *test-anxious students.* At the other end of a continuum of psychological disturbances, two students, labeled *emotionally disturbed,* had very serious emotional problems that severely disrupted their lives. Test anxiety for these students was only one manifestation of their unhappiness, discomfort, and highly generalized psychopathology. In between these extremes there were two students whose test anxiety was caused or exacerbated by a recent crisis; these students were labeled as having experienced a *critical life incident.* Thus, different historical antecedents and life stresses were associated with test anxiety in the three pairs of students who were the subjects of the case studies.

The components of the individual case descriptions are organized as follows: (a) the student's performance on the test anxiety and general anxiety measures, (b) an analysis of the student's test anxiety experiences, (c) a brief developmental history, (d) an evaluation of current situational stresses, and (e) a general description of the student's current psychological functioning as reflected in the psychological test data. The means and standard deviations for the TAI Total scores and scores on the *W* and *E* subscales and the STAI State Anxiety (A-State) and Trait Anxiety (A-Trait) subscales for each pair of students are listed in Table 5.1. The percentile equivalents of these scores for college undergraduates are also listed in this table.

The nature, historical development, and concomitants of test anxiety are described for each student. (These narratives have been modified to exclude personally identifying information; the names of the students in the sample have all been randomly changed.) The brief developmental history touches on each student's relationship with his or her parents, significant life events, and educational experiences that seemed to contribute to the development of the

Table 5.1 Means, standard deviations, and percentile ranks for three groups of students on the Test Anxiety Inventory and State–Trait Anxiety Inventory

	Groups			Total combined groups
Measure	Test anxiety	Critical life incident	Emotionally disturbed	
Trait Anxiety Inventory				
Total				
M	55.00	63.00	49.00	55.67
SD	9.90	14.14	1.41	9.97
%ile Rank[a]	85.00	95.00	75.00	86.00
Worry				
M	21.50	23.50	18.00	21.00
SD	6.36	6.36	2.83	4.90
%ile Rank	90.00	94.50	80.50	89.50
Emotionality				
M	22.50	27.00	20.00	23.16
SD	3.54	4.24	2.83	4.22
%ile Rank	78.00	94.00	67.50	80.00
State–Trait Anxiety Inventory				
T-Anxiety				
M	44.50	45.00	50.00	46.50
SD	10.61	7.07	12.73	8.50
%ile Rank	83.50	79.00	92.00	83.50
S-Anxiety				
M	45.00	42.00	48.00	45.00
SD	4.24	9.90	14.14	8.38
%ile Rank	84.50	75.00	89.50	84.50

Note. TAI = Test Anxiety Inventory; STAI = State–Trait Anxiety Inventory; A-Trait = Trait Anxiety subscale; A-State = State Anxiety subscale.

[a]Percentile ranks for grouped data represent the midpoint between percentile ranks assigned to men and the percentile ranks assigned to women, using the group mean as the raw score for entering the normative data tables.

student's test anxiety and his or her efforts to cope with it. Finally, current situational stresses that involve problems in living, relationships with peers, and contemporary problems affecting relationship with parents are summarized for each student.

Test Anxiety Pair

Test anxiety was the primary problem for these two students. Both of these students experienced high levels of tension and apprehension in the initial interview, and neither showed any consistency in how they coped with stress. However, they appeared to have stable family backgrounds, adequate social skills, and effective coping mechanisms for dealing with most life stresses. The primary motivation of these students in seeking treatment for their test anxiety was self-improvement rather than academic survival. Both students had maintained a level of acceptable academic performance before volunteering for the program.

Jane R., a 20-year-old female junior at the university who was majoring in education, volunteered for the test anxiety program after receiving an announcement that was sent to all dormitory residents. On the TAI, Jane's total score placed her in the 91st percentile for college students; her W and E scores were at the 95th and 82nd percentiles, respectively. In contrast, Jane scored at the 51st percentile for college students on the STAI A-Trait subscale. However, her score at the 80th percentile on the A-State subscale suggested that she was experiencing acute subjective discomfort during testing. On the basis of the information gathered in the interviews and psychological testing, this elevation in A-State appeared to be primarily associated with her decision to seek help for a relatively long-standing problem.

In the initial interview, Jane described her experience of anxiety and her general reactions to tests. As the deadline for an examination approached, she became progressively more preoccupied with anxious anticipation and worry. While taking a test, she experienced heightened tension and apprehension, but this did not result in "blocking" or affect her recall. After completing a test, Jane engaged in self-depreciatory thoughts about her performance until the examination was returned.

Jane reported that she had experienced test anxiety since high school, but did not recall any specific precipitating event or situation associated with her first experience. In high school, Jane's attention became more focused on her academic performance. She was successful in maintaining a B average throughout high school and in her first 2 years of college. She regarded test anxiety as a nagging problem that she wanted to change.

Jane was an only child from an upper-middle-class family. Both parents were college graduates; her father worked as an executive in a large corporation and her mother was an interior designer. Jane had a close relationship with both parents, who, in spite of their busy careers, invested a great deal of time and interest in her. She felt that both parents were affectionate and supportive, and their expectation that she graduate from college was the only pressure they ever put on her.

In high school, Jane was quite popular. She dated regularly, was a majorette, and was elected class treasurer in her senior year. She reported that academics were relatively easy and enjoyable. In college, Jane continued to enjoy her studies and planned to become a teacher on graduation. Her social adjustment was good, and she had a steady boyfriend whom she planned to marry. She reported experiencing only occasional minor conflicts with her boyfriend and her female roommate, which she attributed primarily to being nonassertive. These problems appeared to reflect Jane's reactions to the normal developmental stresses experienced by most students in her age group and were primarily manifested in her tendency to worry and ruminate over minor problems.

Psychological testing indicated that Jane was somewhat defensive and tended to minimize her problems. Under pressure, Jane tended to entertain pessimistic thoughts about the future (worries), and this pattern appeared to be primarily situational rather than an unstable personality characteristic. A conscientious person who maintained high expectations for herself, Jane was self-critical with regard to what she perceived as her own liabilities. She also tended to deny angry feelings and had difficulty accepting and expressing negative affect. Interpersonally, Jane seemed to be outgoing and gregarious, but she was somewhat anxious about being accepted and liked by others. When threatened with rejection, she responded with cautious anticipation and placed on others the burden of making the first move.

In summary, Jane appeared to be a relatively normal, emotionally mature young woman who had little difficulty in establishing and maintaining close interpersonal relationships. Although she tended to ruminate in response to stress, and experienced worry and anxiety about her test performance, her test anxiety appeared to be a relatively circumscribed problem.

The second student in the test anxiety pair was Jim A., a 23-year-old man who had recently transferred from a 2-year college and was a junior at the university majoring in business. Jim volunteered for test anxiety treatment after reading an ad describing the program in the student newspaper.

Jim's TAI Total score was at the 79th percentile, and his scores on the W and E subscales were at the 80th and 74th percentiles, respectively. This pattern of scores was consistent with Jim's self-reported reactions in test situations and suggested that both worry and emotionality responses occurred in examinations. On the STAI, Jim scored at the 92nd percentile on the A-Trait subscale and the 88th percentile on the A-State subscale. His extreme scores on the STAI seemed to reflect a reactive depression that appeared to result from a disconfirmation of his expectations regarding his academic performance.

In the interview, Jim described going "blank" and being unable to retrieve critical information when confronted with test questions that he could readily have answered. This situation made him intensely anxious while taking an exam, and he began to worry about his performance on subsequent test questions. As a result of this pattern, Jim became increasingly self-preoccupied during a test, and his test performance deteriorated. These disruptive test-taking experiences first occurred during Jim's second exam at the university, which was approximately 3 months before he volunteered for treatment.

Jim had never been test anxious before college; he was an A student throughout high school and maintained a B+ average in junior college. In his first exam at the university, Jim received a C even though he had spent many hours in preparation. He was shocked and disappointed with his performance and had anticipated making an A on the exam. As a result, he was taken totally by surprise and began to question his ability to succeed in college. Following this, Jim began worrying about upcoming exams and began blanking out and forgetting answers to questions on other tests. The answers to these same questions were easily retrievable once the exam had been completed and handed in. This problem plagued him for his entire first academic quarter at the university and was the major impetus for seeking treatment.

Exploration of historical antecedents revealed that Jim had a relatively stable family background. He was the oldest of two children and had a sister

2 years younger than he. He saw his parents as fairly permissive and felt he had a good deal of personal freedom to pursue his own goals and interests. His father worked as a plumber and his mother was a housewife. When Jim was 19, his father became paralyzed for life as the result of a job-related accident. To help his family financially in this difficult period, Jim was forced to quit junior college to become employed full-time and was unable to return for 3 years. Eventually, the financial strain lessened when Jim's mother obtained a part-time job and began receiving insurance benefits awarded to his father in connection with the accident. Following this, Jim returned to junior college for a year, after which he enrolled at the university.

Jim described himself both in high school and in junior college as a loner whose primary interest was his studies. He made few friends and spent a great deal of time by himself. It had only been in the past year that Jim began dating on a regular basis and, at the time of these interviews, was dating his first steady girlfriend. Jim stated that doing well in school was the main stress in his life, and he was quite concerned about his "average" performance.

Psychological testing indicated that Jim was experiencing a mild reactive depression and feeling that he could not cope adequately with his problems. He was pessimistic about the future, and his emotional state was characterized by feelings of anxiety and tension. Jim held very high expectations for himself, which were difficult to fulfill in reality. Interpersonally, he was shy and awkward in social situations, but somewhat more comfortable once an intimate (predictable) relationship was established.

For both students in the test anxiety pair, anxiety over test performance seemed to be an extension of their high performance standards in other areas. These students were both highly test anxious and appeared somewhat more prone to experience worry than emotionality in testing situations. Their levels of state anxiety, as measured by the STAI A-State subscale, were high, but on the A-Trait subscale, their performances showed little consistency. Neither of the students in this pair exhibited any gross psychopathology or appeared to be affected by major emotional conflicts.

These two students seemed to fit prevalent conceptions of the "typical" test-anxious student. They appeared to be bright, capable, and highly motivated to do well in an academic setting. They were free from serious psychopathology, and even their test anxiety did not prevent them from passing examinations. These students, however, are probably not representative of the population of students who request help for test anxiety in university counseling settings. For many students, test anxiety is much more debilitating, and they are forced to cope with it in the context of other problems that seriously disrupt the quality of their lives. In the next section, we explore the interplay of life crises and test anxiety for the critical life incident pair.

Critical Life Incident Pair

These two students' test anxiety resulted from, or was exacerbated by, a personal crisis in their lives. Both students in this pair had established some maladaptive patterns of coping with stress and experienced high levels of worry and emotionality in stressful situations. In addition to being test anxious, these students were dealing with a personal or family crisis that threatened their self-esteems. These stresses appeared to increase the value of successful academic performance as a way of proving each student's adequacy. This pattern resulted in an exaggeration of the importance of test performance, which was personalized to reflect each student's self-worth. Although their quality of life was lower as a result of these stresses, both students appeared to have averted a major emotional disorder.

Ted R. was a 25-year-old veteran who was a junior at the university majoring in engineering. He was referred for test anxiety evaluation by the vocational rehabilitation specialist in the counseling center after he expressed having recall problems during tests or examinations. Ted's TAI Total score was at the 99th percentile, indicating that he was an extremely test-anxious individual. His scores on the E and W subscales were at the 98th and 99th percentiles, respectively. On the STAI, he scored at the 90th percentile on the A-State subscale, which was almost identical to his standing on the A-Trait subscale (89th percentile). These scores indicated that in comparison to a normative sample of college students, Ted was a highly anxious individual whose test anxiety appeared to be one manifestation of a generalized pattern of social-evaluative anxiety.

In the initial interview Ted described becoming quite anxious and blanking out or forgetting answers to questions while taking a test. This disruptive experience was confined to test-taking situations, and most of the answers to these same test questions were easily retrievable once the examination was over.

Ted had been experiencing test anxiety for approximately 1 month before seeking treatment. According to his account, he first experienced test anxiety after failing a chemistry exam for which he had studied only minimally. In his next test experience, he received a C on an algebra exam for which he was prepared and on which he felt he should have done better. Again, he described blanking out during the test and recalling the previously inaccessible material by the time he arrived at his home. On two subsequent tests, he reported similar experiences, resulting in a failing grade on one occasion and a near failing grade on the other.

In a brief history, it was learned that Ted was the fourth of seven children and that his family background was relatively uneventful. His father was a civil engineer and his mother was employed part time. Ted described both parents as hardworking but somewhat neglectful, which he attributed to the large size of his family. His parents appeared to be fairly permissive and gave all of their children considerable latitude in making decisions and pursuing their own life goals. Ted expressed feeling alienated and distant from both parents.

Because of the large family size, Ted looked to two of his older brothers as role models. He described having a very close relationship with one brother, John, whom he admired, liked, and wished to emulate. One of the reasons Ted gave for choosing engineering as a major was that his older brother John had majored in engineering at another university. He described John as an engineering genius, even though John had not completed college.

Ted's early precollege education was unremarkable, and he experienced academic success throughout. He had no academic difficulties in junior and senior high school and maintained a B average. Ted had been enrolled at the university for the past 2.5 years and maintained a 2.8 grade point average.

Socially, Ted had been dating one girl exclusively for 4 or 5 months. Although this relationship was stable during most of that period, he felt that it was waning and sensed that they were drifting apart. At the time of the interview, they were dating sporadically, and each seemed more preoccupied with his or her own life. Ted stated that he enjoyed working with his hands and frequently tinkered with bicycles or did repairs on people's homes for spare cash. At the time of the interview, Ted's time was primarily divided between his girlfriend, hobbies, and school.

Before his junior year at the university, Ted began to take his academic pursuits more seriously and felt that his motivation for achievement had never been higher. He had previously been uninterested in school, regarded academics as "just for fun," and had not formulated any educational goals. Ted expressed being upset and perplexed that his new-found interest in achievement was not accompanied by greater academic success.

In the summer before this junior year in college, two things happened that appeared to have contributed directly to Ted's test anxiety. First, as a result of a summer job involving considerable manual labor (which he hated), Ted decided to make a serious commitment to work at school, earn good grades, and obtain an engineering degree. This factor, he said, was motivating him to earn a 4.0 grade-point average in school. The second factor was possibly more important, but was also less consciously perceived by Ted. At about the same time that he was reformulating his educational objectives, his older brother, John (whom Ted admired greatly), had a mental breakdown and was hospitalized for several weeks. At the time of his hospitalization, John, who appeared to be quite delusional and highly anxious, emphasized to Ted that he should stay in school, earn a 4.0 in engineering, and make something of his life. He reminded Ted that he had been a brilliant student and stated that he felt his present condition was the result of not working hard enough in college and making his life something worthwhile.

It appeared that Ted's identification with John and subsequent fear that he too was vulnerable to a similar breakdown influenced his disposition to overpersonalize his test performance. Although there were probably numerous sources of Ted's test anxiety, it seemed clear from his self-report that his brother's hospitalization and subsequent warning had a direct impact on his attitudes toward tests and behavior in testing situations.

Psychological testing indicated that Ted was a conscientious, perfectionistic, highly ordered individual who was self-critical and tended to worry and ruminate over problems. He appeared to be a highly anxious individual whose life was characterized by indecision and tension. His principal defenses seemed to be rationalization and intellectualization, which were only partially successful in binding his anxiety. His test data were consistent with those of persons who feel excessive anger and frustration, which they regard as unacceptable and hence must deny. He also experienced considerable state anxiety as a result of impending stresses for which he felt unable to cope. Interpersonally, he appeared to be somewhat cautious, although he could make friends with ease. His fear of intimate relationships was expressed in a hesitancy to become closely involved with others.

Overall, test and interview data supported the picture of a worried, constricted, moderately neurotic individual who was extremely test anxious and had unresolved identification conflicts with his older brother.

The second case in the critical life incident pair was Dale A., a 23-year-old male junior who had transferred to the university from a community college in New York State. Dale volunteered for test anxiety treatment after reading about the program in the student newspaper.

Dale obtained an overall TAI score at the 87th percentile, indicating that he was highly test anxious. His scores on the E and W subscales were at the 89th and 88th percentiles, respectively. These test results indicated that in testing situations he probably experienced both self-centered worry and heightened emotional responses that interfered with his test performance. His STAI scores were in the 61st percentile on the A-Trait subscale and in the 50th percentile on the A-State subscale. Compared with other college undergraduates, Dale's STAI scores suggested that he was generally anxious, but was apparently able to manage his anxiety in most situations.

In the initial interview, he described the nature of his subjective experiences in test or examination situations as a feeling of panic with associated memory blockage. This occurred primarily in response to test questions that he could not readily answer, and generalized to subsequent questions on the same exam. The consequence of this subjective process was invariably poor test performance. As was the case with the previous student in this pair, Dale remembered the answers he had been blocking once the examination was completed.

In his precollege educational experiences, Dale was an average student and reported no significant feelings of anxiety or dread associated with tests or examinations. His first experience with anxiety in test situations had occurred when he enrolled in junior college. He remembered feeling that he was not smart enough to be in college and began to worry about most forthcoming tests. This pattern continued with decreasing intensity for the 2 years before graduation, but Dale did not feel it interfered with his academic performance.

The problem was exacerbated when he enrolled at the university, and it began to occur during tests, whereas previously it was experienced in anticipation of a test or examination. On one of his first exams at the university, Dale reported severe blocking in association with worry about failure and not having sufficient time to complete the test. As a result, he received a failing grade, although he felt that he had adequately prepared for the test. After receiving information about his performance, Dale immediately began worrying about subsequent tests. He began to approach tests with feelings of panic and responded to these by rushing through questions and engaging in random guessing in an effort to escape from the situation. This pattern led to poorer than expected performance for Dale, and he made several Ds, whereas previously he had maintained a comfortable C average. The recognition that his grades were being adversely affected by anxiety and worry led Dale to apply for the test anxiety program.

His family history revealed that Dale was the second oldest of four boys. His mother had died when he was 16, and his father never remarried. His father's occupation required considerable traveling, and when his father was at home, Dale's relationship with him was unpredictable and characterized by frequent overt expressions of hostility. Dale stated that he never spent much time at home with his father because they always got into fights over everything. His father had a history of alcohol abuse and would come home heavily intoxicated three or four nights a week. This situation usually precipitated verbal and sometimes physical fights between Dale and his father. Dale stated that when his mother was alive, "she protected us from Dad," and her role in the family was that of a moderator; she tended to ease tensions wherever they occurred in the nuclear family. After his mother's death, Dale felt that his relationship with his father had steadily deteriorated.

In high school, Dale had little interest in academics and no aspirations to go to college. After high school, he worked at a wholesale grocery warehouse for several years and attended junior college on a part-time basis. During this time, he lived at home with his father and his youngest brother. Because he had maintained a C average in junior college, he began to feel that it might be possible to continue and graduate from a 4-year university. Though he still had doubts about his ability, he was accepted and enrolled in a 4-year institution in his home state. As a result of a serious physical fight with his father, Dale changed his decision to attend that university and had enrolled at this university instead. He began to feel that obtaining a 4-year degree was important in ensuring that he would not end up like his father.

Dale's social adjustment was characterized by numerous superficial relationships. He was a physically attractive man with good social skills, who appeared at ease in interpersonal situations. He was dating several women at the time of the interview, but did not appear to be emotionally committed to any of them. In his leisure time, he enjoyed sports, like racquetball and touch football, with several male friends.

Psychological testing indicated that Dale relied on denial to avoid unacceptable feelings, impulses, or problem areas. He appeared to be an independent, nonconforming individual, but this was not associated with inappropriate behaviors or significant disturbances in his function. Although he had a history of family conflicts (specifically with his father), he was generally an optimistic and self-confident person. He had some problems with impulse control, but this had not resulted in serious problems for him. Socially, Dale was a pleasant and outgoing person who was cautious and hesitant about forming close attachments for fear of getting hurt or rejected.

In summary, it appeared that his dramatic split with his father and the pressure he felt to make it on his own exacerbated Dale's anxiety over tests to the point that it began to interfere with his getting passing grades. He also believed that there was a significant qualitative difference in the intellectual abilities required to succeed at a university as compared with those needed to achieve in junior college. As academic success became increasingly important to him, so did the frequency with which he began to doubt his intellectual capabilities. Given his history and the importance he placed on academic achievement, Dale apparently was not able to control his responses to test situations as readily.

Both critical life incident students had explicit experiences that seemed to result in an exaggeration of the importance that successful academic achievement held for them. They used different coping styles in dealing with this demand, but neither student avoided the disruptive effects of test anxiety. For Ted, the desire to do well in college was complicated by some unsuccessful test experiences, an unpleasant summer job, and his brother's ominous message. These situations appeared to strain his defenses and heighten his tendency toward rumination and neuroticism. The strength of Ted's identification with his brother complicated his reactions to test situations and led him to exaggerate the negative consequences of failure. In contrast to Ted, Dale was more likely to deny anxiety and was somewhat more prone to impulsive behavior. He was determined to complete college but was plagued by doubts of his ability to succeed. Although he had been mildly test anxious for several years, his father's withdrawal of financial and emotional support greatly exacerbated this problem. Both students in this group appeared to be compulsively driven to succeed in college as a way of coping with a personal life crisis. The negative consequences of test anxiety seemed for them to result from their inability to view tests or examinations realistically.

Emotionally Disturbed Pair

The third pair included two students who were experiencing severe personal–emotional and social problems. Although these students described themselves as test anxious, they were also experiencing significant life disruption and major emotional conflicts. The general level of emotional disturbance suggested by the psychological tests was significantly more severe for these students than for those in the other two pairs.

The first student in the emotionally disturbed pair was Ralph S., a 20-year-old man who was referred for additional evaluation by a career counselor in the center. At the time of his initial contact, Ralph was majoring in political science in preparation for law school and was uncertain about his choice of a major.

On the TAI, Ralph scored overall at the 84th percentile, indicating he was highly test anxious. His scores on the W and E subscales were at the 76th percentile and 84th percentile, respectively, suggesting that he was somewhat more likely to experience emotional reactions to tests than worry. Relative to his TAI scores, he scored at the 61st percentile on the STAI A-Trait subscale. In combination with his test anxiety scores, these results suggest that Ralph was highly test anxious and that his disposition to experience state anxiety in general social situations was somewhat greater than the typical college undergraduate.

In describing his negative reactions to test situations, Ralph expressed his primary problem as being unable to screen out irrelevant information during an exam. When confronted with test questions, he would experience an "informational overload" and ruminate about all possible answers to a question. The inability to reduce the uncertainty inherent in this situation led to his feeling rotten, saying "to hell with it", and responding randomly to test questions. In high school, Ralph recalled feeling test anxious in some classes, but not in others. This pattern continued in college, but the intensity of these feelings became greater there.

There did not appear to be any discernible pattern in the courses or subject areas that made him feel anxious. His anxiety also seemed to be relatively independent of the amount of time spent in preparation for an exam or the importance of a class for completing his major course of study. Although Ralph remembered becoming anxious about tests while in high school, he did not recall his first experience and was unable to identify specific situations that interacted with his feelings of test anxiety. Ralph maintained a C average in both high school and college, but felt that his academic performance did not accurately reflect his intellectual ability and that this disparity was primarily due to test anxiety.

Ralph described being the second of four children and living with both parents until he left home at age 17. He described his father as very successful and a high achiever. When Ralph was 14, his father, who had been a fireman for more than 12 years, was involved in a car accident and was paralyzed and bedridden for 2 years. His father appeared undaunted by this situation, re-educated himself, and became successful at sales. At the time of the interview, Ralph's father owned a small business that was financially profitable.

Ralph stated that his father had pushed him to go to college and make something of himself. Although his father pressured him to excel, he described his relationship with him in positive terms. In contrast, his relationship with his mother was depicted as very poor. According to his account, this relationship was characterized by almost continuous verbal fights throughout his development, and he moved out of the house at age 17 primarily because of the stresses. Ralph stated that his mother clearly favored his younger brother, who "always got what he wanted from her." It appeared that he was quite jealous of his mother's affection for his younger brother, but denied that this was the case when confronted with this possibility.

In high school, Ralph had numerous friends, although he found it difficult to get really close to people. While in high school, he dated occasionally, but never developed a close relationship with a woman. Although he felt his grades were below his actual ability, he experienced no major setbacks in this regard.

In addition to test anxiety, Ralph had several other related problems. Two months before his interview, a woman he had been dating steadily for several weeks abruptly refused to see or speak with him. He had no warning and could not discern any apparent reason for her behavior. In response, he began feeling depressed and started to feel that his friends were also turning against him and deserting him. He was unable to give specific examples to illustrate this, and only alluded to their attitudes as evidence. Ralph felt quite hurt and lonely as a result and began to feel estranged from people.

The depressed affect and associated feelings of rejection and isolation that Ralph experienced appeared to be complicated by his passive style in dealing with hostile feelings and pressing identity conflicts. He described several situations in which he had been angry or annoyed at the behavior of others and felt unable to communicate this to them directly. As a result, he experienced frustration and helplessness, which he dealt with by increasing the emotional distance between himself and these persons for whom he gradually felt contempt.

The other major stress upsetting Ralph at the time centered on feedback he was receiving from other persons regarding certain effeminate gestures that he exhibited. In the past 6 months, the frequency of these kinds of comments had increased. At first, Ralph stated that he was not bothered by homosexual concerns and that these remarks had little impact on him. In a later interview, however, he acknowledged that he had been concerned about these gestures for some time, feared that he might be homosexual, and had experienced considerable anxiety as a result.

On the basis of this brief evaluation, Ralph was referred to a member of the treatment staff for more detailed assessment and psychotherapy. Although he initially followed through on the recommendation, this was short lived, and he discontinued both the test anxiety treatment program and individual therapy after 3 weeks. In the exit interview, his therapist described him as angry and annoyed, feeling that his problems were not that bad and he could handle them by himself. This was the same pattern of dealing with interpersonal stress that Ralph had used in numerous other life experiences.

Psychological testing indicated a strong tendency toward nonconformity in combination with defiant attitudes and values. People with similar test results tend to exhibit emotional passivity and often have unrecognized desires for dependency. These unmet dependency needs in the context of other factors can be expressed in masculine protest behavior or lead to the development of a feminine orientation with accompanying doubts about one's masculinity. Concerns about homosexuality or homosexual "acting out" are also possible expressions. Ralph's test data also suggested an excessive degree of hyperactivity and agitation over minor problems or annoyances. As a result of a low tolerance for frustration, Ralph may have undertaken many projects, but completed only a few of them. His problems were compounded by exceptionally high expectations in virtually all projects he undertook, and failure to complete them led to further anger and frustration. His avenues for expression of these feelings appeared limited, and insight into his emotional difficulties was minimal.

Overall, the test and interview data suggested a rather impulsive, immature, and emotionally unstable young man beset by numerous problems.

The second student in this group was Debbie B., a 19-year-old sophomore who was still undecided regarding her choice of major. Debbie's initial contact with the counseling center was through the clinical intake process, where she identified test anxiety and other personal problems as her presenting complaints.

On the TAI, Debbie obtained a total score at the 67th percentile, indicating that she was moderately test anxious. Although her TAI Total score was low compared with those of the other test-anxious students in our sample, this appeared to reflect her relatively low E subscale score (51st percentile) that was indistinguishable from the population of non-test-anxious college students. Consistent with her tendency to ruminate and make self-critical statements to herself, her TAI W subscale score was at the 85th percentile. On the STAI, Debbie scored at the 98th percentile on the A-State subscale and at the 96th percentile on the A-Trait subscale. This reflected a highly generalized pattern to interpret numerous social–evaluative situations as threatening and to respond to these interpretations with frequent and intense elevations in state anxiety. Her pattern of scores on the STAI suggested that she perceived herself to be in danger and as a result experienced considerable emotional tension and apprehension.

In her first interview she described freezing up while writing papers for courses and worrying in advance of tests about her ability to successfully pass them. During most exams, however, she experienced only moderate levels of tension or apprehension (state anxiety) and did not feel that her test performance suffered greatly as a result. Debbie first experienced test anxiety late in high school and in her first year of college. Although she was able to approximate when she first became test anxious, she was unable to recall the specific occasion or accompanying situational factors. She maintained a C average in high school and obtained a 2.6 grade point average in her first year of college.

A brief history of Debbie's family life revealed that she came from a four-member family and had one sister who was 3 years younger than she. Her parents were college graduates and were both gainfully employed at the time of the interview. Her father was an engineer and her mother had owned a dress shop for some years. She recalled having numerous arguments with her mother and described her as a woman with a bad temper who got angry easily. As a result, Debbie felt her relationship with her mother had gradually become more distant, and she expressed wishing they could be closer. She depicted her father as a very opinionated and difficult person to know and felt emotionally estranged from him. Although she expressed wanting to be closer to both of her parents, she perceived them as wanting to keep her at a distance.

In high school, Debbie began to experiment with marijuana and to associate with a dysfunctional group of friends. Because of this, her difficulties with her parents were exacerbated, and she was placed on restriction much of the time. She felt that her parents always expected a great deal from her academically and put considerable pressure on her to do well in college. She feared disappointing her parents and began worrying about doing well in college and thinking about her academic performance much of the time.

Although Debbie identified test anxiety as her principal concern, she described a number of additional problems that were disturbing her at the time.

In addition to being test anxious, Debbie experienced frequent headaches, had difficulty sleeping, and described periods of hyperventilation and panic that resembled acute anxiety attacks. At the time of the interview, Debbie's parents were in the process of divorcing, and this was producing additional stress for her. In the past, her parents had made many important decisions for her, and she had difficulty making decisions independently. The recognition that her parents would soon be divorced appeared to have heightened her need to rely on them at a time when they were even more preoccupied with their own problems and virtually ignoring her. As a result, she became depressed, began worrying almost constantly about doing well in school, and started to experience intense anxiety that frightened her. In addition, her worry and rumination appeared to generalize to a wide variety of situations and circumstances.

Many of Debbie's interpersonal relationships in high school were superficial, involved moderate drug use, and on one occasion resulted in minor difficulty with the law. Although she dated sporadically, Debbie had no close attachments with men in high school or in college. She had several close girlfriends with whom she had frequent arguments and from whom she felt alienated. Debbie's interpersonal difficulties appeared to result from her compulsive needs to be liked and seek reassurance from others. To gain affection from men, she became sexually indiscriminate and frequently engaged in sexual intercourse with men she knew only casually and for whom she felt little attraction. These episodes were followed by guilt and the recognition that she had not gained the affection she so desperately needed. In response to this, Debbie often got intensely angry at these men, resented them, and had contemplated a homosexual relationship as an alternative to this pattern.

Psychological testing indicated that Debbie experienced chronic psychological problems characterized by tension, apprehension, excessive worry, and rumination. Her self-esteem was extremely low, and she was beset with feelings of inadequacy and inferiority. Her overly passive interpersonal behaviors appeared to reflect strong underlying dependency needs. She showed generally poor judgment in response to stress and was easily overwhelmed by the everyday pressures of living. Although she relied heavily on denial, rationalization, and intellectualization as defenses, these mechanisms were not sufficient to contain her anxiety.

Both students in the emotionally disturbed pair identified test anxiety as their major problem. This was confirmed in the psychological interviews and by their TAI scores. Their pattern of scores on the W and E subscales of the TAI were opposite, but consistent with their respective coping strategies for dealing with perceived stresses. For Ralph, test or examination situations clearly appeared to represent a situation-specific stress that he interpreted as threatening to his self-esteem. His response to the frustration associated with the information overload he experienced in testing situations was characteristic of his general pattern in other areas. Although this coping style appeared to be effective in managing general social–evaluative stresses, the consequences of this pattern in examination situations led to poorer than expected grades on tests or examinations. In contrast, Debbie experienced a more moderate level of test anxiety, and the negative consequences on her academic performance were less pronounced. For Debbie, test anxiety appeared to be less of a situation-specific threat than an extension of her general pattern of chronic tension and rumination. Evaluative stress represented only one of the numerous situations she interpreted as threatening, and her pattern of coping appeared to be relatively consistent throughout.

SAMPLE COMPARISONS

The individual cases considered in this chapter appear to represent distinguishable characteristics. Students in the test anxiety pair exhibited a moderate tendency to worry or ruminate, and their test anxiety seemed to reflect an extension of this general pattern to a situation they identified as threatening. Although highly test anxious, these students obtained total TAI scores that were intermediate between the critical life incident and emotionally disturbed pairs. They also exhibited higher W than E subscale scores. Both students in the critical life incident pair were experiencing stressful life events that were not directly related to test anxiety, but appeared to function as a contributing factor in heightening their levels of test anxiety. As a group, these students had the highest TAI Total, W, and E scores in the entire sample. Although one could speculate on the reasons for the elevated TAI scores, we avoid this temptation, given the small sample size. Last, students in the emotionally disturbed pair were experiencing major emotional conflicts, and their test anxiety experiences seemed to reflect a generally disturbed lifestyle. Although students in this group initially complained of problems with test anxiety, their scores on TAI Total, W, and E subscales were the lowest for the entire sample. This finding was particularly interesting because it occurred in the context of the highest STAI A-Trait and A-State subscale scores for the three pairs. Thus, for the emotionally disturbed pair, scores on the test anxiety and general anxiety measures were consistent with their generalized problems in living.

One of the factors that needs to be briefly explored is the method by which students were selected for this study. It should be understood that the test anxiety treatment program was only one of numerous services offered at the counseling center. As a comprehensive treatment facility for students, the center's counseling services include individual therapy, crisis intervention, career counseling and guidance, and reading and study skills development. The students in our sample were referred from two primary sources, those who were self-referred (volunteered) specifically for the test anxiety treatment program and those who were referred directly for test anxiety evaluation from other professionals on the counseling center staff. The latter students usually sought help for a career or personal problem, and in the interview indicated that test anxiety was a major problem.

In our sample, there was a direct relation between problem severity and the apparent basis for initial contact. Both students in the test anxiety pair volunteered specifically for test anxiety treatment after becoming aware of the program through announcements or other printed media. The modes of entry for the two students in the critical life incident pair were different. For Dale, application to the program was the same as for the two students described previously. Ralph, however, was referred specifically for a test anxiety evaluation by the vocational rehabilitation specialist in the counseling center after the specialist had conferred with him about this problem. Both students in the emotionally disturbed pair were referred to the program by professional counselors on the staff. Thus, there appears to be a relation between the basis for initial contact and problem severity for students who are test anxious. This pattern suggests that students who volunteer for test anxiety treatment in response to program announcements may disproportionately represent only a limited segment of the continuum of psychological problems.

The articulation between client characteristics and treatment techniques is an important aspect of the task confronting psychotherapy research (e.g., Zoller & Ben-Chaim, 1990). In this chapter, we have pointed to some potentially important antecedents and concomitants of test anxiety in college students. Progress in test anxiety treatment could be facilitated by a greater understanding of students who label themselves as test anxious. It is likely that, at a minimum, this will entail a thorough knowledge of etiological factors, personality characteristics, and present stresses. It is our hope that these case presentations have elucidated important dimensions for further research and evaluation.

SUMMARY

In this chapter, we have attempted to take a somewhat in-depth look at the antecedents and concomitants of test anxiety in a college population. On the basis of this brief review, it appears that a wide variety of psychological factors may contribute to a student's experiencing test anxiety. Factor analytic studies of the TAI have demonstrated empirically that even students who identify themselves as test anxious experience different patterns of cognitive and emotional responses to the threat associated with tests or examinations. Although caution should be exercised in generalizing on the basis of such a small sample, the case studies reviewed in this chapter suggest that students who identify test anxiety as a primary concern show little consistency as a group.

6

Test Anxiety, Hemispheric Lateralization, and Information Processing

James D. Papsdorf and Jess H. Ghannam
University of Michigan, Ann Arbor, Michigan, USA

John Jamieson
Lakehead University, Ontario, Canada

In Chapter 5, Anton and Lillibridge looked at psychological antecedents of test anxiety. In this chapter, physiological antecedents are examined. Although research has clearly demonstrated that test anxiety can impair academic performance (Hembree, 1988; Pekrun, 1992; Seipp, 1991), there is as yet little evidence relating anxiety to the neurological and cortical factors that mediate cognitive processing of information. However, reviews by Galin (1974) and Suberi and McKeever (1977) have shown that the two cerebral hemispheres process information quite differently. The left hemisphere, which is the neurological representative of the right side of the body, is characterized by logical approaches to processing verbal information. In contrast, the right hemisphere, the neurological representation of left body processes, is more holistic, global, and spatial, suggesting that the right hemisphere is uniquely involved in processing information associated with emotional stimuli.

The research reported in this chapter investigates the association of test anxiety with right hemisphere utilization. After first considering perceptual, psychophysiological, and neurological evidence of greater activation of the right hemisphere in processing stimuli that evoke emotional reactions, a Right Hemisphere Emotional Specialization and Dissociation (RHESD) model was developed to explain the performance deficits that accompany high levels of test anxiety. On the assumption that lateral eye movements are indicative of hemispheric utilization, the RHESD model was evaluated by examining the eye movement patterns of students in an examlike situation to determine whether a right-hemisphere-determined pattern is more prevalent in high test-anxious students. On the further assumption that hand temperature reflects the influence of the contralateral hemisphere, we evaluate the RHESD model by examining right and left middle digit temperature during the presentation of threatening test-taking imagery.

RIGHT HEMISPHERE AND EMOTIONS

Lesion data first suggested the left hemisphere's unique contribution to verbal processing. Therefore, it is not surprising that lesion data were initially responsible for pointing to the unique functions of the right hemisphere in emotional responding. Goldstein (1939) was so impressed with the marked affect displayed by stroke patients with left hemisphere lesions that he labeled the syndrome *catastrophic reaction*. In describing the behavior of left hemisphere lesion patients, Gainotti (1972) stated, "sometimes a slight stimulus was sufficient to trigger a violent emotional storm, with tears, irritation, vocative utterances and sharp refusals to go on with the examination, but these reactions vanished quickly in a few minutes or even seconds" (p. 47).

These lesion effects have generally been interpreted as resulting from the loss of inhibiting functions in the lesioned hemisphere. The catastrophic reaction associated with a left hemisphere stroke, for example, is assumed to reflect the loss of left hemispheric inhibition of emotional functions located in the right hemisphere. Hecaen et al. (1951) and Denny-Brown et al. (1952) have described a complementary response, an "indifference reaction," displayed by right hemisphere stroke patients. Similar responses have also been observed in nonstroke patients undergoing reversible unilateral hemispheric function suppression by means of the Wada procedure (left or right intracarotid artery injection of sodium amytal).

A growing body of evidence indicates greater right hemisphere participation in the reception, processing, and retention of emotional material. Haggard and Parkinson (1971) used a dichotic listening task and presented nonlesioned subjects with "babble" in one headphone and sensible sentences in the other. They found greater comprehension of the affective qualities of the material with left ear (right hemisphere) presentation. Suberi and McKeever (1977) reported faster reaction times to lateralized tachistoscopic presentations of emotionally expressive human faces in a discrimination task with left visual field (right hemisphere) presentation. Dimond and Farrington (1977) used a specially designed lens arrangement to present three movies to either the left or the right visual field. Although these movies involved a travelogue, a cartoon, and a surgical operation, they were all judged to be more unpleasant and horrifying when projected to the left visual field (right hemisphere) than to the right visual field. There is also evidence from electroencephalogram data that greater right hemisphere activation accompanies emotional imagery. Davidson and Schwartz (1976) observed less parietal alpha in the right hemisphere during emotional imagery production than during nonemotional imagery periods.

The role of the right hemisphere in emotional processing has been impressively demonstrated in research with split-brain patients. Gordon and Sperry (1969) reported that right hemisphere exposure to a nude figure was accompanied by giggling and embarrassment that the subject was unable to explain. Gazzaniga (1970) described the case of a split-brain patient who attacked his wife with his left hand while his right hand came to her assistance.

Hysterical conversion reactions, for example, hysterical paralysis and stocking anesthesia, provide further evidence of greater right hemisphere involvement in processing emotional information. Galin et al. (1977) observed left-sided symptoms for 30 of 42 (71%) females with lateralized conversion reactions. Even for the three left-handed females in their sample, the conversion reaction in each case was on the left side. Similar observations have been reported by Stern (1977) for both right and left-handed women. The conversion symptoms are presumed to reflect the more emotionally active right hemisphere exerting its influence through predominantly crossed sensorimotor pathways.

The above evidence has prompted a number of investigators to theorize about the contributions of the right hemisphere in everyday psychological functioning. Gain (1974, 1977) has suggested, for example, that phenomena identified by the psychoanalytic model can be explained in terms of cerebral specialization. He noted that repression and dissociation may reflect greater right hemisphere functioning, and that primary process thinking, in which images rather than words appear to be the major component, can be identified with the functions of the right hemisphere.

The RHESD Model

In view of the data just considered, we reasoned that a model of relative hemispheric engagement might account for the performance differences observed in students under conditions of low and high test anxiety. Under low-anxiety conditions, according to the RHESD model, there is relatively greater engagement of the left hemisphere—the hemisphere that is specialized for handling verbal comprehension and expression. Because the verbal dimension is usually a major factor in examinations, performance is facilitated. Under high test anxiety conditions, the model assumes that the right hemisphere is relatively more actively engaged. When this less verbally developed hemisphere is more in control, the verbal demands of an examination are less adequately met because academic material encoded in the left hemisphere is more difficult to retrieve.

The studies reported in this chapter were designed to evaluate the validity of the RHESD model. In these investigations, hemispheric activation was inferred from eye movement patterns and digit temperature responses. Anxious individuals were expected to show eye movement patterns indicative of greater right hemisphere engagement. Students with high test anxiety were also expected to show lower left-hand middle digit temperatures during the presentation of threatening test-taking imagery, reflecting greater emotional arousal mediated by the influence of the contralateral hemisphere.

Lateral Eye Movements

When a subject is asked to answer a question requiring thought, for example, "What is the cubic root of 27," he or she will generally gaze to the right or left while composing the answer. The direction of the gaze is thought to be determined by the cerebral hemisphere that is most activated in processing the information being presented (Kinsbourne, 1972). Questions dealing with verbal information generally evoke lateral eye movements (LEMs) to the subject's right, that is, in the direction *away* from the more active hemisphere. In responding to questions of a spatial nature, the eye movements are generally to the subject's left.

The effect of question content on LEMs is most often found in the absence of experimenter–subject eye contact (Gur & Gur, 1975; Harris, 1976). However, when the experimenter maintains eye contact while asking the question, the subject's gaze direction appears to be independent of question content. Gur and Gur (1975) found, for example, that about 80% of a group of 35 male subjects directed more than 70% of their LEMs to either the right or the left. The Gurs suggested that, under conditions of heightened social tension, which experimenter–subject eye contact is presumed to generate, subjects revert to the hemisphere they most frequently use in stressful situations. The RHESD model assumes that those individuals who showed the left LEM pattern were more stressed in this examlike situation.

Two additional observations contributed to our use of the LEM assessment procedure in evaluating the RHESD model of test anxiety. First, Gur and Gur (1975) reported that subjects who showed a left LEM preference (i.e., greater right hemisphere engagement) expressed a larger number of psychosomatic complaints. This finding was consistent with Galin et al.'s (1977) observations that lateralized conversion reactions occur more frequently on the left side. Second, Schwartz et al. (1975) have observed that questions containing emotional content are more likely to elicit left LEMs than nonemotional questions. Thus, the question "Describe your father's face the last time you said goodbye" is more likely to evoke left LEMs than the question "Think of a penny. What direction does Lincoln face?" In replicating Schwartz et al.'s results, Tucker et al. (1977) found that the frequency of left LEMs increases when subjects are stressed, indicating greater right hemisphere involvement under more stressful conditions.

The observations and experimental findings of Schwartz et al. (1975) and Tucker et al. (1977) are consistent with the RHESD model and suggest that, in an experimental test of the model, individuals who are especially tense or anxious during the LEM assessment procedure will show the left eye movement pattern. Moreover, because LEM assessment is similar to an examination, we would expect high test-anxious students to be more likely to show the left LEM pattern.

Lateralized Digit Temperature Response

Although lateral differences in several psychophysiological measures have been reported by a number of investigators (e.g., Bull & Gale, 1975; Varni et al., 1971), there have been few attempts to ascertain whether such differences reflect specialized hemispheric activity. In one of the first investigations of the relation between hemispheric activity and psychophysiological changes, Myslobodsky and Rattok (1975, 1977) recorded electrodermal activity from both left and right fingers while subjects were presented with verbal–numerical (left hemisphere) and visual imagery (right hemisphere) tasks. They found greater right hand electrodermal activity for the verbal–numerical tasks and greater left hand activity for the visual imagery tasks. Thus, greater electrodermal activity was associated with the hand contralateral to the active hemisphere.

Ketterer and Smith (1977) presented subjects with verbal (left hemisphere) or musical (right hemisphere) stimuli and found differences in electrodermal activity similar to those reported by Myslobodsky and Rattok (1975, 1977), but these differences were not statistically significant. Diekhoff et al. (1978) also failed to detect significant lateralized galvanic skin response effects with hemisphere-specific tasks, but significant decreases in electromyographic activity and significant increases in finger pulse volume (increased blood flow) were associated with the contralateral arm and hand, respectively. Because finger temperature varies directly with pulse volume, the finger temperature changes recorded in a given hand appear to reflect the influence of the contralateral hemisphere.

The RHESD model can also be assessed by bilateral monitoring of finger temperature during the presentation of threatening test-related imagery. Boudewyns (1976) has observed that digital skin temperature from the non-dominant hand increases during relaxation and decreases when subjects are threatened with shock. Similarly, Crawford et al. (1977) have reported significant decreases in the temperature of a digit of the dominant hand in subjects discussing anxiety-provoking topics, providing additional evidence that digit temperature can be used as an index of stress. In testing the RHESD model, it was predicted that under visualized exam-stress conditions, temperature reductions in the left middle digit (reflecting the influence of the right hemisphere) would be greater than those in the right middle digit. A second prediction was that this effect would be greater for high test-anxious students.

EXPERIMENT 1: PERSONALITY CORRELATES OF LEM PATTERNS AND DIGIT TEMPERATURE

Papsdorf et al. (1979) assessed the LEMs of 34 right-handed women enrolled during the summer term in an upper division, undergraduate psychology class. These students volunteered to participate in a "test-anxiety study" to receive additional course credit. They ranged in age from 18 to 25 years, with a mean age of 21.3 years. All of the participants had scores of .70 or higher on the Edinburgh Handedness Inventory (Oldfield, 1971), indicating that they were clearly right handed.

Procedure

LEMs were assessed in a sound-attenuating chamber in which the walls were covered with a homogeneous white cloth. Participants were seated at a table directly opposite, and at a distance of 1.2 m from, a male undergraduate experimenter. Each participant was asked a series of 30 questions (Gur & Gur,

1975); the experimenter attempted to maintain eye contact during the question presentation. Following each question, the direction of the first eye movement that subtended an arc of at least 5° was recorded.

Eye movements were scored as left or right if 5° or more lateral component was present. The remaining eye movements were scored as up or down, stares, or nonscorable movements. Stares indicated no break in experimenter–subject eye contact between the end of question presentation and the time the subject began her answer. Nonscorable movements were scored when (a) the subject broke eye contact before question completion or (b) no experimenter–subject eye contact was obtained during question presentation. The participants were not aware that eye movements were being monitored.

Subjects were classified as left movers or right movers if 70% or more of their LEMs were consistently to either the left or the right, respectively. The same criterion was used by Gur and Gur (1975) in classifying their subjects. Women who did not meet the lateral movement criterion were assigned to the bidirectional group. Of the 34 women, 11 were classified as left movers, 8 as right movers, and 15 as bidirectionals.

Following LEM assessment, the women completed several anxiety measures, including the State Anxiety (S-Anxiety) and Trait Anxiety (T-Anxiety) subscales of the State–Trait Anxiety Inventory (STAI; Spielberger et al., 1970), the Test Anxiety Inventory (TAI; Spielberger, 1980), and the Irrational Beliefs Test (IBT; Jones, 1969). In their research with college undergraduates, Spielberger et al. (1978) have reported that TAI Worry (W) subscale scores correlated negatively with academic grades, whereas the correlation between TAI Emotionality (E) subscale scores and grades was essentially zero.

The IBT was developed on the basis of Ellis's (1962) rational–emotive therapy and contained questions such as "It is important to me that others approve of me," "I hate to fail at anything," and "There is a right way to do everything." The participants were instructed to indicate the extent to which they agreed with the IBT statements.

In recording bilateral hand temperature, the participants were seated in a comfortable reclining chair in a temperature-controlled room (22 °C), and Yellow Spring thermistors were lightly taped to the volar surface of the distal phalange of each middle finger. Skin temperature was monitored by means of two Coulbourne Temperature Biofeedback Modules feeding into two B & K Digital Voltmeters. These measures were taken while the participants listened to two audiotapes. The first presented 5 min of progressive relaxation exercises modeled after Bernstein and Borkovec (1973). The second was a test anxiety tape that consisted of an 8-min presentation of progressively more threatening exam-related imagery.

Results and Discussion

The means and standard deviations of the anxiety and irrational beliefs measures for the three LEM groups are presented in Table 6.1. Contrary to expectation, the left movers did not score significantly higher than the right movers on any of these measures. However, the bidirectionals scored signifi-

Table 6.1 Means and standard deviations of self-report measures for Experiment 1

Measure	Left movers (n = 11)		Right movers (n = 8)		Bidirectionals (n = 15)		F
	M	SD	M	SD	M	SD	
Test Anxiety Inventory	37.64	3.82	35.00	5.97	54.33	9.95	23.83***
Worry subscale	12.46	9.97	12.00	2.07	18.67	5.39	11.22***
Emotionality subscale	17.09	2.70	15.88	3.68	25.00	3.05	31.30***
S-Anxiety	37.81	4.95	33.50	5.65	49.67	8.05	18.75***
T-Anxiety	34.27	7.43	33.25	3.88	49.46	9.27	17.08***
Irrational Beliefs Test	265.91	39.95	272.00	16.25	322.13	27.85	16.91***

Note. S-Anxiety = State Anxiety subscale of the State–Trait Anxiety Inventory (STAI); T-Anxiety = Trait Anxiety subscale of the STAI.
***$p < .001$

cantly higher (all $ps < .01$) than either the left or the right movers on all six measures, suggesting that high levels of anxiety and irrational beliefs were associated with the absence of a directional gaze preference.

The failure to find any association between gaze preference and anxiety might reflect motor excitation that caused the highly anxious students to move their eyes more frequently. There are, however, two observations that make this unlikely. First, the initial LEMs following the presentation of each question were recorded, so even if anxious individuals moved their eyes more frequently, this would not explain why the first movement following the question presentation failed to show a consistent direction. Second, when the number of stares was examined for each group, the bidirectionals had a mean of 3.06 compared with means of 1.81 for left movers and 1.75 for right movers. Although not statistically significant, these differences suggest that the bidirectionals tended to maintain eye contact before answering, which was opposite to what would be expected according to a motor excitability hypothesis.

The relation between preferred LEM direction and anxiety was assessed more precisely by determining reflective gaze consistency (RGC) scores for each subject. The RGC scores, which ranged from 50% to 100%, measured the degree to which the participants showed a consistent gaze preference regardless of direction. Correlations between the RGC scores and the anxiety and IBT measures are reported in Table 6.2. The high negative correlations of the gaze consistency scores with the self-report measures indicated that the participants who showed less consistency reported greater anxiety.

The moderate positive correlations between IBT scores and the three anxiety measures that are reported in Table 6.2 were consistent with the correlations reported by Goldfried and Sobocinski (1975). A closer examination of the individual IBT items indicated that students who scored high on the TAI were more likely to report that irrational philosophies, such as "I must do well to enjoy the respect of others," were especially applicable to them. These findings support the use of intervention strategies that attempt to alter anxiety-evoking cognitions, such as Meichenbaum's (1977) cognitive coping and Ellis's (1962) rational–emotive therapy, in the treatment of test-anxious students.

Table 6.2 Intercorrelation matrix of self-report measures and reflective gaze
consistency for Experiment 1

Measure	1	2	3	4	5
1. Test Anxiety Inventory	—	.78**	.75**	.62**	−.79**
2. T-Anxiety		—	.87**	.62**	−.75**
3. S-Anxiety			—	.45**	−.73**
4. Irrational Beliefs Test				—	−.70**
5. Reflective gaze consistency					—

Note. T-Anxiety = Trait Anxiety subscale of the State–Trait Anxiety Inventory (STAI); S-Anxiety = State Anxiety subscale of the STAI.
**$p < .01$.

The data for the bidirectionals were also examined to determine whether LEM direction preference was related to question content. Because the questions contained verbal, arithmetic, and spatial content, it could be argued that bidirectionality could reflect content-related, differential hemispheric activation. Analysis of the individual protocols failed to provide any evidence that the bidirectionals gave more left LEMs to spatial questions and more right LEMs to verbal questions. The finding that question content was unrelated to gaze preference in the present study was consistent with most but not all studies that have used an 'experimenter facing subject' gaze assessment procedure (Ehrlichman & Weinberger, 1978).

Over the course of the 5-min relaxation tape, right digit temperature increased approximately 0.41 °C and left digit temperature increased 0.24 °C; from the end of the relaxation tape to the end of the stress tape, left and right digit temperatures decreased by 0.88 °C and 0.72 °C, respectively. Because the paired *t*-test comparisons of these differences were not statistically significant, the hypothesis that greater left hand reactivity would be associated with stressful test imagery was not supported.

To investigate the relation between digit temperature and test anxiety, the participants were assigned to either high or low test anxiety groups on the basis of a median split of their TAI scores.

Surprisingly, the low test-anxious group had significantly lower temperatures during the entire experiment, but the results of subsequent investigations, in which high test-anxious subjects tended to have lower temperatures, suggested that this was an anomalous finding. Comparisons within the high and low test anxiety groups indicated that, over the relaxation exercise, left and right digit temperature increased 0.51 °C and 0.61 °C, respectively, for the low-anxious subjects and increased 0.004 °C and 0.24 °C, respectively, for the high-anxious subjects. Paired *t*-test comparison showed no significant differences for these temperature changes.

While listening to the stress tapes, low-anxiety subjects showed left and right digit temperature drops of 0.70 °C and 0.62 °C, respectively, and high-anxious subjects showed left and right drops of 1.04 °C and 0.80 °C, respectively, with the difference in the left and right hand digit temperature drops approaching significance ($p = .11$). Although both the high and low test anxiety groups showed slightly greater temperature drops in the left hand during the stress tape, which was consistent with the hypothesis of greater left hand reactivity due to greater involvement of the contralateral right hemisphere, these differential effects only approached statistical significance. Thus, the temperature data yield little support for the RHESD model.

EXPERIMENT 2: LEM PATTERNS, DIGIT TEMPERATURE, AND PERSONALITY CORRELATES OF TEST ANXIETY

The purpose of the second study was to evaluate the generality of the unanticipated finding in Experiment 1 that high test anxiety was especially prevalent among women who failed to show a LEM preference. Whereas the participants in the first study were enrolled in an advanced undergraduate course, the participants in the second study were women who were participating in a widely advertised test anxiety alleviation program. The 31 women in this second sample scored in the right-handed direction on the Edinburgh Handedness Inventory (EHI), with scores ranging from 0.10 to 1.00.

The same LEM and digit temperature assessment procedures described in Experiment 1 were used in this study. Assessment of reflective gaze preference proved to be more difficult, however, because a number of subjects averted their gaze during question presentation or completely avoided eye contact, which resulted in a large number of nonscoreable responses. Therefore, to increase reliability as well as comparability with the first study, only the data for 21 subjects with 15 or more scoreable eye movements were included in the analyses.

Using the 70% gaze consistency criterion, there were 9 left movers, 3 right movers, and 9 bidirectionals in the sample. The means and standard deviations of the anxiety and IBT measures for the three LEM groups are reported in Table 6.3. The results for this more clinical group were similar to those obtained in Experiment 1. The bidirectionals had significantly higher scores on the TAI and the TAI E subscale than did the combined groups (because of the small number of right movers) of left and right movers. Except for the IBT measure, a similar pattern was obtained for the other anxiety measures, but these differences were not statistically significant. Consistent with the results of Experiment 1, examination of LEM direction in bidirectionals failed to yield any suggestion of a content effect, and there were no significant differences between the LEM groups in nonscoreable movements.

Correlations of the self-report measures with RGC scores for participants with more than 15 scoreable eye movements are reported in Table 6.4. The RGC scores correlated negatively and significantly with the TAI as in Experiment 1, but not with the other self-report measures. The STAI T-Anxiety subscale also correlated positively and significantly with the TAI and with the STAI S-Anxiety subscale.

The mean left and right digit temperatures for all subjects in Experiment 2 are plotted in Figure 6.1. During the 5-min progressive relaxation tape, left digit temperature decreased an average of 0.44 °C and right digit temperature

Table 6.3 Means and standard deviations of self-report measures for Experiment 2

Measure	Left movers (n = 9)		Right movers (n = 3)		Left and right combined (n = 12)		Bidirectional (n = 9)		t^a	p
	M	SD	M	SD	M	SD	M	SD		
Test Anxiety Inventory	50.00	13.68	43.66	10.97	48.42	12.89	61.44	11.87	2.37	.03
Worry subscale	19.56	5.39	16.33	6.43	18.75	5.55	21.11	6.83	0.87	ns
Emotionality subscale	20.33	6.12	18.33	2.08	19.83	5.37	27.33	4.21	3.46	.003
S-Anxiety subscale	49.67	10.39	45.00	13.53	48.50	10.78	52.67	10.36	0.89	ns
T-Anxiety subscale	42.22	11.74	51.00	6.24	45.92	10.81	48.56	9.51	0.58	ns
Irrational Beliefs Test	289.29	19.70	289.33	38.80	289.30	19.10	273.14	35.50	1.11	ns

Note. S-Anxiety = State Anxiety subscale of the State–Trait Anxiety Inventory (STAI); T-Anxiety = Trait Anxiety subscale of the STAI.
[a] Comparing left and right combined with bidirectionals

Table 6.4 Intercorrelation matrix of self-report measures and reflective gaze
consistency for Experiment 2

Measure	1	2	3	4	5
1. Test Anxiety Inventory	—	.44*	.40	−.44[a]	−.50*
2. T-Anxiety subscale		—	.60**	.23	.07
3. S-Anxiety subscale			—	.37	−.05
4. Irrational Belief Test				—	.40
5. Reflective gaze consistency					—

Note. T-Anxiety = Trait Anxiety subscale of the State–Trait Anxiety Inventory (STAI); S-Anxiety = State Anxiety subscale of the STAI.
[a]Due to loss of data of 4 subjects, correlation coefficient is not significant.
*p < .05.   **p < .01.

increased 0.37 °C; the difference in the magnitude of these changes was statistically significant ($p < .01$). When considered in the context of the relative inertia of the left hand temperature change in the relaxation condition in Experiment 1, this finding suggested that the right hemisphere may exert a more tonic inhibiting effect on left hand temperature. Because all the subjects of Experiment 2 were high in test anxiety, any performance threat—even

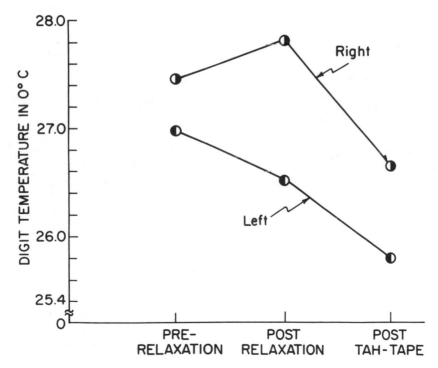

Figure 6.1 Average left and right hand middle-digit temperatures.

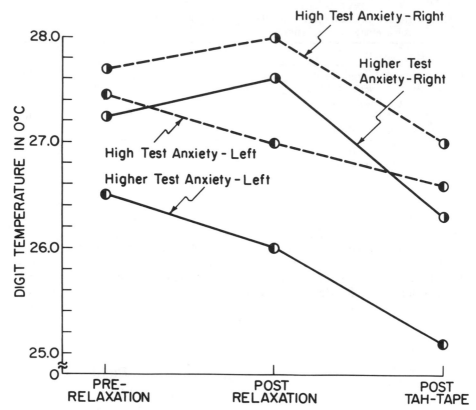

Figure 6.2   Average left and right hand middle-digit temperatures for students with high and very
high test anxiety scores.

asking them to relax—may have been somewhat threatening to right hemisphere functioning.

From the end of the relaxation exercise to the end of the stress tape, right
digit temperature decreased 1.18 °C and left digit temperature decreased
0.71 °C. The difference in these temperature drops was significant ($p < .01$),
a result that was not consistent with the RHESD model.

Paralleling the analysis in Experiment 1, the mean left and right digit temperatures were determined for high and very high test anxiety subjects; the
mean temperatures for these groups are reported in Figure 6.2. The significantly lower hand temperature for the very high (higher) test-anxious participants was more consistent with what has usually been observed in the University of Michigan laboratory than were the results in Experiment 1. Within
groups, the right and left digit temperatures of the high test anxiety students
increased 0.35 °C and decreased 0.45 °C, respectively, and the interaction F
test for these differences was significant ($p < .01$). A similar pattern was also
found for the higher test anxiety participants, with right digit temperature

increasing 0.38 °C and left digit temperature decreasing 0.42 °C; the interaction F test for these differences approached significance ($p < .06$).

During the stress tape, the right and left digit temperature decreased 1.04 °C and 0.41 °C, respectively, for the high test-anxious group, and the difference in these drops was statistically significant ($p < .05$). For the very high test anxiety group, right and left digit temperatures decreased by 1.31 °C and 0.99 °C, respectively; the paired t-test comparison of these differences approached significance ($p < .10$).

GENERAL DISCUSSION AND CONCLUSIONS

The digit temperature data in Experiments 1 and 2 yielded a mixed pattern of results with respect to the predictions of the RHESD model. The stress tape evoked slightly greater left digit temperature drops in high test-anxious subjects in Experiment 1, but this difference was not significant. In Experiment 2, the reverse pattern was observed; the greater drop in right digit temperature during the stress tape was statistically significant for the high test-anxious subjects and approached significance for the very high test-anxious subjects.

Only two temperature findings supported the RHESD model, and these were based on post hoc interpretations; (a) In both experiments there was a greater increase in right digit temperature during the relaxation condition and (b) in Experiment 2, left digit temperature was lower than right digit temperature when the temperatures were compared at the same point in time (see Figure 6.1). These findings are consistent with the hypothesis that because most subjects are somewhat apprehensive in psychology experiment situations, there is relatively greater activation of the right hemisphere.

Although the digit temperature data provide at best limited support for the RHESD model, the LEM data are clearly contradictory. In the two widely divergent female samples, the absence of LEM preferences was associated with high test anxiety. Moreover, in the more heterogeneous nonclinical sample, the absence of LEM preference was also correlated with high trait anxiety and irrational beliefs. These relations did not appear to be attributable to simple motor excitation, nor was there any evidence that the bidirectional women were responding to question content in a consistent manner.

The association of high anxiety with the absence of LEM preference in this study was not consistent with the data briefly reviewed at the beginning of this chapter that led us to postulate the RHESD model as a heuristic device for accounting for temporary exam blocking and impaired exam performance in high test-anxious students. Furthermore, with the exception of the post hoc interpretations already considered, the bilateral digit temperature data were not consistent with the RHESD model, which posits that greater right hemisphere involvement is associated with the processing of emotional information. Thus, it would seem appropriate to reject this model and consider alternative hemispheric models to explain the effects of anxiety on performance.

The data linking high test anxiety with bidirectionality in the reflective gaze assessment procedure suggested an alternative model of interhemispheric competition; it appears that high test-anxious individuals do not consistently use a given hemisphere in coping with test stressors. With each alternation of greater hemisphere engagement, the test-anxious student must start anew, and such flip-flopping would interfere with effective performance. Moreover, poor exam performance generally results in greater concern about doing well and higher performance anxiety scores.

As an example of this type of interhemispheric competition model, consider an administrator who, returning from a lengthy vacation, is faced with a tremendous backlog of paperwork. He first adopts a rational strategy, "I'll do the most important things first" (left hemisphere), but then temporarily allows himself to be overwhelmed by the immensity of the task, "How can I possibly catch up?" (right hemisphere). An example more closely related to test anxiety might involve a student who enters an examination situation with rational statements such as "I've studied hard, I will probably do well" (left hemisphere), but after looking at the first question, which he cannot answer, exclaims, "My God, I'm going to fail!" (right hemisphere).

The relation between test anxiety and LEM preference can also be viewed in terms of competing attention shifts. G. K. Montgomery (1977) has observed that the degree of cardiac deceleration accompanying orientation to an anagram solution problem was less marked in high trait-anxious subjects. Holroyd et al. (1978) found that cardiac variability, which correlates with degree of deceleration, was less marked in high test-anxious subjects. Holroyd et al. suggested that the absence of a sharp decelerative component in the cardiac orientation pattern of high test-anxious subjects may reflect an inability to maintain sustained attention. The difficulty experienced by high test anxious students in focusing attention on a task, as observed by Holroyd et al. (1978), may result from their flip-flopping between right and left hemispheres. If so, the value of the behavioral therapies described in this volume and elsewhere may be enhanced if they help the student to "lock into" one hemisphere or the other.

SUMMARY

Two measures of hemispheric lateralization, finger temperature and lateral eye movement, were used to evaluate right and left hemisphere preference in high and low test-anxious female university students. A significant increase in right digit temperature was found for both groups while they listened to a relaxation tape, indicating greater involvement of the left hemisphere during relaxation. Contrary to expectation, there was little evidence of any difference between the high and low test-anxious students in right hemisphere activation while they listened to a stressful tape. Similarly, the results for the eye movement measure indicated that reflective gaze preferences were unrelated to test anxiety. The findings were interpreted as suggesting that interhemispheric interference, rather than relatively greater activation of the right hemisphere in stressful situations, contributed to the difficulty of high test-anxious students in maintaining attention, and to their poor test performance.

7

Perspectives on Mathematics Anxiety and Test Anxiety

William D. Anton and Mark C. Klisch
University of South Florida, Tampa, Florida, USA

Basic quantitative skills have become increasingly important in the management of daily life. Whereas mathematics was previously necessary for success in the scientific and technical fields, it is now essential in business careers, in the social sciences, and even in the humanities (Stent, 1977). Nevertheless, many students either avoid mathematics or perform well below their actual capabilities because of anxiety aroused by mathematical operations (math anxiety).

Although information on the prevalence of math anxiety in college students is quite limited (Betz, 1978; D'Ailly & Bergering, 1992; Everson et al., 1993), math anxiety appears to be a pervasive problem in university settings. A survey conducted by Richardson (1976) of 400 undergraduates showed that approximately one third experienced extreme levels of anxiety associated with mathematics situations or number manipulations. Betz (1978) studied the prevalence and intensity of math anxiety in a sample of 652 college students; between one fourth and one half of the students in her survey indicated that math made them feel "uncomfortable, nervous, uneasy, and confused" (p. 446).

The relatively higher incidence of math anxiety as compared with test anxiety is surprising. It would seem that math-anxious students would be more difficult to identify than test-anxious students because they can avoid math situations beyond basic coursework, whereas examination situations pervade academic life. A nonmathematics major who is math anxious can design an academic curriculum in which stressful courses involving mathematical problem solving are never encountered. In contrast, it is virtually impossible for the test-anxious student to avoid the examinations that are inevitably associated with academic coursework.

Most research on math anxiety has been directed to assessing its prevalence and the effectiveness of various treatments for reducing its negative effects; relatively little attention has been paid to understanding the nature of math anxiety. However, investigators concerned with the treatment of math anxiety have suggested that it may be functionally similar to test anxiety (Hendel & Davis, 1978). As there appear to be many parallels between math anxiety and test anxiety, current conceptions of test anxiety may be useful in clarifying the nature of math anxiety.

Chapters 5 and 6 examined the psychological and physiological antecedents of test anxiety. In this chapter, the concept of math anxiety is examined and compared with that of test anxiety. The implications of a state–trait anxiety theory for math anxiety are examined and a conception of math anxiety as a situation-specific personality trait is proposed. The principal measures of math anxiety that have been used in empirical research are then reviewed and evaluated. Research on the treatment of math anxiety is then briefly reviewed, and the results of a pilot study designed to assess the effects of a multimodal program for the treatment of math anxiety are reported. The findings in a recent study are described, and directions for future research in math anxiety are explored.

NATURE OF MATH ANXIETY

The empirical investigation of math anxiety was introduced more than two decades ago by Richard M. Suinn and his associates (Richardson & Suinn, 1972; Suinn, 1970; Suinn et al., 1970; Suinn & Richardson, 1971). Richardson and Suinn (1972) defined math anxiety as

feelings of tension and anxiety that interfere with the manipulation of numbers and the solving of mathematics problems in a wide variety of ordinary life and academic situations. Mathematics anxiety may prevent a student from passing fundamental mathematics courses or prevent his pursuing advanced courses in mathematics or the sciences. (p. 551)

Data on the relation between math anxiety and performance on mathematics problems were reported by Richardson and Suinn (1972). In this research, math anxiety was inferred from responses to the Mathematics Anxiety Rating Scale (MARS). The 98 items in this scale describe a wide variety of behavioral situations associated with mathematics. The MARS has been used in several studies to measure individual differences in math anxiety (Richardson & Suinn, 1972; Suinn et al., 1973). In general, these findings indicate that high MARS scores are associated with poor performance on mathematics tests, but Richardson and Suinn do not attempt to explain how high levels of math anxiety interfere with mathematics performance. In contrast, the performance decrements of test-anxious individuals in examination situations have been attributed to blocking, task-irrelevant responding, focusing on internal self-depreciating ideation, processing too much information, or simply worrying about performance.

The relation between math anxiety and other forms of anxiety for college students was investigated in two studies (Betz, 1978; Hendel, 1977). Hendel reported that math anxiety (as measured by the MARS) was substantially correlated ($r = .65$) with a measure of test anxiety. Betz reported that mathematics anxiety, as measured by a modified version of the revised Fennema–Sherman (1976) Mathematics Anxiety Scale (MAS) was significantly correlated ($p < .001$) with trait anxiety ($r = -.28$), as measured by the Trait

Anxiety (A-Trait) subscale of the State–Trait Anxiety Inventory (Spielberger et al., 1970). (As higher levels of math anxiety are indicated by lower scores on the MAS, correlations express a positive relation.) Betz also found that math anxiety was moderately correlated ($p < .001$) with scores on the Test Anxiety Inventory (TAI; Spielberger et al., 1978), which provides subscales for measuring worry and emotionality as components of test anxiety. TAI Total scores correlated $-.42$ with math anxiety; TAI Emotionality (E) and Worry (W) subscales correlated $-.38$ and $-.43$, respectively, with math anxiety.

The results of the Hendel (1977) and Betz (1978) studies suggest that individuals who are high in trait or test anxiety may be similar in some respects to individuals who are math anxious. The positive relation between math and test anxiety could be due to overlap in general item content as both the MARS and the MAS contained items depicting mathematics performance in academic situations or examinations. However, item overlap cannot account for the positive correlation between math anxiety and trait anxiety.

The overlap in item content between measures of math and test anxiety reflects current definitions of math anxiety that include examination situations. It seems likely that some individuals who are presumed to be math anxious may experience feelings of tension and anxiety primarily in math test situations, and that some students labeled as test anxious may manifest these feelings mainly in mathematics examinations. Felsen and Tarudeau (1991) examined anxiety-related gender differences in grade school children and found that the anxiety experienced by girls concerning math performance was related to test anxiety rather than specific to math anxiety. Because there is no clear demarcation between the concepts of math anxiety and test anxiety, this has led to confusion and has resulted in some researchers assuming that "individuals who are mathematics-anxious are also anxious about taking tests" (Hendel & Davis, 1978, p. 431).

Math Anxiety and Test Anxiety

The results of the studies by Richardson and Suinn (1972) and Suinn et al. (1973) have indicated that students identified as math anxious on the MARS performed more poorly on mathematics tasks. However, little attention has been given to clarifying the emotional and cognitive processes associated with math anxiety. In evaluating the appropriateness of test anxiety theory for the understanding of math anxiety, the work of major contributors to test anxiety theory, discussed in more detail in Chapters 1 and 2, is briefly reviewed.

George Mandler and Seymour Sarason (1952, 1953; S. B. Sarason et al., 1952) theorized that test-anxious persons react to the stress associated with evaluative situations by emitting negative self-centered responses that are mediated by a learned anxiety drive. Because these task-irrelevant responses are incompatible with good task performance, high test-anxious persons perform more poorly than low test-anxious persons in evaluative situations.

Liebert and Morris (1967) conceptualized test anxiety as consisting of two major components, worry and emotionality. They described the worry component as "primarily *cognitive concern* about the consequences of failure" (p.

975) and the emotionality component as consisting of autonomic reactions that are evoked by evaluative stress. Morris and Liebert (1969) suggested that worry was associated with performance decrements on intellectual and cognitive tasks. In contrast, emotionality was typically unrelated to task performance, except for students who had low worry scores.

Irwin G. Sarason has been concerned with specifying situational factors and personality characteristics that contribute to the differential performance of high and low test-anxious persons in evaluative situations (I. G. Sarason, 1958a, 1960, 1961, 1965, 1975b; I. G. Sarason & Ganzer, 1962, 1963; I. G. Sarason & Harmatz, 1965; I. G. Sarason & Koenig, 1965). On the basis of this research, Sarason concluded, as stated in Chapter 5, that high test-anxious persons are more self-critical than low test-anxious individuals and are more likely to respond to evaluative situations with personalized, self-derogatory responses that interfere with performance. He described the behavior of test-anxious persons in evaluative situations as follows:

> Test anxiety can be interpreted as the tendency to view with alarm the consequences of inadequate performance in an evaluative situation. In a sense, the highly test-anxious person creates his or her own problem by processing too much information. The job of processing task-relevant information is complicated by maladaptive personalized feedback ("I'm dumb." "What if I don't pass this exam?") (I. G. Sarason 1978, p. 214)

It appears that the concept of test anxiety may be defined in terms of individual differences in the tendency to exhibit maladaptive cognitive and emotional reactions in examination situations. On the basis of the research findings, it appears that test-anxious persons perceive evaluative situations as more dangerous or threatening than individuals who are low in test anxiety, and experience intense elevations in state anxiety and worry when this occurs.

Spielberger et al. (1978) have suggested the relevance of the trait–state distinction in anxiety research for understanding the concept of test anxiety. This view is parsimonious in that test anxiety and trait anxiety are conceptualized within a single theoretical framework in which fewer assumptions are required to account for existent data. On the basis of the available research, Hendel and Davis (1978) have suggested that "mathematics anxiety may be functionally similar to test anxiety" (p. 430). Therefore, it would appear meaningful to explore the implications that trait–state anxiety theory might have for understanding the performance decrements and math avoidance behavior of persons who are math anxious. The relevance of the state–trait distinction in anxiety research and current conceptions of test anxiety as a situation-specific personality trait are considered in the next section.

IMPLICATIONS OF TRAIT–STATE ANXIETY THEORY FOR MATH ANXIETY

Spielberger's (1966b) trait–state anxiety theory is based on Cattell and Scheier's (1961) conceptual distinction between anxiety as a transitory emotional state and as a relatively stable personality trait. The concepts of state and trait anxiety have been defined by Spielberger (1972a) as follows:

> State anxiety (S-Anxiety) may be conceptualized as a transitory emotional state or condition of the human organism that varies in intensity and fluctuates over time. This condition is characterized by subjective, consciously perceived feelings of tension and apprehension, and activation of the autonomic nervous system. . . . Trait anxiety (T-Anxiety) refers to relatively stable individual differences in anxiety proneness, that is, to differences in the disposition to perceive a wide range of stimulus situations as dangerous or threatening, and in the tendency to respond to such threats with S-Anxiety reactions. (p. 39)

Trait–state anxiety theory (Spielberger, 1972a, 1976) provides a conceptual framework for identifying and classifying the principal variables that should be considered in anxiety research (e.g., stress, cognitive appraisal of threat, and psychological defenses) and suggests possible interrelations among these variables. Spielberger proposed that the term *stress* be reserved to denote relatively objective stimulus properties of situations that are characterized by some degree of physical or psychological danger. The term *threat,* however, is used to refer to an individual's subjective perception of a particular situation as dangerous or personally harmful. In general, the appraisal of a particular situation as threatening will depend on the stimulus properties of the situation, the individual's historical experiences with similar situations, and thoughts or memories evoked or reintegrated in the situations. Spielberger's trait–state anxiety theory also recognizes the centrality of the affective and cognitive processes that characterize anxiety states as emotional reactions to stress and specifies the characteristics of stressful stimulus conditions that evoke differential levels of state anxiety in persons who differ in trait anxiety.

As a result of empirical research, two important classes of stimulus situations (stressors) have been identified that produce differential state anxiety reactions in individuals who differ in trait anxiety. In general, high trait-anxious individuals are more likely than low trait-anxious individuals to perceive situations or circumstances in which their personal adequacy is evaluated as more threatening. In other words, stresses that threaten self-esteem (ego threats) evoke state anxiety reactions of greater intensity and duration in high trait-anxious individuals than in low trait-anxious individuals. These differential elevations in state anxiety reactions to evaluative threat have been shown to influence performance on a variety of tasks (e.g., J. P. Denny, 1966; Hodges, 1968; Spielberger et al., 1972; Spielberger & Smith, 1966). Situations involving physical danger, however, do not characteristically evoke differential state anxiety reactions in persons who differ in trait anxiety. Threats of physical danger produce elevations in state anxiety of similar magnitude for high and low trait-anxious persons (e.g., Hodges & Spielberger, 1966; Katkin, 1965; Lamb, 1972).

In the context of trait–state anxiety theory, Spielberger (1972b) conceptualized test anxiety as a situation-specific form of trait anxiety. This conception implies that high test-anxious individuals are more likely to perceive examination stress as threatening and to respond with greater elevations in state anxiety than low test-anxious persons. Intense state anxiety reactions evoked by examination stress appear to correspond to Liebert and Morris's (1967) conception of emotionality as a component of test anxiety. Spielberger et al. (1976) have speculated that worry responses are cued by state anxiety reactions and are analogous to the self-centered interfering responses that characterize the behavior of test-anxious individuals in examination situations.

Although test anxiety theorists (e.g., Liebert & Morris, 1967; Mandler & Sarason, 1952, 1953; Morris & Liebert, 1969; I. Sarason, 1972, 1975b; S. B. Sarason & Mandler, 1952) have emphasized the adverse effects of the worry component of test anxiety, trait–state anxiety theory has focused more on these adverse effects in relation to the activation of strong error tendencies by the high drive levels associated with elevations in state anxiety. Most test anxiety theorists seem to agree that test-anxious persons perceive examination situations as threatening and experience maladaptive cognitions (worry) and intense elevations in state anxiety in these situations. Everson et al. (1993) found that college students experienced more test anxiety in academic subjects they viewed as more difficult. Of special interest, they reported experiencing more anxiety about examinations in math and the physical sciences than in English or the social sciences.

Like test anxiety, math anxiety may be conceived of as a situation-specific personality trait. Trait math anxiety may be conceptualized as reflecting individual differences in the tendency to perceive situations involving the manipulation of numbers and the use of mathematics concepts as threatening. Persons high in math anxiety would respond to these situations with elevations in state anxiety and interfering worry responses. Both worry responses and elevations in state anxiety would seem to adversely affect mathematics performance. Hendel and Davis (1978) have written, "thus, the suggestion by Liebert and Morris (1967) may be relevant. Mathematics anxiety, like test anxiety, may be composed of two major components: (a) cognitive concern about performance (worry) and (b) emotionality" (p. 430).

MEASUREMENT OF MATH ANXIETY

Numerous measures of math anxiety have been used in the published and unpublished research literature. Very little information, however, is available regarding the cognitive, emotional, and behavioral significance of math anxiety measures (Hendel & Davis, 1978). Many of these instruments were developed to measure a specific treatment effect and have not been psychometrically evaluated. Others have been used exclusively with high school age and younger subjects. In this section, only math anxiety measures that met the following three criteria are considered: (a) Some psychometric data have been collected on the instrument, (b) the measure has been used in at least one study in the published research literature, and (c) the instrument has been used with college undergraduates. Only two measures of math anxiety met these criteria.

The published literature referenced J. W. Wilson et al. (1968) as the earliest report on the measurement of math anxiety. The MARS was developed at about the same time by Richard M. Suinn and his associates (Richardson & Suinn, 1972; Suinn et al., 1970) as a unifactor measure of mathematics anxiety. The instrument was constructed to assess the subjective emotional reactions experienced by college students in response to actual occasions requiring number manipulations. Most items describe practical situations involving mathematics, but a few depict mathematics performance in academic test situations (Suinn et al., 1973). The MARS lists 98 situations that students might encounter in their lives. The following are illustrative (Suinn, 1972):

34. Studying for a math test.
42. Checking over your monthly bank statement.
48. Figuring the sales tax on a purchase that costs more than $1.00.
54. Taking an examination (final) in a math course.
86. Opening a math or stat book and seeing a page full of problems.

Subjects are requested to indicate the degree of anxiety aroused in response to each item by checking response options ranging from 1 (*not at all* anxious) to 5 (*very much* anxious; Richardson & Suinn, 1972). A total score is derived by summing the values assigned to each item. High scores reflect high anxiety associated with mathematics.

Normative data on the MARS are available on students from two universities (Richardson & Suinn, 1973; Suinn et al., 1973). Test–retest reliabilities over 2- and 7-week periods were .78 and .85, respectively, in these samples. These reliability coefficients compare favorably with those reported for measures of social, test, and manifest anxiety for comparable time periods (Richardson & Suinn, 1972; Suinn et al., 1970). Internal consistency reliability as measured by coefficient alpha was reported to be .97 for a sample of 397 students (Richardson & Suinn, 1972, 1973), indicating that the items on the MARS cluster around a single homogeneous factor. Item-total correlations were greater than .50 for over half of the correlations for all items (Richardson & Suinn, 1972, 1973). Measures of construct validity have been obtained from correlations between the MARS and the mathematics subtest of the Differential Aptitude Test (DAT). These correlations have ranged from − .32 to − .64, and suggest that higher math anxiety is associated with poorer performance on a math test.

Additional validity data reported in the literature are found in three separate studies (Richardson & Suinn, 1971; Suinn et al., 1970; Suinn & Richardson, 1971) that showed clients requesting treatment for math anxiety had higher MARS scores than the normal standardization sample. These same students showed significant decreases in MARS scores compared with untreated controls following treatment for math anxiety. These studies are considered in greater detail later in this chapter in the Treatment of Math Anxiety section.

The MAS was developed by Fennema and Sherman (1976) to assess the presence of math anxiety in high school students. It consists of 12 items and is one of eight scales composing the Fennema–Sherman Mathematics Attitudes

Scales. The MAS was intended to measure "feelings of anxiety, dread, nervousness, and associated bodily symptoms related to doing mathematics" (Fennema & Sherman, 1976, p. 4). Subjects are required to respond to each item on a 5-point Likert-type scale ranging from 1 (*strongly disagree*) to 5 (*strongly agree*). Scale development procedures for the MAS are summarized by Fennema and Sherman (1977). Split-half reliabilities for each scale in the inventory are equal to or greater than .89.

The MAS was modified by Betz (1978) to make it more appropriate for administration to a college population. Betz reported a split-half reliability coefficient of .92 for a sample of 652 college undergraduates. The following questions are illustrative of the 10 items in the modified scale:

4. I usually don't worry about my ability to solve math problems.
6. I get really uptight during math tests.
9. Mathematics makes me feel uncomfortable and nervous.

Parallels between the measurement of math anxiety and test anxiety are few. The measurement of test anxiety has been more closely articulated with theory (e.g., Alpert & Haber, 1960; Liebert & Morris, 1967; Mandler & Sarason, 1952; I. G. Sarason, 1972; Spielberger et al., 1976, 1978) than has been the case with math anxiety. Numerous studies of test anxiety have appeared in the empirical literature since C. H. Brown (1938a, 1938b) developed the first questionnaire for identifying test-anxious test students more than 40 years ago. The literature on the measurement of test anxiety is considered in greater detail in Part I.

Factor-analytic studies of the Test Anxiety Questionnaire (TAQ) and the Test Anxiety Scale (TAS) have been reviewed by Spielberger et al. (1978). In general, these studies (e.g., Gorsuch, 1966; Richardson et al., 1977; Sassenrath, 1964) have suggested that the TAQ and TAS are factorially complex and in need of significant revision. Factor studies of these measures have been criticized by Spielberger et al. (1978) for failure to include appropriate marker variables to assist in the identification of factors. As a result of this and other problems with factor studies of the TAQ and the 37-item TAS, Spielberger et al. developed a new psychometric instrument for measuring test anxiety, the Test Anxiety Inventory (TAI). More detailed consideration of the development of the TAI may be found in Chapter 3.

The measurement of test anxiety has received much more empirical attention than the measurement of math anxiety. Spielberger et al. (1978) have suggested that the bulk of the evidence is consistent with the assumption that test anxiety is a situation-specific measure of anxiety proneness (trait anxiety) in test situations. On the basis of their empirical studies of the TAI, worry and emotionality appear to be the major components of test anxiety. To the extent that Hendel and Davis's (1978) assumptions are correct, careful attention to the literature on the measurement of test anxiety could be extremely useful in the measurement of math anxiety.

The current definition of math anxiety includes mathematics performance in both practical life situations and examinations. Consistent with this definition, the principal measures of math anxiety include items on math performance in test situations. As was noted earlier, this could be one reason that Betz (1978) found math anxiety to be more highly correlated with test anxiety than with trait anxiety. This overlap in general item content between measures of math anxiety and test anxiety in part reflects current conceptions of math anxiety as a complex phenomenon that includes elements of test anxiety in some instances. More precise measurement of math anxiety will be dependent on refinement of the concept. The item content of both the MAS and the MARS clearly seems social–evaluative in nature and appears to be consistent with Spielberger's (1966a, 1972a, 1975) conception of psychological stresses that threaten self-esteem. Although the situations described vary widely and include math test situations, all items deal with mathematics performance in one form or another. In most descriptions, the element of one's performance being compared with some standard of excellence is either explicitly stated or implied.

TREATMENT OF MATH ANXIETY

Many behavioral therapy approaches used in the management of math anxiety overlap with those reported in the past 3 decades in the treatment of test anxiety. Although treatment procedures for math and test anxiety are similar, the test anxiety treatment literature spans a larger time period and is much more extensive. Borrowing on the apparent similarity between test anxiety and math anxiety, early researchers concerned with the reduction of math anxiety applied procedures originally developed in the treatment of test anxiety (Suinn et al., 1970). Thus, it appears that—from the standpoint of theory, measurement, and now treatment—the literature on test anxiety has relevance for math anxiety research.

Efforts to investigate effective test anxiety treatments far outweigh those in the area of math anxiety in volume, scope, and complexity. The literature on the treatment of test anxiety has been comprehensively reviewed in a paper by Gonzalez (1976), who reported published documents that date as far back as 1933. Many of these studies are considered in the chapters included in Part III. In general, studies have evolved from case reports depicting the application of psychoanalytic psychotherapy (Bergler, 1933) to systematic investigations comparing the effectiveness of alternative treatment strategies (e.g., Anton, 1976; Meichenbaum, 1972). Although many different approaches have been used in the treatment of test anxiety, behaviorally oriented procedures, including systematic desensitization, relaxation, implosion therapy, and cognitively oriented therapy, appear to have most relevance for the treatment of math anxiety. Much of the value of this literature is that it represents a variety of attempts to compare the effectiveness of different therapeutic procedures in the management of a specific problem.

Attempts to develop effective therapeutic approaches for math anxiety have been few. In general, studies have included the application of traditional behavioral therapies (Richardson & Suinn, 1973; Suinn et al., 1970; Suinn &

Richardson, 1971) or have been concerned with the use of cognitive procedures such as rational–emotive therapy (Hendel & Davis, 1978; Kogelman & Warren, 1978; Tobias, 1978).

In treatment studies of math anxiety, the usual procedure is to administer to high math-anxious subjects one of the standard math anxiety measures before and after treatment. In a few of the studies, pre- and postmeasures of mathematics performance are evaluated to assess treatment effectiveness. The major studies investigating the effect of behavioral treatments on math anxiety have been undertaken by Suinn, Richardson, and their colleagues (1971, 1973). However, as with much of the test anxiety research, more attention is given to treatment procedures per se than to the nature of math anxiety.

In the first treatment study of math anxiety reported in the empirical literature, Suinn et al. (1970) compared the effectiveness of marathon desensitization with accelerated massed desensitization in a sample of 13 college students. Their results indicated that both treatments were effective in reducing math anxiety, as measured by scores on the MARS. In addition, both procedures resulted in improved performance on the math form of the DAT, administered under a special 10-minute time limit. No significant differences were found between the two treatments on either of these dependent measures.

Suinn and Richardson (1971) tested the comparative effectiveness of Anxiety Management Training (AMT) and systematic desensitization in the treatment of math anxiety. The goal of AMT is to develop self-control over disruptive anxiety responses through the development of competing responses such as relaxation. The outcome of this training procedure is similar to systematic desensitization in that the subject learns to respond to previously anxiety-evoking cues with feelings of relaxation. Unlike systematic desensitization, AMT does not involve the use of anxiety hierarchies. Both treatments resulted in a reduction of the math anxiety, and no difference between treatment procedures was found. An increase in mathematics performance after treatment occurred only for the AMT group. As in the previous study, the MARS and DAT were used as the dependent measures. Combining elements of the previous two studies, a third experiment examined the relative effectiveness of traditional systematic desensitization, accelerated mass desensitization, and AMT in reducing math anxiety (Richardson & Suinn, 1973). All these treatments were found to be equally effective in reducing math anxiety, but unlike the previous studies, no increase in mathematics performance was found.

On the basis of the findings of these three studies, behavioral treatments seem to be applicable and effective in the reduction of math anxiety. The results of these studies are mixed with respect to improvement in mathematics performance following behavioral treatment. Although the effects of treatment in the first two studies resulted in higher DAT math scores, the absence of similar findings in the last study leaves the treatment–performance relation unclear. An additional problem is found in the measure of mathematics performance used in these studies. Although the DAT is a valid and reliable measure of mathematics performance, the use of an abbreviated version of the mathematics section under special time constraints may serve to weaken the accuracy of the test.

Treatment approaches using rational–emotive techniques (RETs; Ellis & Harper, 1975) have also been reported in the literature. Generally, these treatments are based on the premise that anxiety or emotional disturbance is a result of illogical, "irrational" thinking. By bringing the illogical nature of certain beliefs into awareness, an individual becomes able to discard the beliefs and instill logically sound beliefs in their place. In the treatment of math anxiety, the rational–emotive approach attempts to examine various irrational beliefs that individuals have constructed around mathematics activities. Beliefs such as "some people have a mind for math and some don't" or "there is a best way to do a math problem" serve to increase mathematics anxiety in some individuals, leading to mathematics avoidance or poor mathematics performance. By exploring and dispelling these and similar irrational beliefs in a supportive relationship, math anxiety may be reduced.

Kogelman and Warren (1978) and Tobias (1978) reported initial attempts to incorporate RETs in courses and clinics designed to help math-anxious individuals at Wesleyan University and Wellesley College. Although no systematic research data on the effectiveness of these programs have been reported to date, preliminary results suggest that the RET approach has generally been successful in reducing math anxiety.

A recent study by Hendel and Davis (1978) examined the effectiveness of a multimodal, cognitively oriented program in reducing math anxiety. The authors described this treatment as AMT, as detailed by Richardson (1976). It should be noted that this training is conceptually different from the AMT reported in the earlier study by Suinn and Richardson (1971), which was strictly behavioral in nature. The revised AMT (Richardson, 1976) incorporates "techniques designed to make clients aware of (while teaching them to modify) their maladaptive beliefs and patterns of self-verbalizations that cause specific and general anxiety problems" (pp. 104–105).

In this more recent conception of AMT, Richardson (1976) strongly emphasized rational reevaluation and the learning of behavioral stress management techniques in multimodal treatment. The stress management procedures reported by Hendel and Davis (1978) consist only of a brief introduction to relaxation and desensitization techniques. Sixty-nine women requesting help for math anxiety served as subjects in this study. After first participating in a 3-hour diagnostic clinic, subjects were self-assigned to one of three groups, a no-treatment condition, a special mathematics course, or a combined procedure consisting of AMT in conjunction with the mathematics course. Assessment of math anxiety was carried out pre- and posttreatment, using the MARS test. Although posttest data are available for only 47 of the original subjects, the results indicated that students who received AMT evidenced a greater reduction in MARS scores than students who participated in the course-only or no-treatment control groups. No attempt was made in this study to assess the effect of treatment on mathematics performance. Although these findings support the effectiveness of RET multimodal treatments in reducing math anxiety, methodological difficulties in the Hendel and Davis study weaken this conclusion.

A pilot study by Levinson and Klisch (1978) investigated the effects of multimodal RET treatment on math anxiety and mathematics performance. In this study, a group of 14 self-referred college students were enrolled in a math anxiety reduction workshop. The subjects participated in five 2-hour group sessions, two each week for a period of 2.5 weeks. The program used RET techniques, attempting to bring into awareness, and modify, the subjects' "irrational" beliefs about mathematics. Although students were asked to focus on their subjective responses to mathematics exercises, no skill development procedures were included as part of the program. The MARS test and an informal measure of mathematics performance, constructed for purposes of this study, were administered in a pretreatment session and again in the final treatment session.

Eleven of the original 14 students completed the treatment program. Analysis of pre- and posttreatment MARS scores showed a highly significant decline in the level of math anxiety following the group treatment. A significant increase in the level of mathematics performance was also found. However, in the absence of both an appropriate control group and a valid measure of mathematics performance, these findings are only suggestive.

MATH ANXIETY IN PERSPECTIVE

On the basis of the literature reviewed in this chapter, math anxiety appears to be a widespread phenomenon on college campuses. Math anxiety can have a serious effect on career and occupational choice for individuals who prematurely narrow their options as a result of math avoidance. These effects appear more pervasive for women, who as a group experience higher levels of math anxiety and math avoidance than do men. These considerations underscore the importance of understanding the nature of math anxiety, its measurement, and its treatment.

In this chapter, we have tried to show that math anxiety shares functional similarities with test anxiety and that current conceptions of test anxiety have relevance for understanding the nature of math anxiety. Math anxiety, like test anxiety, would appear to refer to individual differences in a situation-specific personality trait. For the math-anxious person, the manipulation of numbers or mathematics problem solving represents a psychological stress that is interpreted as threatening to self-esteem. Over time, accumulated failure experiences in mathematics problem solving lead to a relatively stable disposition (trait anxiety) to respond to such situations as ego threatening, and a self-perpetuating cycle is established.

Math anxiety can be distinguished from test anxiety by the stimulus properties of situations that are considered dangerous or personally threatening. Whereas math-anxious persons are likely to interpret situations involving the manipulation of numbers and mathematics problems as threatening, test-anxious individuals are more likely to appraise examination situations as personally threatening. The emotional and cognitive processes resulting from the perception of threat are probably similar for math-anxious and test-anxious students. Both are likely to experience interfering worry cognitions and intense elevations in state anxiety in situations they perceive as dangerous or personally threatening. For both math- and test-anxious persons, the consequences of inadequate performance appear to be exaggerated. Whereas test-anxious individuals appear to respond to the evaluative aspects inherent in test situations, persons high in math anxiety seem to respond to the ego-threatening aspects of numerical manipulations.

Obviously, some people experience math anxiety and test anxiety in varying combinations. We propose that individuals who experience math anxiety primarily in an examination context be labeled *math–test-anxious,* provided they do not also experience similar anxiety in non-math-test situations. Math anxiety would appear to be a more appropriate term for individuals whose fear of number manipulations in solving mathematics problems is relatively independent of the context.

Successful reduction of math anxiety as a result of behavioral treatments has been reported with consistency in the experimental literature. Considering the suggested similarities between math and test anxiety, it is not surprising that the treatment of math anxiety seems to have evolved from the research on the successful treatment of test anxiety. As is the case with test anxiety, it seems likely that these behavioral treatments serve to modify the emotional reactions (state anxiety) that are evoked in math-anxious persons in response to situations requiring the use of mathematics.

Reports of cognitively oriented treatments of math anxiety suggest that these approaches may also be effective. Unlike the strictly behavioral treatments, cognitive approaches focus on the identification of distracting irrational beliefs about mathematics that are characteristic of high math-anxious individuals. Dispelling such beliefs lowers math anxiety, as was found by Hendel and Davis (1978), who reported significant reductions in math anxiety following treatments using cognitively oriented techniques. The results of a pilot study (Levinson & Klisch, 1978) add support to these findings.

SUMMARY AND SUGGESTED DIRECTIONS IN MATH ANXIETY RESEARCH

In this chapter we examined the theoretical relationship between math anxiety and test anxiety, and reviewed current research in this area of study. As conceptualized by Spielberger (1972b), test anxiety and math anxiety are situation-specific personality traits. Individuals high in math anxiety are more likely to respond to math threat situations with heightened state anxiety. As has been detailed, significant efforts have been undertaken to quantify and measure math anxiety, and psychometric instruments have proven useful in exploring treatment efficacy. The theoretical issues and empirical findings considered in this chapter suggest that treatments for test anxiety can be successfully adapted to reduce math anxiety.

The effects of the various treatments of math anxiety on mathematics performance require future study. In two behavioral studies, an increase in mathematics performance was found following treatment (Suinn et al., 1970; Suinn & Richardson, 1971), but a third similarly designed study found no such effect (Richardson & Suinn, 1973). A cognitively oriented pilot study conducted by Levinson and Klisch (1978) also reported posttreatment increases in mathematics performance.

A systematic study of the treatment of math anxiety is currently planned to evaluate the effectiveness of multimodal RET procedures. In addition to evaluating the effectiveness of various treatments in reducing math anxiety and improving mathematics performance, interactions among measures of math anxiety, test anxiety, and trait and state anxiety will also be examined. Two measures of math anxiety, the MARS and the Fennema–Sherman (1976) MAS, will be administered pre- and posttreatment to college students who request treatment for math anxiety. The students will be randomly assigned to treatment and waiting-list control groups. Although the MARS has been widely used in previous research, use of both instruments will permit a more accurate and valid assessment of math anxiety. The only constraint on group assignment will be to ensure that the groups are matched on pretreatment levels of math anxiety.

A justifiable criticism of mathematics anxiety treatment studies, as noted earlier in this chapter, is the use of informal or unvalidated measures of math performance. Because the assessment of mathematics performance is critically important, two measures of math performance will be administered, both pre- and posttreatment: the Wide Range Achievement Test and an abbreviated mathematics section of the DAT. The Wide Range Achievement Test is a brief, widely accepted, and well-validated measure of mathematics performance; the abbreviated DAT has proved useful in the studies of Suinn and his colleagues (e.g., Suinn et al., 1970). Although the MARS appears to have considerable promise as a measure of math anxiety in college students, psychometric refinement of math anxiety measures should be pursued. Factor studies that include measures of test anxiety, worry and emotionality, and trait anxiety as marker variables would be helpful in explicating the factor structure of the MARS.

Future research on math anxiety should be directed toward identifying situational factors and personality characteristics that influence the performance of high math-anxious persons engaged in mathematics tasks. Research on the treatment of math anxiety will benefit from the use of valid and reliable measures of mathematics performance, such as the math form of the DAT and the Wide Range Achievement Test. In addition to reducing math anxiety, improving performance in math-anxious students may require a combination of treatment approaches that include training in study and test-taking skills.

8

Anxiety and Test Performance

Samuel Ball
Board of Studies, Carlton, Victoria, Australia

Earlier chapters in Part II explored the antecedents of test anxiety and several approaches to treatment. This chapter examines research that has investigated the relation between anxiety and performance on important tests. The implications that may be drawn from this literature suggest one of three things: (a) Testing organizations and psychologists have been remiss in not putting more effort into investigating an obviously important problem; (b) the relation between test anxiety and test performance is so complex that the strenuous efforts of testing organizations and psychologists have generally failed to untangle the web of interrelations; or (c) researchers know the answer to the question of the relation between test anxiety and test performance, but poor dissemination coupled with political, social, and educational pressures prevent them from admitting what they already know.

Because of its theoretical origins in the psychoanalytic literature, anxiety has tended to be a "bad" construct, that is, anxiety has negative connotations. In the case of fear, the emotional reaction is to an objective, external, realistic danger. With anxiety, the emotional reaction is a less rational and sometimes debilitating response to a situation that is not necessarily harmful. Mental health experts and progressive educators tend to regard anxiety as something to avoid and as a sign that malevolent forces exist in the anxious person's environment. Therefore, test anxiety *must* be bad.

Alpert and Haber (1960) and others (e.g., Pekrun, 1992; Schwarzer & Jerusalem, 1992) have pointed out that anxiety may be either facilitating or debilitating, as detailed earlier in Chapter 2, and both of these possibilities must be taken into account when looking at the relation between test anxiety and performance on important achievement and aptitude tests. There are two important principles that illustrate the complexity of the relation between anxiety and performance.

The first principle involves task difficulty. The more difficult the task, the more likely that anxiety will have undesirable effects. Conversely, the easier the task, the more likely that anxiety will have facilitative effects. A good example of this principle is provided in Kenneth W. Spence's (Spence et al., 1956) classic study that required subjects to learn two different sets of paired-associate, consonant–vowel–consonant (CVC) trigram lists. One list of trigrams was difficult to learn because it involved similar (competing) responses to the stimulus trigrams; the second list of trigrams was easy to learn because there were very few competing responses. Level of drive was inferred from scores on the Taylor (1953) Manifest Anxiety Scale. In accordance with the Spence et al. (1956) predictions from drive theory, high-anxious subjects performed better in learning the easy list and more poorly in learning the difficult list than did low-anxious subjects. Presumably, test anxiety would have similar differential effects on performance, depending on the test's level of difficulty. Thus, test anxiety should have different effects, for example, on math computation than on math problem solving if these activities involve different levels of difficulty.

The second principle is that when a performer is highly intelligent, or has expert skills or high proficiency on a task, anxiety is more likely to enhance rather than to detract from performance. This is clearly related to the previous principle because, from a phenomenological viewpoint, a difficult task will be relatively easy for a person who is very bright or highly proficient (Spielberger, 1966a). For such persons, the task does not involve a variety of competing responses jockeying with each other at the synaptic starting gate. Rather, the task may actually be quite easy so that heightened anxiety simply helps the proficient person to better focus attention on a simple task he or she has previously mastered. The main point here is that test anxiety may facilitate the performance of a bright student who has the major facts and processes of a discipline down cold and may impair the performance for a less able student, especially if he or she is not sure of the basic facts and processes.

Before examining the empirical research on test anxiety and test performance, there is one further point that Spielberger (1966b, 1972a) and Calvo et al. (1992) have drawn attention to, namely, that anxiety can be conceptualized as a relatively transitory state or condition brought on by a particular stimulus, or as a relatively permanent condition or trait that is not particularly dependent on a specific stimulus situation. When it comes to important examinations such as the Scholastic Aptitude Test (SAT), one might reasonably expect both kinds of anxiety to be present, thereby generating larger than usual amounts of anxiety. Thus, research on test anxiety that has been carried out with respect to less important test situations, such as midterm tests in Biology 101 at East Cupcake College or monthly math quizzes in the 8th grade of George Washington Junior High School, may bear little generalizability to the impact of test anxiety on the College Board Examinations and other crucial testing situations.

Another way of formulating the same problem is that the relation between test anxiety and test-taking performance may not be monotonic or linear. Perhaps this relation is curvilinear, and only at extreme levels of fear or anxiety (as experienced by some birds when approached by snakes) is the effect strong (or lethal as in the bird analogy). In a small scale study of over- and under-achievers, Ball (1977) noted that although the mean anxiety level for the two groups was the same, the variances were quite different. An examination of the anxiety score distributions showed that overachievers had a wider range of anxiety scores; they apparently either could not care less or were so anxious they could not perform well. This observation suggests that clarification of the underlying reasons for observed curvilincarity should be an important topic for future research on test anxiety and performance.

A final introductory point—perhaps suggesting a missing link in test anxiety research and theory—is that the overall effects of test anxiety on learning are rarely examined. Instead, only the actual test-taking performance is considered as a dependent variable. It is equally important to ask what effects test anxiety has on studying behavior and consequent learning.

Back in the 1960s, a number of colleges under radical student pressure either suspended exams altogether or reduced their importance by using a pass–fail grading system. Not much systematic research was carried out on this development, now largely gone the way of many radical reforms; however, Bob Feldmesser, a sociologist then at Dartmouth College, showed that student performance tended to deteriorate as the tests were eliminated. In short, whether tests cause debilitating anxiety at the time they are taken or not, they serve, perhaps through facilitating anxiety, to focus student effort during the term—to give students something to work for. To use a personal example, my PhD comprehensives produced a lot of test anxiety for me; they also made me work very hard in going over my notes and books in a way I would never have done if that crucial test requirement had not been present.

To summarize these introductory observations, there is an unsatisfactory state of affairs in which researchers continue to speculate about the relation between test anxiety and performance on crucial examinations such as the SAT. It has also been suggested (a) that test anxiety may be facilitating, at least for some students; (b) that there may be moderator variables, such as the level of difficulty of a test and the proficiency of the test taker, that interact with test anxiety; and (c) that the relation between test anxiety and performance may be curvilinear, that is, increasing test anxiety may enhance test performance up to a certain point, after which greater test anxiety serves to lower performance.

RESEARCH ON TEST ANXIETY, TEST INSTRUCTIONS, AND CREATIVITY

It has been demonstrated in a number of studies that test instructions can influence the degree of anxiety of the test taker. For example, S. B. Sarason et al. (1960) showed that demanding, test-oriented instructions increased anxiety and resulted in performance decrements, especially for students who were already highly anxious. However, when a gamelike situation was used, anxiety was lowered and performance was somewhat improved. Similarly, Gerlach et al. (1964) found that originality increased when the test taker was given clues as to what was being looked for in the test.

Two commonly used instruction techniques have been used to arouse test anxiety: ego-involving instructions emphasizing the evaluative aspect of the test and negative feedback or failure instructions during the test. Both have debilitative effects. According to Liebert and Morris (1967), this negative impact is produced by the cognitive component of anxiety—worry, conscious concern, and fear of consequences—rather than the emotionality (affective) component (see also Topman et al., 1992). Although the instructions for the SAT and other crucial exams are not deliberately anxiety invoking, the indirect evidence cited above suggests that anxiety level is somewhat but not highly related to performance. It has also been shown that test instructions can influence anxiety and performance levels, but usually only to a rather mild degree.

ANXIETY, TEST-ITEM DIFFICULTY, AND ITEM COMPLEXITY

The preponderance of the evidence suggests that low-anxious students do better on more difficult items than do high-anxious students. In a laboratory experiment some years ago, for example, Spielberger and Smith (1966) found that low-anxious subjects had at least an initial superiority over high-anxious subjects on a moderately difficult learning task. However, as learning progressed, the high-anxious students showed greater improvement and were superior to the low-anxious students by the end of the experiment.

It is difficult to categorize impartial examinations, such as the SAT, as involving necessarily complex items. However, because they contain such items this would seem to favor students who were *not* high (at least not very high) in anxiety. Again, however, the evidence does not indicate a large impact or widespread effects. Rather, it seems to suggest that the performance of some students is to some degree affected by anxiety. In general, this kind of research does not usually look for a potentially positive impact of increasing the anxiety level of students who are very low in anxiety.

ANXIETY, APTITUDE, AND ACHIEVEMENT

Most studies have reported a small, negative relation between test anxiety and ability or aptitude (e.g., Mandler & Sarason, 1952; S. B. Sarason et al., 1960), whereas other studies have reported correlations of certainly no more than $-.3$, so less than 10% of the aptitude variance is accounted for by anxiety, and probably no more than 5% on the average. This is nevertheless worth being concerned about: Smoking accounts for only about 3% of the variance associated with longevity and people feel this is important. However, such relations certainly do not explain or account for large differences in performance that are sometimes claimed by educators with a dislike for anxiety as a construct.

Conflicting results have been obtained when the relation between anxiety and achievement has been assessed, but, as indicated earlier in Chapter 2, a general finding is that there is a small negative relation (Hembree, 1988). Walsh et al. (1968), using the Alpert and Haber (1960) Anxiety Scales, obtained a positive relation for facilitating anxiety and a negative relation for debilitating anxiety. Clearly anxiety can have positive as well as negative effects on achievements.

WORRY, EMOTIONALITY, AND TEST TAKING

If one separates out the cognitive or worry component and the affective or emotionality component of test anxiety, one finds that worry varies as an inverse function of performance expectancy (Morris & Liebert, 1970). The greater the expectancy of doing well, the less the worry from pre- to post-examination. The lower the expectancy, the greater the worry. The emotional component does not seem to be affected systematically by expectancy.

It has been found that the importance of a test elevates the worry score and also influences the effects of negative feedback. Negative feedback produces increments in anxiety mainly under high test-importance conditions. Moreover, students tend to produce their own feedback; they generally know whether an exam is important and how they are doing on it without having to be told. These conclusions are based on indirect evidence that students who have done well on the Preliminary SAT, and who have excellent school records, worry less in taking the SATs than their less talented, less hard-working fellow students. It would seem that the effects of worry, as a component of test anxiety, may perhaps reinforce the effects of talent and hard work to a degree, helping to differentiate between able students, who tend to be confident, and less able students, who tend to worry more. If anything, this would tend to improve the validity of tests such as the SAT, and again warns one that research on relatively unimportant tests may produce findings that are not generalizable to crucial kinds of examinations.

IMPACT OF TEST ANXIETY ON TEST PERFORMANCE

One might think that this would be the largest section of this chapter, that is, that there was a mass of research evidence on the actual impact of test anxiety on performance on crucial tests. Actually, this section is quite short.

Some time ago, French (1962) properly criticized research that simply showed that anxiety accompanies low test scores. He argued that this proves nothing about the part that anxiety plays in bringing about the low scores. French administered the SAT examinations (Math and Verbal Scales) under ordinary conditions, under conditions in which the students were led to feel relaxed, and under conditions in which the students were made to feel anxious. He then correlated the SAT scores obtained under these three conditions with the students' grades and compared the correlations. Correlations for the SAT Verbal and Math scales are reported in Table 8.1 and indicate, if anything, that relaxed testing conditions lowered the correlational concurrent validity, at least for the Math SAT.

A complex simultaneous equations analysis was conducted to determine the effects of anxiety on the obtained SAT scores. Scaled scores were computed

Table 8.1 Correlations with grades of the Scholastic Aptitude Test (SAT) Verbal and Mathematics scales given under ordinary, relaxed, and anxiety-producing conditions

Condition	SAT Verbal Scale	SAT Math Scale
Ordinary	.53	.49
Relaxed	.53	.46
Anxiety producing	.52	.50

to allow for practice and fatigue effects, which were confounded with the relaxed and anxious conditions. The effects of anxiety on the SAT were minimal, as can be seen in Table 8.2. It is interesting that the female students obtained a 10-point increase on the Math SAT in the anxiety condition. French's (1962) explanation of this finding seems quite reasonable: He suggested that the female students in the relaxed condition may not have exerted much effort, because they tend to dislike math. However, they tried harder in the anxiety condition, so that anxiety produced a positive impact. However, it should be noted that the standard error of measurement of the SAT is about 30 points, so the anxiety effect appears minimal.

In a further analysis of the data, the students were divided into three groups: below average, average, and above average. The effects of anxiety were then calculated separately for these groups. Even when the SAT items were difficult (i.e., for the below average group), decrements in performance were not associated with anxiety, leading French (1962) to conclude that anxiety was not an important determinant of SAT scores.

Of course, one could argue that French's (1962) results reflected an average impact and that the performance of some individuals was greatly facilitated by anxiety, whereas the performance of others was severely hurt by anxiety. It could also be argued that the relaxed condition was confounded experimentally in French's work with the low importance of the test. If this were so, French's results might reflect a conservative estimate of the debilitating effects of anxiety on the SAT, but there is little evidence to support this conjecture. Nor is it reasonable to assume that a different experimental design or statistical analysis would produce radically different results.

Table 8.2 Estimated effects of anxiety on Scholastic Aptitude Test (SAT) Verbal and Math scores

Students	SAT Verbal Scale		SAT Math Scale	
	N	Anxiety effect	N	Anxiety effect
Males	661	1	575	−2
Females	427	−11	373	10
Total	1,088	−4	948	3

SUMMARY AND CONCLUSIONS

This chapter began with speculation about the impact that test anxiety might have on the SAT and other crucial academic measures. An indication of the complexity of the theoretical issues was noted as the relevant literature was reviewed. For some students, at least, test anxiety may be facilitative; test difficulty and test importance are factors to be considered; and linear relation may not provide true representations of the data.

Selected research evidence—mainly indirect evidence—was then examined. If the impact of test anxiety is intense and widespread, then the research evidence has yet to show it. The possibility that test anxiety produces an intensely negative impact for a few students cannot be refuted; if it does, however, it probably also produces a mildly positive impact for many students, resulting in relatively little overall impact. Or test anxiety may have a mildly negative impact for most students; that is, if it is widespread, the effect is probably mildly negative.

The present state of affairs concerning test anxiety research suggests that (a) researchers have been remiss in not putting more effort into the area; (b) the questions and relations are so complex that researchers have a great deal more work to do, but that this is no reflection on them; or (c) researchers already know many of the answers, but social and educational pressures, the Zeitgeist, prevent those answers from being heard. There is probably some truth to all three of these statements. In general terms, however, it would seem that test anxiety is not the main reason that underprepared groups of students do poorly on certain tests. Nor is test anxiety the cause of a general debility in students' performances on major examinations.

III

RESEARCH ON THE TREATMENT OF TEST ANXIETY

9

Systematic Desensitization, Study Skills Counseling, and Anxiety-Coping Training in the Treatment of Test Anxiety

Hector P. Gonzalez
University of South Florida, Tampa, Florida, USA

Achieving one's educational and professional goals generally depends on academic performance. Therefore, it is not surprising that most students experience anxiety both before and during examinations. As a consequence of their emotional reactions during tests, the level of achievement of many of these students is substantially lower than would be expected on the basis of their intellectual aptitude.

The problem of test anxiety is widespread, and the loss to society of the creative contributions of otherwise able students is considerable. Over the past three decades, a number of treatment strategies have been used with test-anxious students, and the development of new treatment techniques continues to proliferate (see Vagg & Spielberger, Chapter 14, for a review of the various treatment components presented in this chapter and Chapters 10–13.). Although systematic desensitization has been used more often than any other single approach (Hembree, 1988; Spielberger & Vagg, 1987), a wide range of behavioral methods have been used in the treatment of test-anxious clients, including relaxation training (Bedell, 1976; Chang-Liang & Denny, 1976), anxiety-management training (Richardson & Suinn, 1974), covert reinforcement (Finger & Galassi, 1977; Wisocki, 1973), vicarious desensitization (D. R. Denny, 1974), massed desensitization (Richardson & Suinn, 1974), implosive therapy (Cornish & Dilley, 1973; R. E. Smith & Nye, 1973), study counseling (Allen, 1971, 1973; Annis, 1986; Gonzalez, 1976), cognitive behavior modification (Goldfried et al., 1978; Holroyd, 1976; Meichenbaum, 1972), and computer-assisted treatment (Buglione et al., 1990).

In early studies of the treatment of test-anxious students, it was generally assumed that reducing test anxiety would facilitate improvement in academic performance (Spielberger et al., 1976). Although most behavioral approaches

This chapter is based in part on the author's doctoral dissertation, submitted to the Department of Psychology of the University of South Florida. The research was conducted under the supervision of Professor Charles D. Spielberger and was supported in part by a grant from the Advanced Research Projects Agency, U.S. Department of Defense (MDA 9-3-77-C-0190), awarded to C. D. Spielberger and W. D. Anton.

have been effective in reducing test anxiety, research findings have indicated that improvement in grades is only rarely achieved (Allen et al., 1980; Gonzalez, 1978a). Furthermore, because test anxiety treatment studies have primarily been concerned with the effectiveness of specific behavioral techniques in reducing anxiety (Wine, 1971), the fact that reductions in test anxiety have not resulted in improvement in academic performance tends to be largely ignored.

Combinations of systematic desensitization and various forms of group counseling have been used in a number of studies to reduce test anxiety and improve grades. In many of these studies, group counseling procedures designed to teach study skills, to facilitate coping with anxiety in test situations, or both were successful in reducing test anxiety and improving grades (e.g., Allen, 1971; Cohen, 1969; Doctor et al., 1970; Gonzalez, 1976; Katahn et al., 1966; McManus, 1971; Mitchell & Ng, 1972). However, despite this remarkable consistency in the research findings, a closer examination of the individual studies in which some combination of desensitization and group counseling was used reveals serious methodological problems.

The chapters in Part II looked at the antecedents, correlates, and consequences of test anxiety. In Part III, various approaches to treatment are described. This chapter reports the findings of an investigation of the effects of desensitization, study counseling, and anxiety-coping training on the test anxiety and academic performance of test-anxious university students. Before describing this study, research on the effectiveness of behavioral interventions for the treatment of test anxiety is examined. Then, research on the effects of test anxiety treatment on academic performance is reviewed.

EFFECTS OF BEHAVIORAL TREATMENTS ON REDUCING TEST ANXIETY

The findings in most studies of systematic desensitization with test-anxious students have consistently indicated that desensitization is effective in reducing test anxiety (Hembree, 1988). In several desensitization studies that failed to obtain a reduction in test anxiety (e.g., Donner & Guerney, 1969; Johnson & Sechrest, 1968; Lomont & Sherman, 1971), there were significant methodological problems. Donner and Guerney (1969), for example, had a 43% attrition rate, and Lomont and Sherman (1971) had the only study among those reviewed in which students received remuneration for their participation. Although there are also methodological problems in some desensitization studies in which reductions in test anxiety were found (Gonzalez, 1978a), there is, nevertheless, substantial evidence that desensitization is effective in reducing test anxiety (Hembree, 1988).

The effectiveness of study counseling in reducing test anxiety has been evaluated in a number of studies, with treatment procedures that have varied from structured behavioral methods to more traditional approaches that involved discussing feelings and attitudes about studying and exams (Gonzalez, 1976). In most of these investigations, study counseling alone was not effective in reducing test anxiety, but in those studies in which group counseling was combined with desensitization, some reduction in test anxiety was usually found (Hembree, 1988).

In summary, study counseling was most likely to result in a reduction in test anxiety when combined with structured behavioral techniques for teaching students how to observe, measure, and change their study behavior and how to prepare for and take examinations (e.g., Allen, 1971, 1973; Gonzalez, 1976). Reductions in test anxiety are also more likely to be found when students are explicitly informed that improving their study habits would reduce their anxiety and improve their grades. The importance of enhancing student expectations for therapeutic gain should not be underestimated in treatments designed to reduce fear and anxiety (Lick & Bootzin, 1975).

EFFECTS OF BEHAVIORAL TREATMENTS ON ACADEMIC PERFORMANCE

Students' grade point averages (GPAs) have been used most frequently to assess academic performance in test anxiety treatment research. Because GPA can be influenced by many different factors (Lin & McKeachie, 1970; Pervin, 1967), the sensitivity of GPA as a measure of treatment effectiveness has been questioned (Allen, 1971; Lavigne, 1974). Nevertheless, there is substantial evidence that combining desensitization with group counseling can lead to improved academic performance (e.g., Allen, 1971; Mitchell & Ng, 1972). However, in most studies of the effects of desensitization on academic achievement no improvement in grades was found (Gonzalez, 1978a).

In one desensitization study in which improved grades were found (Donner & Guerney, 1969), the desensitization procedures failed to reduce test anxiety. As previously noted, however, there was also excessive attrition in this study (43%). Similarly, R. E. Smith and Nye (1973) found that desensitization reduced test anxiety and improved GPA, but there was also a very high attrition rate (37%) in their desensitization group. In a third study (Meichenbaum, 1972), no information was provided on how pretreatment GPA was defined, for example, cumulative GPA, GPA for prior quarter, and so forth, which makes it difficult to evaluate its findings.

In studies with excessive attrition, improvement in GPA could be due to the fact that those students who fail to improve are those most likely to drop out of treatment. Because desensitization training is designed to reduce test anxiety and thereby facilitate academic achievement, findings of improved GPA in the absence of any reduction in test anxiety are paradoxical (Donner & Guerney, 1969). In such studies, improvement in academic performance in the absence of any reduction in test anxiety cannot logically be attributed to treatment effects. In sum, there is little evidence that desensitization alone is effective in improving academic performance.

In studies in which study counseling alone was used as a treatment for test anxiety, only Allen (1973) found improvement in GPA. It should be noted, however, that the mean pretreatment test anxiety level of Allen's subjects was about the same as that of students in a normative sample at the same college. Beneke and Harris (1972) found that procedures similar to those used by Allen were effective in increasing the GPA of nonanxious college students. Therefore, although study counseling alone may be effective in improving the academic performance of students with low to moderate test anxiety, there is little evidence that study counseling alone can improve the GPA for high test-anxious students.

In a number of studies in which desensitization was combined with group counseling in the treatment of test-anxious students, significant improvements in GPA were found (Hembree, 1988). However, Gonzalez (1978a) failed to find improvement in GPA in a treatment group that received desensitization plus study counseling (D + SC). This finding was surprising because the treatment that Gonzalez used was effective in decreasing test anxiety and in improving study habits in previous research. A major difference between Gonzalez's D + SC treatment and the study counseling procedures used in previous studies was that Gonzalez emphasized topics related to study skills in his discussion period while providing only minimal training in coping with anxiety. In most previous studies, some time was devoted to the discussion of anxiety during examinations and the use of relaxation as a means for coping with anxiety.

Another important difference between Gonzalez's (1978a) study and previous investigations in which desensitization was combined with group counseling was the length of the academic term. Gonzalez conducted his study at a university that operated on the quarter system, whereas most of the studies in which improvements in GPA were observed were conducted at institutions that operated on a semester term (e.g., Allen, 1971; Cohen, 1969; Doctor et al., 1970; Katahn et al., 1966; Mitchell & Ng, 1972). In the single study conducted in the context of a quarter system in which improvement in GPA was found (McManus, 1971), treatment was initiated at the beginning of the quarter, whereas Gonzalez did not initiate treatment until the 5th week of the 11-week academic term. Thus, there was relatively little time in Gonzalez's study for the reduction in test anxiety and the improvement in study habits to have any influence on grades.

In summary, the combination of systematic desensitization with some form of group counseling is the only test anxiety treatment technique that has been consistently effective in reducing test anxiety and improving academic performance. Unfortunately, these studies do not identify the components of the treatment programs that were primarily responsible for the observed improvements in GPA. In all but one of the seven desensitization plus group counseling studies, both study skills training and discussions about coping with anxiety were used. Thus, study skills training, teaching students how to cope with anxiety, or both could have produced the observed improvement in academic performance. Furthermore, study habits were not measured, and there were serious methodological flaws in some of these studies, such as high attrition, failure to assess test anxiety, and the use of nonequivalent control groups (Gonzalez, 1978a; Paul, 1969).

EFFECTS OF DESENSITIZATION IN COMBINATION WITH STUDY COUNSELING OR ANXIETY COPING TRAINING IN THE TREATMENT OF TEST-ANXIOUS STUDENTS

This study investigated the relative effectiveness of desensitization in combination with study counseling or anxiety-coping training in the treatment of test-anxious students (Gonzalez, 1978a). A no-treatment group controlled for test–retest effects and the passage of time. The subjects were 46 undergraduate students under 30 years of age who requested treatment for test anxiety at a university counseling center. None of the students were receiving any type of psychological treatment at the time the study was initiated.

In a pretreatment testing session, the students were given the Test Anxiety Scale (TAS; I. G. Sarason, 1972), the Test Anxiety Inventory (TAI; Spielberger et al., 1978), the Study Habits (SH) subscale of the Survey of the Study Habits and Attitudes (W. F. Brown & Holtzman, 1965), and the Effective Study Test (EST; W. F. Brown, 1964). On the basis of pretreatment SH subscale scores, the students were divided into above and below average study habits groups. Male students who scored above the SH median score of 40 were assigned to good SH group [$N = 10$]; those with scores below the median were assigned to the poor SH group [$N = 11$]. To have groups of comparable size, female students who scored at the SH median of 42 were randomly assigned to the good [$N = 15$] or poor [$N = 14$] SH group. Students with good and poor pretreatment study habits were assigned to one of the following experimental conditions: (a) desensitization plus study counseling (D + SC, $N = 18$), (b) desensitization plus anxiety-coping training (D + ACT; $N = 19$), and no treatment control (NTC; $N = 9$). Sex, scholastic ability, the student's personal schedule, credit hours for which the student was currently enrolled, and number of hours of work per week at the time of the experiment were also taken into account in assigning subjects to the three experimental conditions. Before treatment, the experimental groups did not differ on any of the outcome measures.

The students in the NTC condition participated in the pretreatment testing session and were informed that they could not be offered treatment until the next academic term. Approximately 1 week before the posttreatment testing session, the students in the NTC condition were contacted by mail and asked to participate in this session at which appointments for treatment during the next term would be given.

There were four treatment groups, each consisting of 8 to 10 students. Two treatment groups received D + ACT, and two received D + SC. Treatment was initiated in the 3rd week of the 11-week academic term. The therapist was an advanced graduate student in clinical psychology, with substantial training and experience in the behavioral treatment techniques that were used.

The treatment groups met twice weekly in the same room over a period of 4 weeks, for a total of eight treatment sessions. Each treatment session lasted approximately 75 min. During the treatment sessions, the students reclined in lounge chairs while they received relaxation training and desensitization. The procedures were recorded on preprogrammed audiotapes, which were the same as those used by Anton (1975) and Bedell (1975).

In the first treatment session, after the therapist and the students introduced themselves, the therapist gave a brief explanation of the treatment rationale. The students were informed that they would be learning how to cope with the anxiety they experienced in testing situations. This was followed by relaxation training, which consisted of brief tension-release cycles for different muscle groups, ending with a period of undisturbed relaxation. The initial session concluded with a 10-min discussion of difficulties experienced during relaxation training that prevented the student from achieving a relaxed state. At the conclusion of the session, the students were encouraged to practice the relaxation exercises at home. Beginning with the second session, different procedures were followed for the D + ACT and the D + SC treatment groups.

D + ACT Treatment

In the second and third sessions, the D + ACT groups spent the first 15 min discussing their progress and the problems they encountered when practicing the relaxation exercises at home. Identifying muscles that became tense in stressful situations and muscle groups that the students were not able to relax during training were also discussed. The final 50 min of these sessions were devoted to progressive relaxation of different body areas, followed by a period of undisturbed relaxation. At the conclusion of the third session, the students were encouraged to use the relaxation skills they had recently learned to help them cope with anxiety-provoking situations encountered in their daily life.

Beginning with the fourth session, the D + ACT treatment group focused on discussion of the successes and failures experienced by these students in using relaxation to cope with anxiety. Many students reported that they used the relaxation techniques to cope with the anxiety in a variety of stressful situations, for example, in class presentations or driving a car in heavy traffic, in addition to taking a test. Some students reported that they used relaxation to help them fall asleep, to alleviate headaches, and to wait more patiently. The students in the D + ACT treatment condition were encouraged to talk about their experiences in attempting to cope with anxiety in all of these situations.

Following the discussion period in Sessions 4 through 8, the relaxation training was reduced from 50 min to 10 min, and 40 min of each treatment session was devoted to systematic desensitization. In Session 4 and continuing through Session 7, 6 items of the 29-item standard test anxiety hierarchy were presented in each session; 5 anxiety hierarchy items were presented in the finals session.

D + SC Treatment

The D + SC groups received the same relaxation training and desensitization procedures as the D + ACT groups. The essential difference between these conditions was that the first 15 min of Sessions 2 through 8 for the D + SC groups were devoted to study skills training, whereas students in the D + ACT group spent this time discussing their experiences in practicing and using relaxation exercises to cope with anxiety-provoking situations.

The study skills training procedures used in this study were essentially the same as the study counseling techniques used by Gonzalez (1976), as adapted from Allen (1972) and Groveman et al. (1975). The following topics were discussed: motivational factors that interfere with academic performance, functional analysis of study behavior, self-monitoring and graphing of study behavior, positive reinforcement and the Premack principle, improvement of reading efficiency, and how to prepare and take examinations. (Note that the Survey, Question, Read, Recite, and Review method of improving reading skills was used in this study for improvement of reading efficiency.) Students were given brief lecture notes, charts, and study guidelines describing the materials that were covered in the study skills training session.

All students participated in a posttreatment group testing session, which was conducted in the same room as the pretreatment session. The same tests that were given in the pretreatment testing session were readministered in the posttreatment session. Cumulative GPAs and the GPA for the term during which the treatment took place were obtained for each student from the official records of the university registrar.

EFFECTS OF TREATMENT ON TEST ANXIETY

The mean pre- and posttreatment TAS and TAI scores for the D + ACT, D + SC, and NTC groups are presented in Figure 9.1. Statistical analysis of these data indicated a significantly greater reduction in TAS and TAI scores for the D + ACT group than for either the D + SC or the NTC groups, which did not differ from one another. The findings for the D + ACT condition were essentially the same as those reported in six previous test anxiety treatment studies in which similar desensitization plus anxiety-coping training procedures were used (Allen, 1971; Cohen, 1969; Doctor et al., 1970; Katahn et al., 1966; McManus, 1971; Mitchell & Ng, 1972) and with the results of almost all studies in which desensitization alone was effective in reducing test anxiety.

Failure to find any reduction in test anxiety for the D + SC condition was puzzling because the combination of desensitization with some form of study counseling had been effective in reducing test anxiety in most previous studies. In this study, the students in the D + SC group received the same desensitization procedure as the D + ACT group and were also given lectures on study skills and notes and charts to help them monitor their study habits. However, the study counseling component differed from the procedures used in previous studies, and these differences may have contributed to the negative results.

In contrast to previous studies in which a combination of desensitization and study counseling was effective in reducing test anxiety, in this study the D + SC treatment devoted little time to interaction between the students and

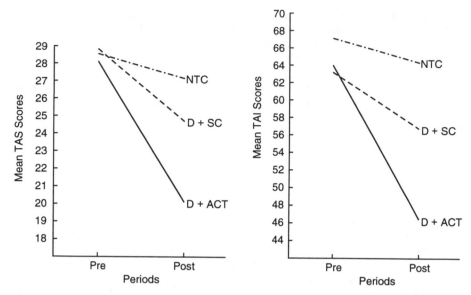

Figure 9.1 Pre- and posttreatment Test Anxiety Scale (TAS) and Test Anxiety Inventory (TAI) mean scores for the desensitization plus anxiety-coping training (D + ACT), desensitization plus study counseling (D + SC), and no treatment control (NTC) groups.

the therapist. This omission was intentional because one of the goals of the study was to investigate the relative influence of study skills training and anxiety-coping training. On the basis of the literature, we expected that the D + SC treatment would reduce test anxiety and improve study habits, but the procedures for helping students improve their study habits may have detracted from the effectiveness of the desensitization procedures. Study counseling appeared to increase the students' awareness of poor study behavior and may have contributed to continuing apprehension and worry about taking tests while attenuating expectations for therapeutic success.

The findings for the TAI Emotionality (E) and Worry (W) subscales were quite similar to the results obtained for the TAS and TAI total scores. The mean pre- and posttreatment E and W subscale scores for the D + ACT, D + SC, and NTC groups are presented in Figure 9.2. Statistical analysis indicated that students in the D + ACT treatment condition showed significant reductions in E and W subscale scores, whereas the D + SC treatment was not effective in reducing either emotionality or worry. Although the effects of behavioral treatments on the worry and emotionality components of test anxiety have as yet received little attention in the literature, Finger and Galassi (1977) have reported that relaxation, covert positive reinforcement, or a combination of these treatments resulted in similar reductions in worry and emotionality as measured by the Liebert and Morris (1967) Worry–Emotionality Questionnaire.

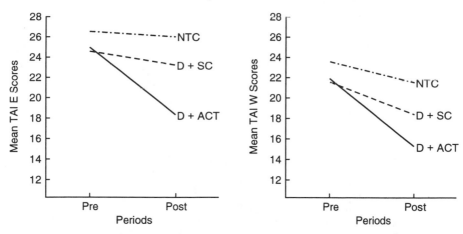

Figure 9.2   Pre- and posttreatment Test Anxiety Inventory (TAI) Emotionality (*E*) and Worry (*W*) mean scores for students in the desensitization plus anxiety-coping training (D + ACT), desensitization plus study counseling (D + SC), and no treatment control (NTC) groups.

EFFECT OF TREATMENT ON STUDY HABITS AND KNOWLEDGE ABOUT STUDY METHODS

Improvement in study habits was expected in the D + SC group on the basis of positive findings in three previous studies (Doctor et al., 1970; Gonzalez, 1976; Mitchell & Ng, 1972) in which similar procedures were used. However, neither the D + ACT nor the D + SC treatment conditions improved study habits as measured by the W. F. Brown–Holtzman (1965) SH subscale. The relatively brief time devoted to study counseling in the D + SC treatment condition probably contributed to the negative findings. In Gonzalez's (1976) study, the D + SC treatment group spent 30 min in study skills training, and substantial improvement in the SH scores was found. Furthermore, almost half of this time was devoted to discussions about study methods and difficulties in implementing newly learned skills. In this study, a total of only 15 min per session was devoted to study counseling, and most of this was consumed by didactic presentations. Thus, there was little time for the students to interact with the therapist.

The mean pre- and posttreatment scores on the EST for students in the D + ACT, D + SC, and NTC groups are presented in Figure 9.3, in which it can be noted that EST scores for students in all three experimental conditions increased. However, statistical analyses revealed that the D + SC treatment group showed a significantly greater improvement in knowledge of effective study procedures than did the students in the other two groups, which did not differ in EST scores. The increase in EST scores in the D + SC treatment group may be interpreted as evidence that the study counseling procedures were

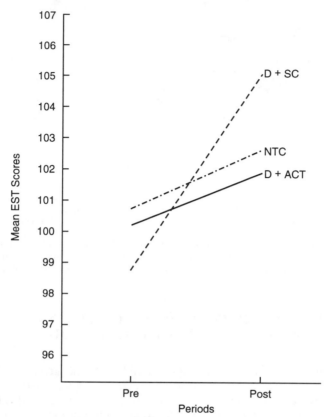

Figure 9.3 Pre- and posttreatment mean Effective Study Test (EST) scores for students in the desensitization plus anxiety-coping training (D + ACT), desensitization plus study counseling (D + SC), and no treatment control (NTC) groups.

effective in communicating information to students regarding appropriate methods of studying.

The finding that scores on the EST increased in the D + SC treatment condition, while there was no improvement in study habits, suggested that the students were learning useful information about study procedures but either were not sufficiently motivated or did not know how to use this information. The conclusion of Groveman et al. (1975), based on a review of the literature on study skills counseling and behavioral self-control approaches for improving study behavior, is worth noting: "If clients are to improve substantially, the therapist must get them to keep using the techniques they learned in therapy" (p. 11). It would seem that group discussion, modeling and practice of techniques, and intensive review of assigned homework must be incorporated into the treatment package to develop and maintain effective study behaviors.

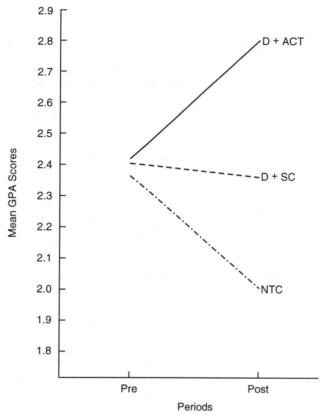

Figure 9.4 Pre- and posttreatment grade point average (GPA) means for students in the desensitization plus anxiety-coping training (D + ACT), desensitization plus study counseling (D + SC), and no treatment control (NTC) groups.

EFFECTS OF TREATMENT ON ACADEMIC PERFORMANCE

The pre- and posttreatment GPA means for students in the D + ACT, D + SC, and NTC conditions are presented in Figure 9.4. These data were evaluated by a least-squares analysis of variance (ANOVA). The significant Groups × Periods effect reflected the fact that the D + ACT group showed a significant increase in GPA from the pre- to the posttreatment period, whereas the GPAs for the D + SC and the NTC groups declined. The improvement in GPA for the D + ACT treatment was consistent with the finding that this treatment was effective in reducing test anxiety, emotionality, and worry. Fourteen of the 19 students in this condition showed an increase in academic performance. The failure to find any improvement in academic performance in the D + SC condition was contrary to theoretical expectations but consistent with the finding that this treatment was not effective in reducing test anxiety or improving study habits.

Although improvement in GPA for the D + ACT treatment group was not expected in this study, it was consistent with the results of six previous studies that combined desensitization with some form of group counseling. Although the D + ACT treatment procedure in this study differed from those in previous studies in that there were no discussions regarding study methods or habits, the students were encouraged to use relaxation as an anxiety-coping technique, and considerable time was devoted to discussions in which information on successes and failures in using relaxation for coping with anxiety was reported.

On the basis of previous research (Gonzalez, 1976), students with good study habits who showed a substantial reduction in test anxiety were expected to have greater improvement in academic performance than students who experienced little or no reduction in test anxiety. To test this hypothesis, the data for the students in the D + ACT and D + SC groups were combined and then divided into two groups on the basis of the amount of reduction in test anxiety that was shown by each student. This was accomplished by computing TAI change scores (Δ TAI) for each student by subtracting posttreatment TAI scores from pretreatment TAI scores and adding a constant of 20 to avoid negative values (The TAI was used in defining the high and low test anxiety reduction groups because it was considered to be a more sensitive measure of test anxiety than the TAS. The TAI has a wider range and greater variability in scores than the TAS.) Four groups were thus formed on the basis of SH and Δ TAI scores. Students with good study habits (SH subscale scores above the median) who had a Δ TAI score above 34 constituted the good SH–large TAI reduction group. Students in the good SH–small TAI reduction group had SH subscale scores above the median and Δ TAI scores below 29. Similarly, students in the poor SH–large TAI group scored below the SH median and had Δ TAI scores above 34 and students in the poor SH–small TAI group had Δ TAI scores below 29.

The pre- and posttreatment GPA means for students with good and poor pretreatment SH scores and large or small reductions in TAI are reported in Figure 9.5. These data were analyzed by means of a 2 × 2 × 2 least-squares ANOVA in which study habits and reduction in TAI scores were the between-subjects variables and periods was the within-subjects variable. This analysis yielded a significant SH × TAI Reduction × Periods interaction effect, which is depicted in Figure 9.5. Although the good SH–large TAI reduction group showed the predicted large increase in GPA, the good SH–small TAI reduction group declined in GPA, and the two poor study habits groups showed little change. Except for the substantial drop in GPA for the good SH–small TAI reduction group, these findings were consistent with the results previously reported by Gonzalez (1976), who also found that students with good study habits and substantial reductions in test anxiety showed the greatest increase in GPA.

In summary, the D + ACT treatment in this study was effective in reducing test anxiety and its worry and emotionality components, as compared with the D + SC and NTC conditions, for which test anxiety remained essentially un-

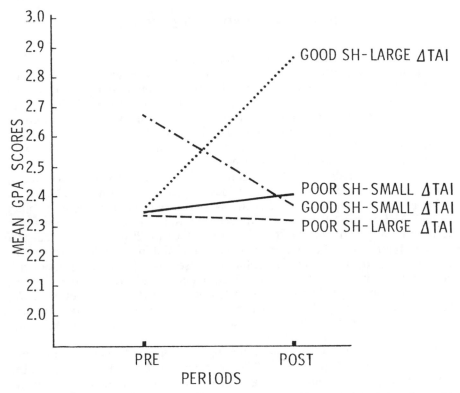

Figure 9.5   Pre- and posttreatment grade point average (GPA) means for treated students with good and poor study habits (SH) and large and small reductions in their scores on the Test Anxiety Inventory (Δ TAI).

changed. Contrary to expectation, study habits for students in the D + SC group remained essentially unchanged, as did those for students in the D + ACT and the NTC groups. The D + SC treatment was effective in improving knowledge about effective study procedures, whereas no improvement in EST scores was found for the D + ACT group. The D + ACT treatment was effective in improving grades, whereas there was no improvement in the academic performance of the D + SC treatment; the latter treatment was also ineffective in reducing test anxiety and improving study habits. When the treatment groups were combined, students with good pretreatment study habits and large reductions in test anxiety showed the greatest improvement in grades, indicating that substantial reductions in test anxiety facilitate the academic performance of students with good study habits.

DISCUSSION AND CONCLUSIONS

Research on the treatment of test-anxious students has demonstrated that desensitization and other single behavioral treatments are effective in reducing test anxiety, but there is little evidence that this reduction in anxiety results in improvement in academic performance. In contrast, in most of the studies in which desensitization was combined with some form of group counseling, improvements in GPA were obtained. The success of these combined treatment approaches has been attributed to improvement in study habits along with reduction in test anxiety (Mitchell & Ng, 1972).

Because study habits correlate negatively with test anxiety (e.g., Wittmaier, 1972) and positively with academic achievement (W. F. Brown & Holtzman, 1965) and appear to contribute to academic performance independent of ability (Lin & McKeachie, 1970), it would seem essential to take study habits into account in the treatment of test anxiety. Over the past 20 years, numerous test anxiety treatment studies have been conducted, and in many of these investigations some form of study counseling was used as a treatment component. Yet, study habits were actually measured in only a few studies (e.g., Annis, 1986; Doctor et al., 1970; Garcia, 1975; Gonzalez, 1976; Mitchell et al., 1975; Mitchell & Ng, 1972). Thus, a major shortcoming in test anxiety treatment research has been the failure to measure and attempt to improve the faulty study habits of test-anxious students.

It has been previously established that test-anxious students have poor study habits (Desiderato & Koskinen, 1969; Wittmaier, 1972) and that they tend to devote less time to actual studying than less anxious students (Allen et al., 1972). For the test-anxious students who participated in the study described in this chapter, the pretreatment mean score on the EST was 99.22, which is within the average range of 99 to 105 for college freshmen (W. F. Brown, 1964). In contrast, the mean score of these students on the SH subscale was 40.66, which is at the 30th percentile level for college freshmen (W. F. Brown & Holtzman, 1965). Thus, the students in this study had about average knowledge of effective study methods but were well below average in using their knowledge. These findings suggest that procedures for the treatment of test-anxious students should include training in self-control techniques to improve study habits.

In most of the test anxiety treatment studies that found improvement in grades, students were encouraged to use relaxation as a means for coping with anxiety during examinations and other stressful situations. Furthermore, the motivation to use relaxation techniques during examinations is apparently enhanced by group discussions in which students report their experiences of success and failure with these techniques in a variety of stressful situations. In effect, the group discussions seemed to stimulate the students to try out the newly learned anxiety-coping techniques and to persist in using these techniques during examinations and other stressful situations.

Meichenbaum (1972) and Holroyd (1976) used cognitive behavior modification strategies in the treatment of test-anxious students, and significant reductions in test anxiety and improvement in grades were found in both studies. Although the treatment techniques used by these investigators appeared to facilitate academic performance by alleviating or reducing the intensity of worry cognitions, Meichenbaum's and Holroyd's cognitive strategies also placed a strong emphasis on encouraging and motivating the test-anxious students to actively cope with a variety of stressful situations.

Group discussions and counseling with test-anxious students appear to facilitate cognitive restructuring (Goldfried et al., 1978) while reducing the tendency for these students to experience self-doubts and self-depreciating thoughts in evaluative situations. To the extent that group discussions reduce the amount of time that test-anxious students spend in ruminating about personal shortcomings and perceived inadequacies (Schwarzer & Jerusalem, 1992), students will be able to devote more attention to the task at hand (e.g., studying and taking tests) and to concentrate better during examinations.

A comprehensive treatment program for test anxiety requires careful evaluation of the students' motivation to actively cope with anxiety-arousing problems and the extent to which worry cognitions and intense emotional reactions interfere with studying and academic performance. In motivating test-anxious students and teaching them to use specific treatment techniques, group discussions of the students' experiences in using these coping skills appear to be an essential component of the treatment process. Study habits must also be taken into account, and study skills training and self-control behavioral programs should be offered for students with poor study habits.

SUMMARY

This study investigated the relative effectiveness of desensitization in combination with either study counseling or anxiety-coping training in the treatment of test-anxious students with good and poor study habits. The participants were 46 undergraduate students with good and poor study habits who requested treatment for test anxiety. They were assigned to one of three groups: D + SC, D + ACT, or NTC. Each treatment group met for 75 min, twice a week over a 4-week period for a total of 8 sessions.

The D + ACT, D + SC, and NTC groups did not differ on any of the outcome measures before treatment. The D + ACT treatment condition was effective in reducing test anxiety from pre- to posttreatment. No significant changes in test anxiety scores were found for the D + SC group, which did not differ from the NTC group.

The D + SC treatment was effective in improving knowledge about effective study procedures, as expected, whereas no improvements in these scores were observed in the D + ACT group. Contrary to expectation, study habits for students in the D + SC group remained essentially unchanged, as did the SH subscale scores for students in the D + ACT and the NTC groups.

The D + ACT treatment was effective in improving grades, whereas results for the D + SC treatment did not differ from those for the NTC group. These results were consistent with the finding that the D + ACT treatment was effective in reducing test anxiety, in contrast with the D + SC treatment, which did not reduce anxiety.

Students in the D + ACT group were encouraged to use relaxation as a means of coping with anxiety. The motivation of these students to use relaxation techniques during examinations appeared to be enhanced by group discussions of success and failure experiences with these techniques in a variety of stressful situations. The group discussions also appeared to facilitate cognitive restructuring, which reduced the tendency for the test-anxious students to experience self-doubts and self-depreciating thoughts in evaluative situations.

When the treatment groups were combined, students with good pretreatment study habits and large reductions in test anxiety showed the greatest improvement in grades. These findings provide evidence that a substantial reduction in test anxiety leads to improvement in the academic performance of students with good study habits.

10

Cognitive Therapy, Study Counseling, and Systematic Desensitization in the Treatment of Test Anxiety

Benjamin Algaze
University of South Florida, Tampa, Florida, USA

Numerous studies of the treatment of test-anxious students have been conducted with the expectation that alleviating test anxiety would improve academic performance (Spielberger & Vagg, 1987). A variety of therapeutic approaches have been used in these studies, including systematic desensitization, study counseling, and cognitive therapies (Algaze, 1980; Gonzalez, 1978a). Of these treatments, systematic desensitization has been used more often than any other approach (Spielberger et al., 1976).

Although systematic desensitization has been consistently effective in reducing test anxiety, there is little evidence that this treatment alone improves academic performance. However, in combination with study counseling, systematic desensitization has been effective not only in reducing test anxiety, but also in improving academic achievement, as shown in the preceding chapter by Gonzalez. Because study counseling alone does not lead to improvement in the grades of test-anxious students (e.g., Allen, 1971; Hembree, 1988; Mitchell & Ng, 1972), it would seem essential to include some form of study skills training in combination with systematic desensitization to improve the academic performance of test-anxious students.

Wine's (1971) review of the literature on test anxiety, which attributed the performance decrements of test-anxious students to disturbances of attention and cognitive factors, provided the impetus for research on cognitive approaches to the treatment of test anxiety. In the 1970s, the effectiveness of cognitive treatments for reducing test anxiety and improving academic performance was investigated in a number of studies (e.g., Bruch et al., 1974; Goldfried et al., 1978; Hahnloser, 1974; Holroyd, 1976; Lavigne, 1974; Meichenbaum, 1972; Scrivner, 1974; Thompson, 1976; Vagg, 1978; Wagaman, 1975). Although the results of these studies are not entirely consistent, congitive

This chapter is based on the author's doctoral dissertation, submitted to the Department of Psychology of the University of South Florida. The research was conducted under the supervision of Professor Charles D. Spielberger and was supported in part by a grant from the Advanced Research Projects Agency, U.S. Department of Defense (MDA 903-77-C-0190), awarded to C. D. Spielberger and W. D. Anton.

therapy, either alone or in combination with systematic desensitization, was effective in both reducing test anxiety and improving grades in the more adequate, better controlled studies (e.g., Holroyd, 1976; Meichenbaum, 1972).

Research on the nature and measurement of test anxiety provides additional justification for cognitive treatment approaches. This research (e.g., Lam & Hong, 1992; Liebert & Morris, 1967; Morris & Liebert, 1970; Schwarzer & Jerusalem, 1992; Spielberger, 1980), as discussed earlier in Chapters 1 and 2, suggests that test anxiety consists of two interrelated components: worry and emotionality. Worry is defined as cognitive concern and self-preoccupation with one's performance, ability, or adequacy. Emotionality refers to heightened emotional and physiological arousal during examinations. Although measures of worry generally correlate negatively with academic performance, no consistent relation has been found between emotionality and performance (Doctor & Altman, 1969; Liebert & Morris, 1967; Morris & Liebert, 1970).

Following the lead of Liebert and Morris (1967), Spielberger (1980) and his colleagues (Spielberger et al., 1978) have emphasized worry and emotionality as components of test anxiety. Test anxiety is conceptualized as a situation-specific anxiety trait; high test-anxious students tend to perceive evaluative situations as more threatening and to respond with greater elevations in state anxiety (worry and emotionality) in these situations than do low test-anxious students.

Morris and Liebert (1970) have suggested that "worry may be alleviated through cognitively oriented counseling or study skills training" (p. 325). However, in most test anxiety treatment studies, systematic desensitization has been used to modify the emotional reactions of test-anxious students; the students' cognitive ruminations and worry reactions have largely been ignored (Spielberger et al., 1976). Because worry is negatively correlated with grades whereas emotionality is not related (for a more detailed discussion, see Chapter 1), it would seem especially important to reduce or eliminate worry in order to facilitate academic achievement.

Cognitive therapies seem uniquely appropriate for eliminating the negative ruminations (worries) of test-anxious students, whereas systematic desensitization is more appropriate for reducing emotionality (Morris & Liebert, 1970; Spielberger et al., 1976). However, in five cognitive test anxiety treatment studies in which worry and emotionality were treated simultaneously, no consistent treatment effects were found in two studies (Hahnloser, 1974; Scrivner, 1974), one study reported that cognitive and emotionality-focused treatments reduced both worry and emotionality (Finger & Galassi, 1977), and worry and emotionality were not even measured in two studies (Meichenbaum, 1972; Osarchuck, 1976). It has also been shown that an emotionality-focused treatment, when enriched with anxiety-coping training, reduced both components of test anxiety (see the study reported by Gonzalez, Chapter 9).

The findings in research on the treatment of test anxiety suggest that a treatment package that combined cognitive therapy, systematic desensitization, and study counseling should be especially effective in reducing test anxiety and improving academic performance. This combination of treatment components has never been evaluated with test-anxious students. The goals of this study were to evaluate cognitive therapy (CT) alone and in combination with systematic desensitization (SD) and study counseling (SC) in the treatment of test-anxious college students. Before describing the procedures and results of this study, the research literature on cognitive approaches in the treatment of test anxiety is reviewed and evaluated.

COGNITIVE TREATMENT OF TEST ANXIETY

Studies evaluating the effectiveness of cognitive therapies in the treatment of test anxiety can be divided into three general categories. One group of studies used cognitive therapy alone in treating test anxiety. A second group used cognitive therapy (CT) in combination with other treatment components such as systematic desensitization (SD) or study counseling (SC). The third group consisted of several studies that compared CT alone with combinations of CT and other treatment components.

The effectiveness of CT alone for reducing test anxiety and improving academic performance has been investigated in five studies (Bruch et al., 1974; Goldfried et al., 1978; Scrivner, 1974; Thompson, 1976; Wagaman, 1975). Although significant reductions in test anxiety were found in all but one study (Thompson, 1976), there was no improvement in grade point average (GPA) or performance on cognitive–intellectual tasks that could be attributed to the cognitive treatment in any of these studies.

Two studies (Lavigne, 1974; Meichenbaum, 1972) combined CT with other approaches in the treatment of test anxiety. Lavigne (1974) compared a combined treatment—CT, SC, and relaxation training—with desensitization alone and a waiting-list control group. The combined and desensitization treatments both produced significant reductions in test anxiety relative to the control group. There was also a tendency for the students who received these treatments to show improved performance on a cognitive intellectual task (the Wonderlic Personnel Test), but this improvement was not statistically significant. Neither treatment group showed any improvement in GPA.

Meichenbaum (1972) carried out the first well-controlled study using CT in the treatment of test anxiety. Meichenbaum's "cognitive therapy" was actually a combination of two approaches: it included coping imagery and modified systematic desensitization (MSD). When this combined treatment (CT + MSD) was compared with desensitization treatment and a waiting-list control group, the combined treatment resulted in greater reduction in test anxiety, greater improvement in grades, and better performance on two cognitive–intellectual tasks (Digit Symbol Test and Raven Progressive Matrices). Desensitization was also more effective than no treatment in reducing test anxiety and in improving grades, and it was just as effective as the combined treatment for improving performance on the cognitive–intellectual tasks.

A major limitation in the Lavigne (1974) and Meichenbaum (1972) studies was that the experimental design did not permit clarification of which component in the combined treatment condition was primarily responsible for the observed effects. This issue was addressed in three studies in which CT alone was compared with treatments in which CT was combined with SD, other treatment components, or both (Hahnloser, 1974; Holroyd, 1976; Vagg, 1978).

Hahnloser (1974) compared CT alone with a combination of CT and relaxation training, and relaxation training alone, in the treatment of test anxiety. He found that the combined treatment was the most effective in reducing test anxiety, but none of the treatments led to any improvement in academic performance.

Holroyd (1976) investigated the relative effectiveness of each of the components in Meichenbaum's (1976) CT + MSD treatment of test anxiety. In this study, Holroyd compared CT alone, SD alone, and CT + SD with pseudotherapy and no-treatment control (NTC) groups. He found that CT alone was more effective than any other treatment for reducing test anxiety and state anxiety and for improving GPA, but that SD alone, CT + SD, and pseudotherapy also reduced test anxiety and improved GPA relative to the NTC condition. However, only the CT and CT + SD conditions in Holroyd's study resulted in improved performance on a cognitive–intellectual task (Digit Symbol Test). Although the CT-alone treatment exhibited clear superiority over the other approaches, all of Holroyd's treatments, including the SD and pseudotherapy control conditions, resulted in improved grades.

Vagg (1978) evaluated the effectiveness of CT and biofeedback in the treatment of test-anxious college students with good and poor study skills (see also the study reported by Vagg and Papsdorf in Chapter 13). The CT treatment alone, and combined with biofeedback, produced significant reductions in test anxiety and its worry and emotionality components, as measured by the Test Anxiety Inventory (TAI; Spielberger, 1980). No changes in test anxiety were found for the biofeedback treatment alone or for the NTC groups. In addition, Vagg found that students with good study skills had higher pretest GPAs than students with poor study skills and tended to show more improvement in GPA as a result of treatment.

In summary, CT reduced test anxiety in 9 of the 10 treatment studies that were reviewed, but improvement in grades or performance on cognitive–intellectual tasks was found in only 2 of these investigations (Holroyd, 1976; Meichenbaum, 1972). Thus, the literature is inconclusive with regard to the effectiveness of cognitive therapies in improving academic performance, but procedural variations among the studies, the diversity of the treatments, and the methodological problems that were noted in some of the studies no doubt contributed to these equivocal findings.

In test anxiety treatment studies that have attempted to treat worry or emotionality, the research findings have not supported the expectation that cognitive and emotionality-focused treatment approaches would have different effects on these components. Because worry is negatively correlated with grades and emotionality is not, reductions in worry should facilitate achievement (as outlined earlier in Chapter 2). A combination of CT + SD should reduce both the worry and the emotionality components of test anxiety, and these treatments combined with SC might be an optimal approach for improving the academic performance of test-anxious students.

COGNITIVE THERAPY, SYSTEMATIC DESENSITIZATION, AND STUDY COUNSELING IN THE TREATMENT OF TEST ANXIETY

This study was undertaken to compare four approaches to the treatment of test anxiety and its worry and emotionality components. The treatment conditions were (a) CT alone, (b) CT + SC, (c) CT + SD, and (d) CT + SC + SD. An NTC condition was also included to evaluate test–retest effects and the passage of time.

On the basis of previous research findings, it was expected that the four treatments, which all included a CT component, would reduce test anxiety and worry. The two treatments with an SD component (CT + SD and CT + SC + SD) were expected to reduce emotionality more than the treatment conditions that did not include this component (CT and CT + SC). Similarly, the treatment conditions with an SC component (CT + SC and CT + SC + SD) were expected to improve study habits more than the treatments without this component (CT and CT + SD). Although all four treatments were expected to improve grades, the CT + SC + SD treatment was expected to be more effective than the other conditions.

Subjects and Test Instruments

The subjects were undergraduate students who requested treatment for test anxiety at the University of South Florida Counseling Center. Most of the students learned about the study through campuswide announcements of the availability of a test anxiety treatment program, but some students spontaneously came to the counseling center seeking assistance for their test anxiety problems.

A total of 85 students expressed interest in the program. Individual half-hour interviews were conducted with these students to determine if they met the following criteria for being included in the study: (a) full-time undergraduate student under 30 years of age who had completed at least one term at the university, but who was not a final-term senior; (b) GPA below 3.5; (c) not receiving any type of psychological treatment at the time of the study; and (d) not working more than 20 hr per week on a paid job. The 62 students who met all of these criteria were invited to attend a pretreatment group testing session. Of the eligible students, 45 attended the testing sessions and were the subjects for this study.

Three test anxiety scales were used as treatment outcome measures. These were I.G. Sarason's (1972) Test Anxiety Scale (TAS), Liebert and Morris's (1967) Worry–Emotionality Questionnaire (WEQ) Worry and Emotionality scales, and Spielberger's (1980) TAI, which has subscales to measure worry (W) and emotionality (E) as components of test anxiety (see Chapter 1).

The Trait Anxiety (A-Trait) subscale of the State–Trait Anxiety Inventory (STAI; Spielberger et al., 1970) was used to measure anxiety proneness, that is, the disposition to respond with elevations in state anxiety under a wide range of threatening conditions. Extensive data on the reliability and validity of the STAI A-Trait scale are reported in the test manual (Spielberger et al., 1970).

The W. F. Brown–Holtzman (1965) Survey of Study Habits and Attitudes (SSHA) was used to measure study habits and study attitudes. The Study Habits (SH) subscale assesses specific study habits such as promptness in completing assignments, freedom from distraction, and effective study procedures. The Study Attitudes (SA) subscale measures students' attitudes toward academic tasks, feelings about the fairness of professors, and beliefs about the purpose of education. Reliability and validity data and norms for the SSHA are reported in the test manual (W. F. Brown & Holtzman, 1965).

Four measures of GPA were obtained from official university records. These were cumulative GPA before treatment, GPA for the quarter immediately before treatment, GPA for the quarter in which treatment took place, and GPA for the quarter following treatment. The GPAs were based on the allocation of 4 quality points for each credit hour for which the student received an A, 3 points for a B, 2 for a C, 1 for a D, and 0 for an F.

Procedure

In group-testing sessions conducted 5 to 7 days before the initiation of treatment, the subjects were given the SSHA, TAS, TAI, STAI A-Trait, and the WEQ Worry and Emotionality subscales, in the order indicated, with standard instructions for each scale. Subjects were then divided into good and poor study habits groups on the basis of their pretreatment SH subscale scores. Students who scored above 38, the median SH score, were assigned to the good study habits group ($n = 22$); those who scored 38 or below were assigned to the poor study habits group ($n = 23$).

The students in the good and poor study habits groups were assigned, on the basis of their available free time, to one of the following experimental conditions: (a) CT ($n = 8$), (b) CT+SC ($n = 8$), (c) CT+SD ($n = 8$), (d) CT+SC+SD ($n = 8$), and (e) NTC ($n = 13$). In assigning the subjects to the various conditions, the investigator attempted to match the experimental groups on pretreatment test anxiety and GPA.

The students in the NTC group were notified that more students had signed up for the program than could be treated during the current term and that they would be offered treatment in the following term. They were also informed that they would be asked to participate in another group-testing session near the end of the term, at which time the appointments for future treatment would be scheduled.

The four treatment groups met twice each week over a period of 4 weeks, for a total of eight sessions. Each session lasted approximately 2 hr and was conducted in the same room by the investigator, an advanced graduate student in clinical psychology with extensive supervised experience with behavioral approaches to the treatment of test anxiety.

The initial treatment session began with a brief description of the rationale for treatment, followed by introductions among the students. The CT procedures, which were essentially the same as those developed by Meichenbaum (1972), were then introduced to all four treatment groups. Before this investigation, the experimenter–therapist obtained experience in several pilot studies in applying the CT procedures described in Meichenbaum's Therapist's Manual. These procedures were designed to (a) make the test-anxious students aware of the anxiety-engendering thoughts or task-irrelevant cognitions they experienced while studying for or taking tests and (b) train them to cope with anxiety and distracting thoughts by practicing coping skills imagery exercises to help them focus their attention on the task and away from negative ruminations. The students were taught to concentrate on positive thoughts before a test and to develop the habit of instructing themselves to attend to the task while studying or taking tests. The students were then informed of the general goals of cognitive treatment and the specific goals of the particular treatment condition to which they were assigned. After this point in the first session, the procedures for the four treatment groups differed as described below.

CT. After discussing the nature of the negative thoughts that are experienced in evaluative situations, the therapist clarified how these negative ruminations can lead to poor test performance. This discussion continued for 35 min, after which there was a 75-min "placebo" discussion of the students' feelings about professors, the courses they liked best or least, or any other topic of interest. The content of the placebo discussions was unrelated to any of the therapeutic approaches; these discussions were designed only to equate for the total time of each session for the four treatment groups.

The final step in the initial session for the CT condition consisted of the homework assignment. For the first assignment, the students were instructed to continue to analyze the negative thoughts they experienced during any test they took before the next session and to be prepared to report their observations.

Over the course of the next six sessions, the same general pattern was followed in the CT treatment condition. The first 15 min was spent in discussing experiences and observations relating to the homework assignment, followed by 35 min in which the therapist administered the CT procedures. These sessions all ended with the placebo discussion and the assignment of the homework. The topics covered in Sessions 2 to 7 in the CT condition were (a) the situations and contexts in which negative thoughts and feelings were experienced; (b) the self-defeating, irrational, and "self-fulfilling prophecy" aspects of negative cognitions; (c) the emotional reactions that were elicited by these thoughts; (d) how to change negative thoughts into positive cognitions that supplant students' worries; (e) the importance of concentrating on the task while studying for or taking tests; and (f) learning and practicing coping skills imagery exercises (see Meichenbaum, 1972, and Algaze, 1980, for more complete details of these exercises).

In the final treatment session for the CT condition, the topics covered in all preceding sessions were reviewed. At the conclusion of this session, the students were informed of the date, time, and place for the posttreatment group testing session to which they were assigned.

CT + SC. The CT + SC group received the same CT procedures given to the CT group, as described above. In addition, this group received SC similar to that used by Allen (1972), as modified by Garcia (1975) and Gonzalez (1976). Session 1 of the CT + SC treatment began with a 35-min discussion of the motivational factors that interfere with studying and academic performance, followed by a 35 to 40-min placebo discussion, after which the homework assignment was given.

During the next six sessions, the CT + SC group spent approximately 35 min of each session discussing the following study skills topics: (a) functional analyses of study behavior, (b) positive reinforcement and the Premack Principle, (c) monitoring and graphing study behaviors, (d) improving reading efficiency (The Survey, Question, Read, Review, and Recite system was used to help improve reading proficiency in this study.), and (e) how to prepare and take examinations. The students were given notes, charts, and study guidelines for each of these steps and were instructed to review these materials as part of the homework assignments.

In the final treatment session, the CT + SC group reviewed and discussed the CT and SC topics covered in the preceding seven sessions. At the conclusion of this session, the students were informed of the date, time, and place for the posttesting session to which they had been assigned.

CT + SD. The CT + SD group received the same CT procedures as the CT group, followed by 30–35 min of SD treatment, 5 min of undisturbed relaxation, and 35 min of placebo discussion. The SD procedures were presented by means of preprogrammed audiotapes while the students reclined in lounge chairs, and the procedures were essentially the same as those used by Anton (1975) and Bedell (1975). The homework assignment for this condition was the same as for the CT condition, but in addition the students were instructed to practice relaxation for at least 15 min every day.

In the final session, the CT topics that had been discussed in the preceding sessions were reviewed, and ways of effectively using the SD treatment to cope with anxiety were discussed. The time, date, and place of posttreatment testing session to which students had been assigned was announced at the end of the session.

CT + SC + SD. This group received all of the treatments described above. The CT procedures were delivered first in each session, followed by the SC and SD treatment procedures. There was no placebo discussion. The homework assignments for this condition included all of the assignments given to the other treatment groups.

In the final session, CT and SC topics covered in the previous seven sessions were reviewed and ways of using the SD treatment to handle anxiety were discussed. At the end of the session, the time, date, and place of the posttesting session to which these students were assigned was announced.

The two posttreatment testing sessions were conducted 1–3 days after termination of treatment in the same room as the pretreatment testing. The same tests given in the pretreatment testing session were readministered in the posttreatment testing. After the testing was completed, all students in the NTC group who expressed interest in receiving treatment were given appointments for future treatment and dismissed. The students who had participated in the treatment groups were then informed about the purposes of the study and debriefed.

RESULTS

The data analyses are based on 38 subjects who participated in all facets of the study and whose performance was not contaminated by having engaged in other treatment activities. The number of subjects in each of the five experimental conditions was approximately equal (8 in CT, CT + SC + SD, and NTC; 7 in CT + SC and CT + SD). Of the 45 subjects who completed the pretreatment testing, 2 dropped out of the experiment because of scheduling conflicts (1 each in the CT + SC and CT + SD groups). Four subjects in the NTC group failed to report for the posttreatment testing sessions, and 1 additional NTC subject was dropped because she had enrolled in a study skills course while the study was in progress.

Effects of Treatments on Test Anxiety and Trait Anxiety

The pre- and posttreatment means and standard deviations for the test anxiety measures of students with good and poor study habits are presented in Table 10.1. The data for the TAS and TAI measures were evaluated in 5 × 2 × 2 least-squares analyses of variance (ANOVAs) in which the five experimental conditions, good and poor study habits, and pre- and posttreatment periods were the independent variables. The results for the TAS and TAI measures were quite similar; for both measures, the periods main effects ($p <$ .001) and the Groups × Periods interactions ($p <$ .01) were statistically significant.

Because there were no statistically significant effects involving the study habits variable, the data for subjects with good and poor study habits were combined. The TAS and TAI pre- and posttreatment mean scores for subjects in the five experimental conditions are graphed in Figure 10.1. As can be noted, substantial reductions in test anxiety were found for all four treatment groups, whereas the test anxiety scores for the NTC group remained essentially unchanged. Subsequent analyses of the TAS and TAI data showed that all treatment conditions significantly ($p <$ .01) reduced the scores for both test anxiety measures as compared with the NTC group and that the four treatment groups did not differ in the amount of reduction in test anxiety.

The data for the TAI W, TAI E, WEQ Worry, and WEQ Emotionality measures were also evaluated in 5 × 2 × 2 least-squares ANOVAs. For the two worry measures, the periods main effects ($p <$ .001) and the Groups × Periods interactions ($p <$ .05) were statistically significant. Because there were no significant effects involving the study habits variable, the data for good and poor study habits groups were combined and the Groups × Periods interactions for the TAI W and WEQ Worry measures are plotted in the left-hand side of Figures 10.2 and 10.3, respectively. As can be noted, the worry scores

Table 10.1 Pre- and posttreatment means and standard deviations for the Test
Anxiety Scale (TAS), the Test Anxiety Inventory (TAI), and the State–
Trait Anxiety Inventory Trait Anxiety (STAI A-Trait) subscales for
students in the five experimental conditions

Treatment condition and study habits	TAS		TAI		STAI A-Trait	
	Pre	Post	Pre	Post	Pre	Post
CT + SC + SD ($n = 8$)						
Good ($n = 3$)						
M	27.0	13.0	64.0	37.0	42.7	34.0
SD	2.7	11.5	10.6	20.4	6.7	10.4
Poor ($n = 5$)						
M	28.4	14.4	61.4	37.8	50.8	41.0
SD	5.4	6.6	14.3	7.9	6.6	9.0
CT + SC ($n = 7$)						
Good ($n = 3$)						
M	30.7	11.0	59.0	32.0	45.3	33.3
SD	3.1	10.8	6.0	16.5	9.3	11.6
Poor ($n = 4$)						
M	26.8	10.3	59.0	27.5	45.0	33.0
SD	8.1	7.3	15.5	7.9	3.6	12.2
CT + SD ($n = 7$)						
Good ($n = 3$)						
M	26.3	10.0	52.3	33.0	48.3	48.7
SD	9.5	9.5	19.7	9.2	4.6	8.4
Poor ($n = 4$)						
M	30.0	14.8	64.8	35.0	51.5	37.5
SD	2.2	6.3	4.3	11.9	11.9	7.4
CT ($n = 8$)						
Good ($n = 4$)						
M	28.5	19.5	63.0	47.5	39.3	38.5
SD	6.5	12.7	16.2	25.2	8.3	10.7
Poor ($n = 4$)						
M	31.8	19.3	63.0	42.8	48.0	39.8
SD	2.2	6.3	8.8	14.4	8.5	5.0
NTC ($n = 8$)						
Good ($n = 4$)						
M	23.0	23.3	51.0	53.3	40.5	39.5
SD	6.6	7.1	12.7	13.7	8.2	7.2
Poor ($n = 4$)						
M	28.5	29.8	64.5	59.5	53.5	47.5
SD	4.8	2.6	13.6	9.1	7.1	9.7

Note. CT = cognitive therapy; SC = study counseling; SD = systematic densitization; NTC
= no treatment control; Pre = pretreatment; Post = posttreatment.

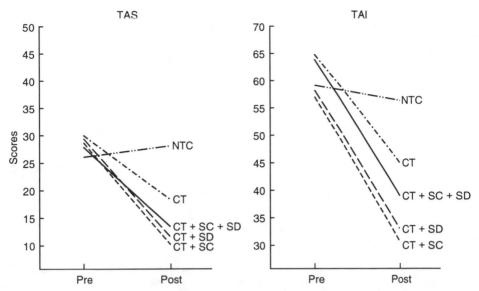

Figure 10.1   Pretreatment (Pre) and posttreatment (Post) Test Anxiety Scale (TAS) and Test Anxiety Inventory (TAI) mean scores for the four treatment conditions and the no-treatment control (NTC) group. CT = cognitive therapy; SC = study counseling; SD = systematic desensitization.

for all four treatment groups decreased, whereas the NTC group showed little change on these measures. Subsequent ANOVAs for the worry measure showed that three of the four treatments (CT + SC, CT + SD, and CT + SC + SD) significantly ($p < .01$) reduced the scores on both worry scales as compared with the control group, but these treatments did not differ from each other in these effects. Paradoxically, the effects of the CT-alone treatment in reducing worry were apparently weaker than the other treatments.

The results for the emotionality data were quite similar to the findings for the worry measures; the periods effects ($p < .001$) and the Groups × Periods interactions ($p < .01$) were significant for the TAI E subscale and the WEQ Emotionality scale. All four treatment groups showed substantial reductions in emotionality relative to the NTC group, as can be seen in the right-hand sides of Figures 10.2 and 10.3. Subsequent ANOVAs also indicated that the CT-alone condition was also weaker than the other treatments in reducing WEQ Emotionality scores; the posttreatment difference between the CT and the NTC groups on this measure only approached significance ($p < .08$).

The STAI A-Trait means and standard deviations for students with good and poor study habits are also reported in Table 10.1. These data were evaluated in a 5 × 2 × 2 ANOVA in which only the periods main effect was statistically significant ($p < .001$), indicating that all five experimental conditions showed comparable reductions in trait anxiety. Because there were no significant Groups × Periods interactions and the NTC group also showed a significant reduction in A-Trait, apparently none of the treatments were effec-

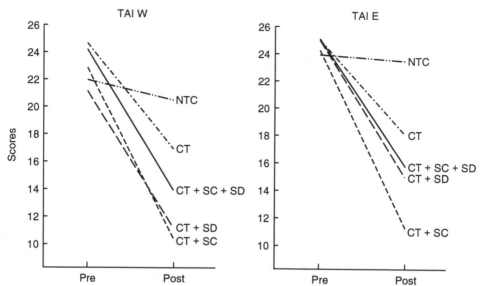

Figure 10.2 Pretreatment (Pre) and posttreatment (Post) Test Anxiety Inventory and Worry (*W*)
and Emotionality (*E*) mean scores for the four treatment conditions and the no-
treatment control (NTC) group. CT = cognitive therapy; SC = study counseling;
SD = systematic desensitization.

tive in reducing trait anxiety. In contrast, the TAI *W* and *E* subscales and
WEQ Worry and Emotionality Scales scores were consistently reduced by
three of the treatments (CT + SC, CT + SD, and CT + SC + SD) and the CT
condition appeared to have some effect in reducing worry and emotionality,
but this treatment was weaker than the other three, as can be noted in Figures
10.2 and 10.3.

Effects of Treatment on Study Habits and Attitudes

In the analyses of the effects of treatment on study habits and study attitudes, the data for each measure were evaluated in 5 × 2 ANOVAs in which
treatment conditions and periods were the independent variables. The significant periods effects ($p < .001$) and Groups × Periods interactions ($p < .02$)
that were found for both measures are graphically presented in Figure 10.4.
As can be noted in the left half of Figure 10.4, the SH subscale scores for all
four treatment groups increased substantially, whereas the SH subscale scores
for the NTC group were essentially unchanged. In the right-hand portion of
the figure, it can be seen that the two groups that included the SC treatment
component (CT + SC and CT + SC + SD) showed greater increases in SA subscale scores than did the treatment groups without the SC component (CT and
CT + SD), whereas the SA subscale scores of the NTC group decreased slightly
from pre- to posttreatment.

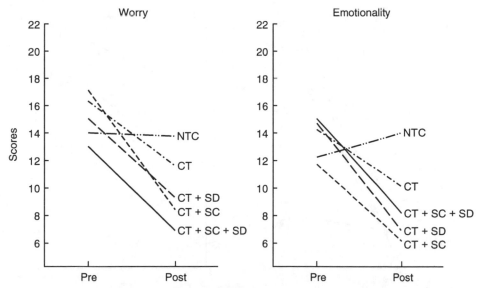

Figure 10.3   Pretreatment (Pre) and posttreatment (Post) Worry–Emotionality Questionnaire Worry and Emotionality subscale scores for the four treatment conditions and the no-treatment control (NTC) group. CT = cognitive therapy; SC = study counseling; SD = systematic desensitization.

In comparing the SH subscale scores of each of the four treatment groups with those of the NTC group in 2 × 2 ANOVAs, the Groups × Periods interactions were significant ($p < .01$) for all four treatment groups. For the SA data, significant Groups × Periods interactions were found only for the two treatment groups that included the SC component (CT + SC. $p < .001$; CT + SC + SD, $p < .05$). However, in subsequent 4 × 2 ANOVAs of the SH and SA subscale scores, in which the four treatment conditions were compared with each other, only the periods main effects were significant ($p < .001$), suggesting that the four treatment conditions were equally effective in increasing SH and SA subscale scores and did not differ from each other in these effects.

It was predicted that the SC treatment component would be more effective than the other treatments in improving study habits. Therefore, to have more subjects for evaluating this prediction, the CT + SC and CT + SC + SD groups were combined and compared with the combined CT and CT + SD groups. The pre- and posttreatment SA and SH subscale scores for subjects in the combined groups were evaluated in 2 × 2 ANOVAs. For the SA data, the periods main effect ($p < .001$) and the Groups × Periods interaction ($p < .05$) were statistically significant, indicating that the combined treatment groups that included the SC component improved study attitudes more than did the treatment conditions that did not include SC, as can be seen in Figure 10.5. For the SH data, only the periods main effect ($p < .001$) was statistically significant. Thus, both combined treatments improved study habits and study

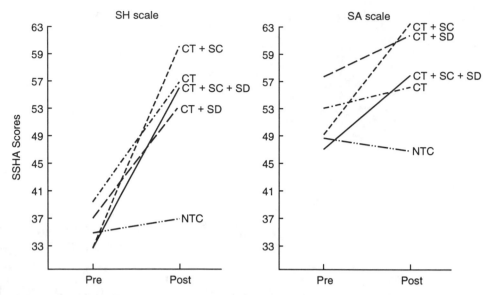

Figure 10.4 Pretreatment (Pre) and posttreatment (Post) mean Study Habits (SH) subscale and Study Attitudes (SA) subscale scores for the four treatment conditions and the no-treatment control (NTC) group. CT = cognitive therapy; SC = study counseling; SD = systematic desensitization.

attitudes, but the combined treatments with the SC component improved study attitudes more than the treatments that did not include this component.

Effect of Treatment on GPA

In evaluating the effects of treatment on grades, cumulative GPAs and grades for the quarter before treatment were both used as the pretreatment measures, and grades for the quarter during which treatment took place comprised the posttreatment measure. The pre- and posttreatment means and standard deviations for these GPA measures are reported in Table 10.2. When the previous quarter's grades were used as the pretreatment GPA measure and the effects of treatment on GPA scores were evaluated in $5 \times 2 \times 2$ ANOVAs similar to those used in the preceding analyses, only the periods main effect approached significance ($p < .10$); no significant effects or trends were obtained by using cumulative GPA as the pretreatment GPA measure.

The absence of statistically significant Groups $\times$ Periods interactions in the analyses of the GPA indicates that the treatments in this study failed to improve grades, but this may be due in part to the small number of subjects ($n = 3$–5) in each cell. Because a major goal of this study was to compare the relative effectiveness of CT with CT + SD in the treatment of test anxiety, the data for the two treatment groups that included an SD component (CT + SD and CT + SC + SD) were pooled. The combined CT + SD treatment conditions

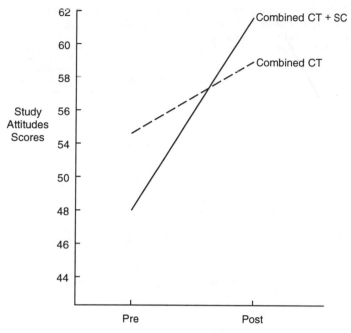

Figure 10.5   Pretreatment (Pre) and posttreatment (Post) Study Attitudes (SA) subscale scores for the combined CT and CT + SC treatment conditions. CT = cognitive therapy; SC = study counseling.

were then compared with the combination of treatment conditions not including an SD component (CT alone and CT + SC) and with the NTC group. The pre- and posttreatment GPA means for the three conditions are graphed in Figure 10.6 in which grades for the academic quarter immediately before treatment were used as the pretreatment GPA measure. It can be seen that the combined CT + SD groups showed a substantial increase in GPA, whereas the combined CT groups remained relatively unchanged and the NTC group increased only slightly. However, the Groups × Periods interaction for the 3 × 2 ANOVA based on these data only approached statistical significant ($p <$ .08).

Effects on GPA of the combined CT and CT + SD treatments were further evaluated in 2 × 2 ANOVAs in which each experimental condition was compared with the other. A significant Groups × Periods interaction ($p <$ .05) was found in the ANOVA comparing the combined CT + SD with the CT conditions, reflecting a larger increase in GPA for the combined CT + SD group, as can be seen in Figure 10.6. However, there were no statistically significant effects in the ANOVAs comparing each combined treatment group with the NTC group, indicating that the combined treatment conditions did not differ from the control group.

In the final analyses of the GPA data, possible long-term effects of treatment were evaluated. The GPA means and standard deviations for the term following

Table 10.2 Pretreatment, posttreatment, and follow-up means and standard deviations for the grade point averages (GPAs) of students in the five experimental conditions

Treatment condition and study habits	Cumulative GPA Pre	Qt. GPA		
		Pre	Post	Follow-up
CT + SC + SD (n = 8)				
Good (n = 3)				
M	1.87	1.59	2.43	1.91
SD	0.37	0.89	0.45	—
Poor (n = 5)				
M	2.34	1.77	2.55	2.46
SD	0.47	0.89	0.72	0.83
CT + SC (n = 7)				
Good (n = 3)				
M	2.31	2.41	1.92	1.81
SD	0.74	0.53	1.24	2.56
Poor (n = 4)				
M	1.87	1.88	1.96	2.78
SD	0.98	0.96	0.54	0.47
CT + SD (n = 7)				
Good (n = 3)				
M	2.14	2.19	2.77	3.07
SD	1.36	1.40	0.73	0.07
Poor (n = 4)				
M	2.51	1.82	2.44	2.07
SD	0.36	1.39	0.61	0.94
CT (n = 8)				
Good (n = 4)				
M	2.39	2.39	2.61	2.96
SD	0.69	0.68	0.67	0.81
Poor (n = 4)				
M	2.02	2.02	1.78	2.23
SD	0.98	0.98	0.95	0.91
NT C (n = 8)				
Good (n = 4)				
M	2.42	2.10	2.16	2.96
SD	0.87	0.81	1.03	0.48
Poor (n = 4)				
M	1.88	1.91	2.11	2.49
SD	0.96	1.02	1.03	0.18

Note. CT = cognitive therapy; SC = study counseling; SD = systematic densitization; NTC = no treatment control; Pre = pretreatment; Post = posttreatment.

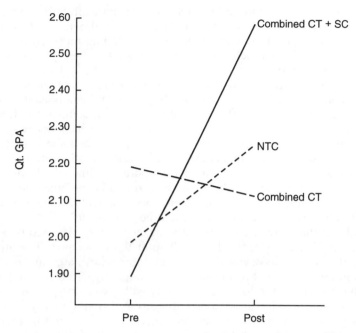

Figure 10.6   Pretreatment (Pre) and posttreatment (Post) mean grade point average (GPA) scores for the combined CT and CT + SD treatment conditions and the no-treatment control (NTC) group. CT = cognitive therapy; SD = systematic densitization.

treatment were reported in Table 10.2. Because 8 students did not enroll in courses during the follow-up term, these data are based on only 30 subjects. In $5 \times 2 \times 3$ least-squares ANOVAs for each of the pretreatment measures similar to those carried out in the preceding analyses, no statistically significant effects were obtained. Thus, there was no evidence that the treatments had any long-term effects.

In summary, the results indicated that no single treatment condition was effective in improving GPA, perhaps due in part to the small number of subjects in each group. However, when the treatment groups that contained the SD component were combined and compared with the treatment groups without SD, the combined CT + SD conditions appeared to have a greater impact in improving grades than the treatment conditions that did not include SD.

DISCUSSION

This study investigated the relative effectiveness of four cognitive approaches to the treatment of test anxiety. All four treatments significantly reduced test anxiety, as measured by TAS and TAI scores, relative to an NTC group; there were no differences among the four treatments in this effect. These findings were generally consistent with the results reported in 9 of 10 previous investigations in which some form of cognitive therapy was used in the treatment of test anxiety.

On the basis of theoretical expectations, cognitive and emotionality-focused treatments should have different effects on the worry and emotionality components of test anxiety, but these differences have never been demonstrated. In this study, all four treatments were effective in reducing worry, which was expected as each treatment included a cognitive component, but the hypothesis that treatments which included an SD component would reduce emotionality more than treatments without this component was not supported. Although all four treatments were equally effective in reducing both worry and emotionality regardless of whether they included the SD component, the treatment condition that consisted of CT alone appeared weaker than the other treatments.

The results of this study are consistent with the findings reported by Finger and Galassi (1977) and by Gonzalez in Chapter 9 and seem to indicate that cognitive and emotionality-focused treatment approaches have similar effects on worry and emotionality. Finger and Galassi have suggested that any treatment which is effective in reducing test anxiety will have corresponding effects on both worry and emotionality because the arousal (emotionality) and cognitive (worry) components of test anxiety interact and occur together as a single process (see also Lam & Hong, 1992). The results of this study and the findings reported in test anxiety literature appear to support Finger and Galassi's hypothesis.

All four treatments in this study also appeared to be equally effective in improving study habits as compared with the NTC group, but only the treatments that included the SC component produced a significantly greater improvement in study attitudes. The treatments that included the SC component were expected to be more effective in improving study habits, but the finding that treatments which did not include this component also improved study habits and attitudes was surprising. This may have resulted from that fact that, in the context of the placebo discussions, students in the groups without the SC component shared information about their study habits even though the therapist attempted to redirect the discussion away from such topics. This type of discussion may have helped some students to improve their study habits.

Gonzalez (see Chapter 9) has demonstrated that it may be more important to motivate students to use their current knowledge of study methods than to train them in new studying procedures. The finding in this study that SC treatment produced significant improvements in study attitudes suggests that these treatments may have improved the students' motivation to study.

In the analyses of this study's GPA data, the treatment groups failed to show any greater improvement in grades than did the NTC group. However, the failure to obtain any improvement in grades could have resulted in part from the small number of subjects in each of the treatment groups, especially in the analysis of the follow-up data.

Holroyd (1976) has reported that CT alone was more effective than CT + SD for improving academic performance. In this study, the combined CT + SD condition tended to produce greater improvement in GPA than the combined treatments without the SD component. A major difference between the two studies was that Holroyd's investigation was conducted in an institution operating on a semester system, whereas this study was conducted at a university that operated on a quarter system. The final exams in Holroyd's study occurred a month after treatment was completed, whereas the final exams in this study were held the same week that treatment was concluded. It is possible that CT + SD approaches have a greater immediate effect in improving grades, whereas the CT treatments alone may have a greater long-term impact on grades. Furthermore, the subjects in Holroyd's study had a longer period of time in which to practice the anxiety coping skills they learned during treatment before they were faced with the stressful final exams.

A second major difference between this investigation and the studies of Holroyd (1976) and Meichenbaum (1972) is that different test anxiety measures were used in selecting the subjects and evaluating treatment outcome. Holroyd and Meichenbaum used Alpert and Haber's (1960) Anxiety Achievement Test (AAT), whereas the TAS and the TAI were used in this study. The AAT Debilitating Anxiety subscale identifies students whose test anxiety adversely affects their academic performance, whereas the TAS and the TAI identify students who experience emotional responses and worry cognitions during tests that may or may not influence performance. It is possible that test-anxious students selected for treatment on the basis of high AAT scores may be more motivated to control their anxiety because their grades are affected by test anxiety.

Meichenbaum's (1972) and Holroyd's (1976) findings that their cognitive treatments improved GPA may have resulted from selecting test-anxious students who were more motivated to improve their academic performance, and who would, therefore, obtain greater benefits from any therapeutic approach that was used. The fact that Holroyd's and Meichenbaum's SD treatments also resulted in improved academic performance, which is an atypical finding in the test anxiety literature, supports this interpretation. Moreover, Holroyd's finding that a pseudotherapy placebo condition was also effective in improving grades provides further evidence that his treatment effects were due in part to his subjects' greater motivation to improve their academic performance.

The results of this investigation provide evidence that cognitive treatment alone reduces test anxiety, and they are generally consistent with most studies in the test anxiety treatment literature. When cognitive treatment was combined with other therapeutic approaches, the effects of the combined treatments were somewhat stronger than CT alone, especially the combination of cognitive treatment and SD for improving academic performance. Thus, the combination of cognitive treatment with emotionality-focused treatments such as SD seems to provide the most effective treatment for students with test anxiety.

SUMMARY

This study investigated the relative effectiveness of four cognitive behavior modification approaches to the treatment of test anxiety: CT ($n = 8$), CT + SC ($n = 7$), CT + SD ($n = 7$), and CT + SC + SD ($n = 8$). An NTC ($n = 8$) group was also included in the experimental design to control for test–retest effects and the passage of time. Each treatment group met for a total of eight 2-hr sessions over a 4-week period. The impact of treatment was evaluated for each of the following outcome measures: (a) the TAS, (b) the TAI, (c) the Liebert and Morris WEQ, (d) the STAI A-Trait, (e) the SSHA SH and SA subscales, and (f) GPA.

All four treatments were effective in reducing test anxiety as measured by the TAS and TAI. Worry and emotionality scores for both the TAI and the WEQ were also reduced for the CT + SC, CT + SD, and CT + SC + SD treatments, as compared with the NTC group. Worry and emotionality scores were also reduced for the CT groups, but the effect was weaker than for the other treatments. None of the treatments led to reductions in STAI A-Trait scores.

The two treatment conditions that included a study counseling component (CT + SC and CT + SC + SD) significantly improved SSHA study attitudes as compared with the two treatments without this component (CT and CT + SD); a similar but nonsignificant trend was also noted for the study habits variable. These results suggested that the primary effect of study counseling was to improve the students' motivation to study rather than to teach them new study skills.

None of the treatment conditions resulted in significant improvement in GPA. However, the two treatment conditions that combined CT with SD (CT + SD and CT + SC + SD) showed greater improvement in GPA than the cognitive treatments without the systematic desensitization component (CT and CT + SC).

The results of this study provide evidence that cognitive treatment alone reduced test anxiety; when cognitive treatment was combined with other therapy components, these effects were stronger. The results further suggested that the combination of cognitive treatment and systematic desensitization was more effective for improving academic performance than was cognitive treatment alone.

11

Comparison of Cognitive Therapy and Rational–Emotive Therapy in the Treatment of Test Anxiety

Tucker M. Fletcher and Charles D. Spielberger
University of South Florida, Tampa, Florida, USA

In research on the treatment of test anxiety, systematic desensitization has been used more often than any other therapeutic approach (Spielberger et al., 1976). Although systematic desensitization is generally effective in reducing test anxiety, there is little evidence that this form of behavior therapy helps students to improve their test performance or to raise their grade point average, as was noted by Gonzalez in Chapter 9 and by Parker, Vagg, and Papsdorf in Chapter 12. One reason for this may be that systematic desensitization is designed to modify the emotionality component of test anxiety, and this component is unrelated to performance. As detailed in Chapter 2, it is worry during tests that has been found to be negatively correlated with performance (Spielberger et al., 1978). Therefore, therapeutic procedures directed toward reducing the worry component of test anxiety should be more effective than systematic desensitization in helping students to improve their academic achievement.

In 1972, Meichenbaum introduced cognitive behavior modification (CBM), a form of cognitive therapy (CT) that has proven successful in reducing test anxiety and in facilitating academic achievement. Meichenbaum's treatment procedures were designed to eliminate the worries of test-anxious students by having them engage in thoughts and behaviors that were incompatible with the generation of task-irrelevant worry cognitions. However, as Holroyd (1976) has noted, this treatment also included elements of systematic desensitization. When Holroyd compared Meichenbaum's CBM with a similar cognitive treatment that did not include any elements of desensitization, he found that the "pure" cognitive treatment was more effective in reducing test anxiety and improving academic achievement than was the CBM treatment.

Meichenbaum (1972) has also acknowledged that his cognitive procedures included elements of Ellis's Rational–Emotive Therapy (RET), which is primarily concerned with modifying irrational beliefs that may lead to worry

The research reported in this chapter is based on the master's thesis of the first author, which was conducted under the supervision of the second author. This research was supported, in part, by a grant to C. D. Spielberger and W. D. Anton from the Advanced Research Projects Agency, United States Department of Defense (MOA 903-77-C-0190).

responses. Because RET was confounded with cognitive therapy in the procedures used by Meichenbaum and Holroyd, it is not possible to determine which aspects of the cognitive treatments used in these studies actually contributed to the improvements in test performance and academic achievement.

The major goal of this study was to evaluate the effectiveness of a modified version of the cognitive procedures used by Meichenbaum and Holroyd in which the RET elements were removed. This treatment was compared with a form of Ellis's RET especially adapted for the treatment of test-anxious students. Before describing this investigation, the findings in previous studies in which cognitive techniques were used to treat test anxiety are briefly reviewed, and the specific procedures used by Meichenbaum and Holroyd are described in greater detail.

STUDIES USING COGNITIVE TREATMENTS OF TEST ANXIETY

The therapeutic effects of various cognitive treatments on test-anxious students have been demonstrated in numerous studies (e.g., Hembree, 1988), a number of which were described earlier by Algaze in Chapter 10. RET has proved as effective as cognitive therapy in reducing test anxiety (e.g., McMillan, 1974; A. G. Montgomery, 1971).

Although test anxiety was reduced by cognitive treatment in most studies, this has resulted in improvement in grades or test performance in relatively few studies (e.g., Holroyd, 1976; Meichenbaum, 1972; Showalter, 1974). As Showalter failed to find any reduction in test anxiety, it is unlikely that the improvement in performance in this study could have resulted from the treatment procedures. However, improved performance that could be attributed to treatment was found in at least two studies (e.g., Meichenbaum, 1972; Holroyd, 1976).

In addition to the elements of Ellis's (1962) RET, the CT treatment procedures used by Meichenbaum (1972) and Holroyd (1976) were designed to eliminate worry cognitions and to modify the self-centered, self-derogatory, attentional focus of test-anxious students. In this study, these procedures are collectively referred to as cognitive therapy prime (CT') to distinguish them from the CT procedures used by Meichenbaum and Holroyd. The key elements of the CT' procedures are described in the following section in which they are examined and compared with a form of Ellis's RET especially adapted for the treatment of test anxiety.

CT' and RET in the Treatment of Test-Anxious Students

The CT' procedures used in this study were essentially the same as the CT procedures used by Meichenbaum (1972) and Holroyd (1976) except that all elements of systematic desensitization and RET were eliminated. The two major phases of the cognitive treatment process have been described by Meichenbaum as follows:

The first is to have the clients become aware of the negative self-statements they are emitting which contribute to their maladaptive behavior. The second phase of cognitive behavior modification is to have the clients develop skills in producing incompatible thoughts and behavior. (p. 50)

Thus, the main goal in CT′ is to displace the worries of test-anxious students with thoughts and behaviors that are incompatible with their occurrence. The test-anxious students are first trained to be sensitive to the negative thoughts ("self-statements") that they experience in testing situations. In the second phase of CT′ treatment, the students are trained to respond to their own negative self-statements as "bell ringers" that remind them to produce task-relevant thoughts and behaviors that are incompatible with their worry cognitions.

In CT′ treatment, the student is taught to produce three types of task-relevant cognitions: (a) self-instructions (e.g., "Just take one question at a time"), (b) coping self-statements (e.g., "Don't worry. Worry won't help anything"), and (c) self-reinforcing statements (e.g., "It's working. I can control how I feel!"). In addition to these cognitive maneuvers, the students are directed to engage in task-relevant behaviors (e.g., working actively on the test itself) that are incompatible with the generation of negative self-statements.

In summary, CT′ procedures operate directly on the worry cognitions that are experienced in testing situations. These procedures provide test-anxious students with relatively simple, straightforward cognitive techniques that help them to cope with the worry and emotional reactions that they experience during examinations.

The fundamental premise of RET is that emotional problems result from the underlying irrational beliefs that an individual holds about some event or situation. Therefore, the RET therapist challenges the irrational beliefs and faulty assumptions of test-anxious students rather than attempting to directly alleviate their worries and emotional reactions as would the CT′ therapist. In RET, the main therapeutic thrust is to teach clients how to challenge and dispute their own irrational beliefs so that they can replace them with more realistic ones.

Although the procedures used in CT′ and RET are quite different, both treatments appear to have the potential to reduce test anxiety and improve academic achievement. The CT′ procedures are more narrowly focused on modifying worry cognitions in test situations. Therefore, these procedures should be more effective than RET in reducing the worry cognitions experienced by test-anxious students during examinations. By reducing worry, CT′ should also be more effective than RET in improving academic performance.

Alternatively, RET would be expected to help test-anxious students in problem areas that would not be helped by CT′. For example, by altering test-anxious students' irrational beliefs (e.g., "education is a waste of time" or "my true value as a human being depends on my academic performance"), RET might contribute to improved attitudes toward school work and the strengthening of students' self-concepts. To the extent that RET enhances the test-anxious students' self-concepts, it would make them less vulnerable to situations that pose threats to self-esteem, and this would lead to a reduction in trait anxiety.

METHOD

The subjects in this study were 66 undergraduate students who responded to campuswide announcements of the availability of a test anxiety treatment program at the University of South Florida Counseling Center. Each of these students was interviewed individually to determine if he or she met the following criteria for participation in the study: (a) completed at least one quarter of academic work, but not a last quarter senior and (b) not currently receiving any type of psychological treatment. The mean age of the 60 students (37 women and 23 men) who met these criteria was 23.6 years.

Experimental Measures

The Test Anxiety Inventory (TAI), which has Worry (W) and Emotionality (E) subscales, and the State Anxiety (S-Anxiety) and Trait Anxiety (T-Anxiety) subscales of the State–Trait Anxiety Inventory (STAI) were administered to all subjects in pre- and posttreatment testing sessions. The psychometric properties of the TAI are described by Spielberger et al. (1978; see also Chapter 4). Detailed information about the STAI is reported in the Test Manual (Spielberger et al., 1970).

The Irrational Beliefs Test (IBT; Jones, 1969) is based on Ellis's (1962) list of 11 commonly held irrational beliefs. It consists of 100 items that describe 10 of these beliefs. This test has been used to evaluate irrational beliefs in studies of social, speech, and test anxiety (Goldfried & Sobocinski, 1975; Trexler & Karst, 1972; Vagg, 1978). Test–retest reliability of the IBT ranges from .88 to .92.

Study attitudes were measured by the W. F. Brown–Holtzman (1965) Survey of Study Habits and Attitudes (SSHA). The Weschler (1955) Digit Symbol Test (DST) as modified by M. A. Brown (1969), which was used by Meichenbaum (1972) and Holroyd (1976), and the Inference Subscale of the California Test of Mental Maturity (CTMM; Sullivan et al., 1957) were used as measures of intellectual performance. To increase the amount of stress in taking the CTMM, the time limit for completing this test was shortened from 8 to 7 min.

Procedure

During the brief initial interview of approximately 15 min duration, the STAI S-Anxiety subscale was administered to the students. At the end of the interview, the students who were eligible to participate in the study were assigned to one of five pretreatment testing sessions that were conducted over a 2-week period before the initiation of treatment. In these sessions, the students were informed that test anxiety was sometimes caused by low IQs and that they would be given two brief IQ tests to determine if this might be the problem in their particular case. After completing the CTMM and the DST tests, the students were administered the STAI S-Anxiety subscale with retrospective instructions to respond in terms of "how you felt while taking the two tests you just finished." The remaining tests were then administered in the following order: the TAI, IBT, SSHA, and STAI T-Anxiety subscale.

Following the pretreatment testing sessions, each student was assigned to either the CT' ($n = 19$) or the RET ($n = 21$) treatment conditions or to the no-treatment control (NTC) group ($n = 20$). Analysis of pretreatment test scores indicated that the three experimental conditions were well matched before treatment on all outcome measures.

Treatment Conditions

Students in the CT' and RET conditions were assigned to four treatment groups. There were two groups for each condition and 9 or 10 students in each group. All of the treatment sessions were conducted by the same therapist in the same room, twice weekly, for 3.5 weeks (7 sessions). Each session lasted approximately 90 min.

CT' treatment. The CT' treatment procedures were designed (a) to teach the students that the anxiety they experienced during tests (and in other evaluative situations) was caused by the negative self-statements (worry cognitions) they experienced in these situations; (b) to train the students to become more sensitive to and aware of negative self-statements at the time they occurred, and (c) to do this so that they could use the occurrence of negative self-statements as cues (bell ringers) to remind them to produce thoughts and behaviors that were incompatible with the generation of additional negative self-statements.

Over the course of the seven treatment sessions, the following specific points were discussed: (a) specific negative self-statements that the students experienced during tests and the anxiety that resulted from these self-statements, (b) the wide range of evaluative situations in which the students experienced negative self-statements, (c) the bell ringer method for coping with test anxiety, (d) examples of positive self-statements that might help the students to cope with anxiety on their own, (e) Meichenbaum's (1977) list of suggested self-coping statements, and (f) self-coping statements generated by the students themselves.

RET treatment. The RET procedures used in this study were adapted from the general RET procedures described by Ellis (1962, 1973). These procedures were organized into four distinct steps or phases:

1. The students were taught Ellis's ABC theory of emotional disturbance, which holds that unpleasant emotional consequences (C) do not result from some activating event (A), but are produced by irrational beliefs (B) that the individuals hold about A.
2. Ellis's concept of the value of a human being was given special attention because it was felt that many of the negative emotions experienced by test-

anxious students resulted from their tendencies to irrationally depreciate their self-worth because of poor academic performance.

3. An overview of Ellis's (1962, p. 61) 11 "common irrational beliefs that cause emotional disturbances" was presented and discussed. This was done to help the students identify one or more of these irrational beliefs as contributing to their feelings of anxiety and, thereby, to motivate greater involvement in the treatment process.

4. Students were given in-depth instruction on how to "challenge, dispute, and change" those irrational beliefs that were judged most likely to contribute to the students' test anxiety.

Shortly after the final treatment session, the same experimental measures were readministered in posttreatment group-testing sessions. After the students had completed the tests, they were debriefed and informed that the DST and the CTMM had been given to assess the impact of anxiety on test performance.

RESULTS

In reporting the findings of this study, the effects of treatment on test anxiety and trait and state anxiety are examined first. The effects of treatment on changes in irrational beliefs and study attitudes are then reported. Finally, the effects of treatment on the two measures of intellectual performance are evaluated.

Effects of Treatment on Anxiety

The pre- and posttreatment means and standard deviations for the TAI, its W and E subscales, and the STAI T-Anxiety subscale are reported in Table 11.1 for students in the CT', RET, and NTC conditions. The data for each measure were evaluated separately in analyses of variance (ANOVAs) in which experimental conditions and pre- and posttreatment periods were the independent variables. The Conditions × Periods interactions and the periods main effects were significant for all four measures; the conditions main effect was also significant for the W subscale.

The Conditions × Periods interactions for the TAI Total, E, and W subscale scores are graphed in Figures 11.1 and 11.2. For the students who participated in the CT' and RET treatment conditions, the scores on all three measures declined, whereas the scores for students in the NTC condition showed little change. To clarify the source of the interaction for the three test anxiety measures, the CT' and RET conditions were compared with the NTC condition and with each other in subsequent 2 × 2 ANOVAS. In the comparisons of the CT' and RET treatments with the NTC group, the Conditions × Periods interactions were significant for all three test anxiety measures. However, only the periods main effect was significant in the comparison of the two treatment

Table 11.1 Pre- and posttreatment means and standard deviations for the TAI Total, Worry, and Emotionality subscales and the STAI T-Anxiety subscale for the cognitive therapy, rational–emotive therapy, and no-treatment control conditions

| | TAI | | | | | | T-Anxiety | |
| | Total | | Worry | | Emotionality | | | |
Treatment	Pre	Post	Pre	Post	Pre	Post	Pre	Post
CT' (*n*=19)								
M	55.73	34.33	20.58	12.05	24.26	14.05	44.16	24.11
SD	13.86	7.07	6.16	3.05	6.24	3.44	8.71	6.67
RET (*n*=21)								
M	56.91	39.05	21.62	14.24	24.10	16.29	45.95	35.71
SD	10.54	10.83	5.00	4.40	4.80	5.29	11.52	9.72
NTC (*n*=20)								
M	55.15	50.75	20.90	19.50	21.65	21.15	41.00	39.40
SD	11.23	13.29	5.84	5.86	4.25	6.06	7.60	10.46

Note. TAI = Test Anxiety Inventory; STAI = State–Trait Anxiety Inventory; T-Anxiety = Trait Anxiety; CT' = cognitive therapy prime; RET = rational–emotive technique; NTC = no treatment control; Pre = pretreatment; Post = posttreatment.

159

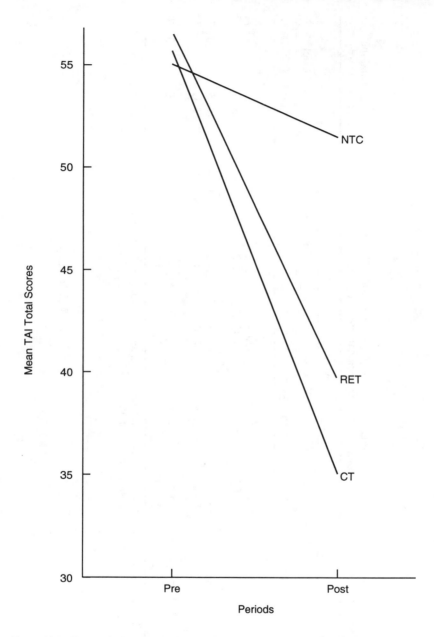

Figure 11.1 Pre- and posttreatment mean Test Anxiety Inventory (TAI) Total scores for subjects in the cognitive therapy prime (CT′), rational–emotive technique (RET), and no treatment control (NTC) conditions.

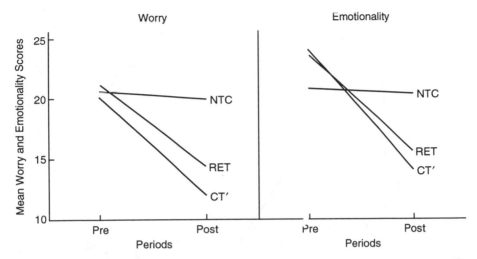

Figure 11.2   Pre- and posttreatment mean Worry and Emotionality scores for the cognitive therapy prime (CT′), rational–emotive technique (RET), and no treatment control
(NTC) conditions.

groups with each other, indicating that the CT′ and RET treatments were
equally effective in reducing test anxiety.

The Conditions × Periods interaction for the T-Anxiety subscale scores is
graphed in Figure 11.3. Although the T-Anxiety scores for students in the CT′
and RET treatment conditions declined, there was little change in the T-
Anxiety subscale scores of students in the NTC condition. To clarify the source
of this interaction, the CT′ and RET conditions were compared with the NTC
condition and with each other in subsequent 2 × 2 ANOVAS. The Conditions
× Periods interactions were significant when the CT′ and RET conditions
were compared with the NTC condition. Only the periods main effect was
significant when the CT′ and RET treatment conditions were compared with
each other. Thus, the results for the trait anxiety measure were quite similar
to the findings for the test anxiety measures.

The STAI S-Anxiety subscale was administered at the time the subjects
were initially interviewed and then readministered during the pre- and posttreatment testing sessions. The means and standard deviations for the S-Anxiety subscale during these administrations are reported in Table 11.2 for the
three experimental conditions. The three conditions did not differ in level of
state anxiety during the initial interview, as was previously noted.

To establish that the subjects in all three experimental conditions reacted
to the threat manipulation in a comparable manner, a 3 × 2 unweighted means
ANOVA was performed in which conditions and testing periods (interview vs.
pretest) were the independent variables. Only the periods main effect was
statistically significant, indicating that the stress provided by the testing situation evoked comparable increases (9 to 10 points) in level of state anxiety in
all three experimental conditions, as can be seen in Table 11.2.

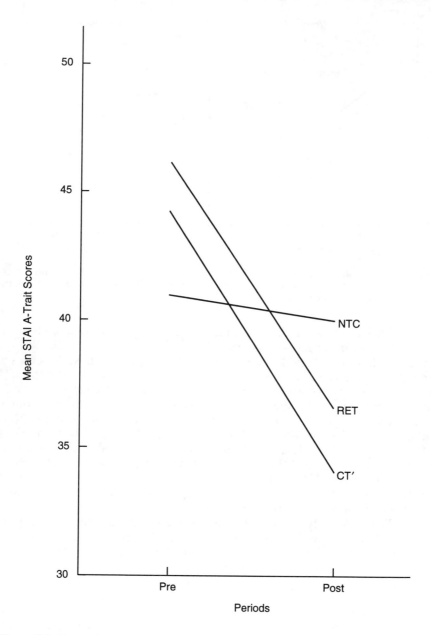

Figure 11.3 Pre- and posttreatment mean State–Trait Anxiety Inventory Trait Anxiety subscale (STAI T-Anxiety [A-Trait]) scores for the subjects in the cognitive therapy prime (CT′), rational–emotive technique (RET), and no treatment control (NTC) conditions.

Table 11.2 Means and standard deviations for the interview S-Anxiety, the pretreatment S-Anxiety, and the posttreatment S-Anxiety for the cognitive therapy, rational–emotive therapy, and no-treatment control conditions

	A-State subscale score		
Treatment	Interview	Pretreatment	Posttreatment
CT′ (n = 19)			
M	43.16	52.37	31.90
SD	10.45	11.76	6.67
RET (n = 21)			
M	44.19	54.14	37.95
SD	11.33	9.60	8.16
NTC (n = 20)			
M	41.20	51.55	40.60
SD	8.08	13.37	8.92

Note. S-Anxiety = State anxiety; CT′ = cognitive therapy prime; RET = rational–emotive technique; NTC = no treatment control.

To determine the effects of each treatment on state anxiety, the pre- and posttreatment S-Anxiety subscale scores of students in the three experimental conditions were evaluated in a 3 × 2 ANOVA. The significant Groups × Periods interaction obtained in this analysis is graphed in Figure 11.4. Students in the CT′ condition experienced a greater decline in state anxiety from the pre- to the posttreatment period than did the students in the RET and NTC groups. To clarify the source of this interaction, the CT′ and RET conditions were compared with the NCT condition and with each other in separate 2 × 2 ANOVAS. The Groups × Periods interaction was significant in the comparison of the CT′ condition with the NTC condition and approached significance in the RET versus NTC comparison ($p < .10$), but was not significant when the CT′ and RET groups were compared with each other.

Effect of Treatment on Irrational Beliefs and Study Attitudes

Pre- and posttreatment means and standard deviations for the IBT scores of students in the CT′, RET, and NTC conditions are reported in Table 11.3. The data for this measure were evaluated in a 3 × 2 unweighted means ANOVA in which treatment conditions and pre- and posttreatment periods were the independent variables. The conditions and periods main effects were statistically significant as was the Conditions × Periods interaction, graphed in Figure 11.5. The interaction effect reflected the fact that the RET group showed a larger decrease in irrational beliefs from the pre- to the posttreatment period than did the other groups.

To further clarify the source of the Conditions × Periods interaction for the IBT measure, the CT′ and RET conditions were compared with the NTC condition and with each other in subsequent 2 × 2 ANOVAS. In these analyses, the Conditions × Periods interactions were significant for the comparisons of the RET group with the CT′ and the NTC groups, but the CT′ and

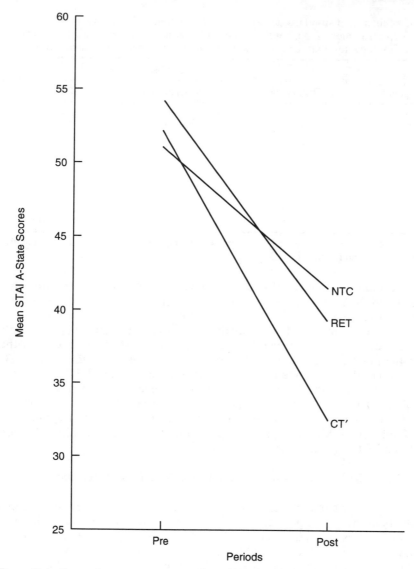

Figure 11.4 Pre- and posttreatment mean State–Trait Anxiety Inventory Trait Anxiety subscale (STAI S-Anxiety [A-State]) scores for subjects in the cognitive therapy prime (CT′), rational–emotive technique (RET), and no treatment control (NTC) conditions.

NTC groups did not differ from each other. These findings indicate that only the RET treatment produced a significant reduction in irrational beliefs.

Pre- and posttreatment means and standard deviations for the Study Attitudes (SA) subscale scores of the students in the CT′, RET, and NTC conditions are also reported in Table 11.3. The data for each of these measures were

Table 11.3 Pre- and posttreatment means and standard deviations for the IBT and the
SA subscale of the SSHA for the cognitive therapy, rational–emotive
therapy, and no-treatment control conditions

	IBT		SSHA SA	
Treatment	Pre	Post	Pre	Post
CT' (n = 19)				
M	287.63	257.68	57.32	61.84
SD	29.18	45.26	15.21	16.54
RET (n = 21)				
M	286.24	222.95	52.76	57.24
SD	32.91	35.44	15.82	16.28
NTC (n = 20)				
M	291.00	271.45	60.60	58.55
SD	44.62	27.31	13.63	17.52

Note. IBT = Irrational Beliefs Test; SA = Study Attitudes; SSHA = Survey of Study Habits
and Attitutdes Scale; CT' = cognitive therapy prime; RET = rational–emotive technique; NTC
= no treatment control; Pre = pretreatment; Post = posttreatment.

evaluated separately in 3 × 2 ANOVAS in which experimental conditions and
pre- and posttreatment periods were the independent variables. The CT' and
RET conditions showed slight increases in SA subscale scores, whereas the
NTC condition showed a slight decline, as can be noted in Table 11.3, but there
were no statistically significant effects in the ANOVA for this measure.

Effects of Treatment on Intellectual Performance

The pre- and posttreatment means and standard deviations for the CTMM
and the DST are presented in Table 11.4. The data for each of these measures
were separately evaluated in 3 × 2 unweighted means ANOVA, in which
treatment conditions and pre- and posttreatment periods were the independent
variables. No statistically significant effects were found for the DST scores as
a function of treatment.

For the CTMM data, only the periods main effect was statistically significant, indicating that all groups improved on this measure, as can be noted in
Table 11.4. As the scores for the NTC group increased as much as those for
the CT' and RET groups, the improvement in the CTMM scores cannot be
attributed to treatment. Thus, the treatment conditions had no systematic
influence on the two measures of intellectual performance.

DISCUSSION

In this study, the CT' and RET treatments reduced test anxiety when compared with the NTC condition, for which there was no change in any of the
test anxiety measures. Although it was expected that the CT' treatment would
be more effective than RET, the finding that both treatments were equally

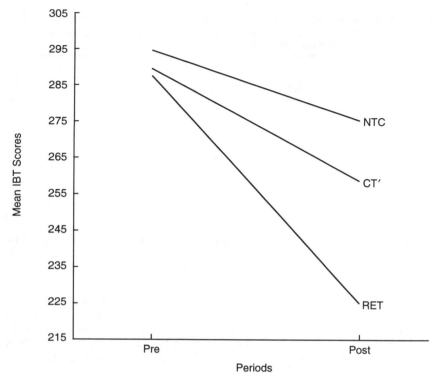

Figure 11.5 Pre- and posttreatment mean Irrational Beliefs Test (IBT) scores for subjects in the cognitive therapy prime (CT′), rational–emotive technique (RET), and no treatment control (NTC) conditions.

effective in reducing test anxiety was quite consistent with the results reported in a number of studies in which a variety of cognitive treatments were used (see Table 11.1, p. 159). The fact that both treatments reduced worry and emotionality was also consistent with the results of previous studies in which it was found that whenever test anxiety was reduced, irrespective of the nature of the treatment, there was a reduction in both worry and emotionality (Algaze, 1980; Cooley, 1977; Finger & Galassi, 1977; Gonzalez, 1978a; Hahnloser, 1974; Vagg, 1978).

The CT′ treatment in this study reduced state anxiety as expected, and the drop in state anxiety in the RET condition also approached significance ($p <$ .10). Although the CT′ condition appeared to be more effective than RET in reducing state anxiety, this difference was not statistically significant. These results were generally consistent with the findings in previous studies in which cognitive treatments reduced state anxiety in test situations (Algaze, 1980; Holroyd, 1976).

The CT′ and RET treatments in this study were both effective in reducing trait anxiety. This was consistent with the results of five previous test anxiety studies in which cognitive treatments were used (Fabick, 1976; Goldfried et

Table 11.4 Pre- and posttreatment means and standard deviations for the CTMM and DST for the cognitive therapy, rational–emotive therapy, and no-treatment control conditions

	CTTM		DST	
Treatment	Pre	Post	Pre	Post
CT′ (n = 19)				
M	11.05	12.05	56.68	53.73
SD	2.25	1.78	9.52	10.48
RET (n = 21)				
M	10.76	11.86	56.57	59.71
SD	2.00	1.49	11.68	12.17
NTC (n = 20)				
M	11.15	12.25	56.70	56.60
SD	2.82	1.16	13.95	12.76

Note. CTMM = California Test of Mental Maturity; DST = Digit Symbol Test; CT′ = cognitive therapy prime; RET = rational–emotive technique; NTC = no treatment control; Pre = pretreatment; Post = posttreatment.

al., 1978; Reister, 1975; Vagg, 1978; Wagaman, 1975). Although cognitive treatment studies failed to reduce trait anxiety in two studies (Algaze, 1980; McMillan, 1974), no reductions in trait anxiety were found in any of the six studies in which systematic desensitization was used in treating test-anxious college students (Anton, 1975; Bedell, 1976; Donner & Guerney, 1969; Garcia, 1975; Gonzalez, 1978a; Mitchell & Ingram, 1970). Thus, the cognitive therapies appear to be more effective than systematic desensitization in reducing the trait anxiety of test-anxious students.

The RET treatment in this study was also effective in reducing irrational beliefs, whereas no difference was found between the CT′ and the NTC condition for this treatment outcome measure. Other investigators have also reported that irrational beliefs as measured by the IBT were reduced by RET in the treatment of test anxiety (Vagg, 1978), speech anxiety (Trexler & Karst, 1972), and social anxiety (Goldfried & Sobocinski, 1975).

The CT′ treatment was expected to be more effective than RET in facilitating performance on cognitive–intellectual tasks. Although there was no improvement in scores on the DST or the CTMM that could be attributed to treatment, the failure to obtain improvement in measures of intellectual performance in this investigation was consistent with a majority of the studies reported in the literature. In 15 studies in which cognitive treatments were used, either alone or in combination with other techniques (see Table 11.1), only Meichenbaum (1972) and Holroyd (1976) found performance gains on intellectual tasks that could be attributed to treatment.

A possible explanation for Meichenbaum's (1972) and Holroyd's (1976) results is that the therapists in these investigations were more effective than the therapists in other studies. However, this seems unlikely because Meichenbaum and Holroyd's therapists were graduate students. A more plausible explanation relates to the fact that the cognitive treatment procedures used by

Meichenbaum and Holroyd included elements of RET in addition to the CT' procedures. Thus, the combination of CT' and RET treatments may be more effective in improving performance on intellectual tasks than either treatment alone.

The finding in this study that RET was almost as effective as CT' in reducing test anxiety may be interpreted as evidence that this treatment modified the test-anxious students' irrational beliefs about tests (e.g., "if I do poorly on a test, I am a worthless person") so that these students no longer perceived the testing situation as highly threatening. Thus, although RET appears to help students to reevaluate testing situations so that they are perceived as less threatening, CT' may help students to cope with anxiety experienced in a threatening situation by teaching them to replace maladaptive negative self-statements with task-relevant thoughts and behaviors.

A major advantage of CT' is the relative ease with which these techniques can be administered. Very little time is required to explain the rationale underlying the CT' procedures and to teach students how to apply them. The students in the CT' condition in this study were thus able to apply the therapeutic techniques at an earlier stage in treatment, and they had more time during the treatment sessions for discussing their experiences in using these procedures. In contrast, the RET treatment required a great deal of time for the therapist to carefully describe one principle before proceeding to the next. Consequently, there was considerably less time during the treatment sessions for discussing applications of the RET principles.

The cognitive treatments used in this study were expected to have greater impact on worry than emotionality, but this was not the case. Indeed, the findings were similar to those reported in other test anxiety treatment studies in which both worry and emotionality were reduced regardless of whether the treatment was cognitively or emotionality oriented (Algaze, 1980; Cooley, 1977; Finger & Galassi, 1977; Gonzalez, 1978a; Hahnloser, 1974; Parker, 1977; Vagg, 1978). Lazarus and Averill (1972) have suggested that worry stimulates emotional arousal, which then keys off additional worry cognitions. According to this view, any treatment that effectively reduces either worry or emotionality will modify both components of test anxiety.

SUMMARY

The relative effectiveness of CT' and RET in the treatment of test-anxious college students was investigated in this study. Sixty undergraduate students who requested treatment for test anxiety at a university counseling center were randomly assigned to CT' or RET treatment conditons or to a NTC group. The treatment groups met twice weekly over a period of 3.5 weeks (7 sessions).

The following outcome measures were used to evaluate the relative effectiveness of the CT' and RET treatments: (a) the TAI, (b) the STAI, (c) the IBT, (d) the SA subscale of the SSHA, (e) the DST, and (f) the Inference Subscale of the CTMM. The experimental groups were well matched on all measures before treatment.

The CT' and RET treatments were equally effective in reducing test anxiety. Both treatments also reduced trait anxiety. Although CT' appeared to be more effective than RET in reducing state anxiety in a test situation, only the RET treatment reduced the irrational beliefs of test-anxious students. Neither CT' nor RET improved study attitudes or test performance.

Given the relative ease of administering the CT procedures, as compared with more complex RET techniques, this treatment approach appears especially well suited for modifying the worry and emotionality components of test anxiety. However, the combination of CT and RET seems to hold greater promise for long-term improvements in academic performance.

12

Systematic Desensitization, Cognitive Coping, and Biofeedback in the Reduction of Test Anxiety

John C. Parker, IV, Peter R. Vagg, and James D. Papsdorf
University of Michigan, Ann Arbor, Michigan, USA

In an age of ever-increasing technological development, in which specialization and advanced training have become more and more important, the specter of academic failure and concerns regarding academic performance are among the most common sources of stress for college students (e.g., Hembree, 1988; Pekrun, 1992; I. G. Sarason, 1959, 1978; Scipp, 1991; Spielberger & Vagg, 1987). According to McKeachie (1951),

> *The college student who looks toward the front of the classroom sees personified in his instructor the grades which will determine whether he can remain in school, enter graduate school, or obtain a good position upon graduation. It seems reasonable to suppose that he enters the classroom with some anxiety, for grades represent a major gateway in his path toward his major vocational and social goals . . . probably the greater focus of student anxiety is the course examination. (p. 153)*

Most students have the ability to do reasonably well on examinations, but because of anxiety many of them fail to perform at a level commensurate with their intellectual ability (Alpert & Haber, 1960; Paul & Eriksen, 1964; Schwarzer & Jerusalem, 1992; Spielberger, 1962; Wine, 1971). Students report that the anxiety associated with tests elicits varying degrees of fear, tension, muscular contractions, headaches, nausea, and restlessness, as well as a reduced ability to think clearly and remember material. The effects of test anxiety may not be noticed by a student until his or her mind goes blank on encountering a difficult question in a testing situation, but the student may previously have experienced many other effects of test anxiety without being aware of them. Considering the suffering involved, along with the potential loss to society of valuable contributions by talented students, effective treatment of test anxiety is extremely important from personal, economic, and social viewpoints.

This chapter is based on the first author's Ph.D. dissertation (Parker, 1977), which was conducted under the supervision of the third author. The first and second authors were primarily responsible for the preparation of the manuscript. We would like to thank the staff of the Reading and Learning Skills Center at the University of Michigan for their assistance in carrying out this research.

Early approaches to the treatment of test-anxious students involved individual or group counseling of a dynamic nature (Chestnut, 1965; Spielberger & Weitz, 1964; Spielberger et al., 1962). In the 1960s, the growing popularity of behavioral techniques stimulated numerous applications of Wolpe's (1958) systematic desensitization in test anxiety treatment studies (e.g., Katahn et al., 1966; Paul & Eriksen, 1964). In general, the research findings indicate that systematic desensitization leads to reductions in test anxiety and, in some instances, to improved academic performance, as reported by Gonzalez in Chapter 9 and Algaze in Chapter 10 (see also Vagg & Spielberger, Chapter 14).

Although systematic desensitization has proved to be an effective treatment for reducing test anxiety, there is strong disagreement in regard to Wolpe's (1958) theoretical explanation of desensitization as operating by the principle of reciprocal inhibition, as reflected in the following statement:

> If a response antagonistic to anxiety can be made to occur in the presence of anxiety-evoking stimuli so that it is accompanied by a complete or partial suppression of the anxiety responses, the bond between these stimuli and the anxiety responses will be weakened. (p. 71)

Thus, according to Wolpe, desensitization involves a relatively passive process of deconditioning in which the relaxation responses are inherently antagonistic to the automatic arousal associated with levels of anxiety.

Goldfried (1971), Wine (1971), Meichenbaum (1972), and Spielberger (1980; Speilberger et al., 1978, 1979) have argued that a cognitive mediational interpretation of test anxiety provides a better explanation of the efficacy of systematic desensitization than does reciprocal inhibition. According to these theorists, systematic desensitization evokes a cognitive coping process that enables the test-anxious student to learn anxiety-reducing skills.

Three approaches to systematic desensitization were evaluated in this study. One treatment, which is referred to as *standard systematic desensitization* (SSD), used Jacobson's (1938) procedures to provide explicit training in progressive muscle relaxation.

A second treatment, which is referred to as *biofeedback-assisted systematic desensitization* (BASD), used biofeedback to provide information about tension in specific muscle groups. Because biofeedback treatments typically do not specify any explicit procedures for relaxing the muscles, no information on how to relax was given to the subjects assigned to this condition.

The third treatment consisted of the same biofeedback and systematic desensitization techniques that were used in the BASD condition, but subjects assigned to this treatment were also instructed to "maintain the image associated with the tension and cope with it." This treatment is referred to as *biofeedback-assisted cognitive coping* (BACC) desensitization.

The major goal of the study was to compare the relative effectiveness of these three treatment approaches to desensitization in reducing test anxiety. If progressive relaxation training of the major muscle groups is the critical variable, then the SSD treatment should be superior to all other conditions in terms of anxiety reduction. If the cognitive coping element is critical, the BACC condition should lead to the greatest reduction in anxiety. If the critical element in anxiety reduction comes from biofeedback about the levels of tension or relaxation in the frontalis muscles, then the two groups receiving biofeedback (BASD and BACC conditions) should be associated with the greatest reductions in anxiety. Another possibility is that knowledge of how to relax or cope is a critical element. If so, the SSD and BACC conditions should be more effective than the BASD condition, because they provide information about how to use the techniques to cope with the stress of the examination situation, and biofeedback by itself does not. Finally, if the way the relaxation is induced makes no difference, all three treatments should be equally effective in reducing anxiety.

METHOD

The subjects were 32 students (16 men and 16 women) at the University of Michigan who responded to newspaper or poster advertisements for a test anxiety program. All of the students had scores of 30 or greater on the Debilitating Anxiety Scale of the Alpert–Haber (1960) Anxiety Achievement Test (AAT), which placed them in the upper 20% of the test score distribution. The average age of the students was 22.5 years.

Eight students were randomly assigned to each of the three treatment groups and to the no-treatment control (NTC) group. Within each group, the students were assigned at random to one of two male graduate student therapists. Both therapists had substantial previous experience with relaxation and desensitization techniques.

Experimental conditions, therapists, and pre- versus posttreatment testing were the independent variables in a $4 \times 2 \times 2$ experimental design. The relative effectiveness of the three treatment approaches was evaluated by comparing their effects on five self-report measures and two physiological measures of test anxiety. The specific measures that were used as dependent variables in this study are described briefly below.

Self-Report Measures

1. *Test Anxiety Scale* (TAS). The TAS is a true–false questionnaire developed by I. G. Sarason (1972) to measure individual differences in the disposition to emit internal self-oriented, self-deprecatory responses under evaluative conditions. (The Test Anxiety Questionnaire was also administered as part of this investigation and was not included here because of redundancy with the TAS and TAI.)
2. *Test Anxiety Inventory* (TAI). The TAI is a 20-item self-rating scale that was designed to measure test anxiety as a situation-specific personality trait (Spielberger, 1980). Subjects are instructed to rate themselves on the frequency that they experience symptoms of test anxiety during examination

situations. In addition to a test anxiety score, which is based on all 20 items, the TAI has Worry (*W*) and Emotionality (*E*) subscales.

3. *State–Trait Anxiety Inventory* (STAI). The STAI consists of two 20-item subscales for measuring trait anxiety (T-Anxiety) and state anxiety (S-Anxiety) (Spielberger et al., 1970). In completing the T-Anxiety subscale, subjects are asked to report how anxious they generally feel. In responding to the S-Anxiety subscale, subjects are instructed to report the intensity of their feelings of anxiety "right now, at this moment."

Physiological Measures

Electromyographic (EMG) recording. The electromyograph recorded from the frontalis (forehead) muscle provided an objective index of skeletal muscle relaxation. High electrical activity corresponds to the muscle tension associated with anxiety, and low levels are associated with relaxed states (Budzynski & Stoyva, 1969). The EMG responses were measured by means of three cutaneous surface electrodes (Narco, Model 710 0009) connected to a Coulbourn Hi Gain Bioamplifier (Model 575-01), which served to filter the electrophysiological input. The connection of the thermal and EMG electrodes, also discussed earlier in Chapter 6, is shown schematically in Figure 12.1.

The bioamplifier produced a continuous raw signal that was fed into a contour-following integrator (Coulbourn Model 576-01). High and low cutoffs were 1000 Hz and 90 Hz, respectively. At the 2,000-millisec. setting, the integrator provided a signal, which was the arithmetic average of the peak amplitudes over a 2-s time period. This signal was channeled to a voltage controlled oscillator (Coulbourn Model 524-05), which changed frequency as a function of the integrator output level. The oscillator output was fed into a Coulbourn Audio Mixer-Amplifier (Model 582-24) and then to a pair of stereo headphones, producing a tone stimulus that varied proportionally to the electromyograph recorded from the frontalis muscle. A readout of muscle tension level was also obtained on a B and K Digital Voltmeter (Model 280) directly from the contour-following integrator.

Thermographic recording. The temperature from the middle joint of the middle finger of each subject's nondominant hand was recorded to provide an indirect measure of peripheral blood flow. Tension or anxiety restricts the peripheral blood flow and leads to a decrease in finger temperature; a reduction in tension produces the opposite effects (Boudewins, 1976; Taub, 1975).

Pre- and Posttesting

The following pretests were individually administered: (a) the STAI, (b) the TAS, and (c) the TAI. After completing these paper-and-pencil tests, the subject was taken into the treatment room and seated in a comfortable reclining chair. The electrodes were then connected, and baseline data were collected for 5 min. Following this, the students listened to a 9-min recorded tape that instructed them to imagine the various stages involved in preparing for and taking a test (R. S. Shapiro, 1976).

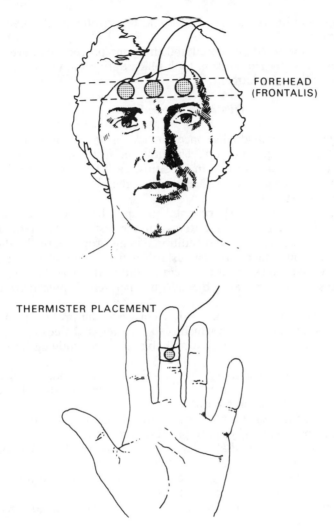

Figure 12.1 Electrode placement for electromyographic and thermal measurements.

EMG and temperature readings were taken immediately before and 2 s after each taped auditory stimulus that described specific steps in preparing for and taking a test. At the completion of the tape, each student was asked to take the Otis and Lennon (1965) test, which was given with standard instructions. EMG and temperature data were collected at 1-min intervals during this test.

At the end of the pretesting session, each subject was informed of whether he or she was assigned to a treatment or a control group, and an appointment was scheduled for either treatment or posttesting. Students assigned to the control group were informed that they would be provided with treatment the following semester.

The same tests were administered and the same procedures were followed in the posttest session. This session took place during the week immediately after the completion of treatment.

Treatment Procedures

Each subject met individually, once each week for 7 consecutive weeks, with one of the two experimenters. The first and last sessions were used for pre- and posttesting; the five interim sessions, each lasting approximately 90 min, were the treatment sessions. Members of the NTC group attended only the pre- and posttesting sessions.

Session 1. For all three experimental groups, the first session began by having the subject suggest specific items for the test anxiety hierarchy. The items suggested by the subjects and additional items proposed by the therapists were evaluated, and a hierarchy was established in terms of the amount of anxiety they evoked. The standard 12-item hierarchy that was developed based on this process was used for all subjects. This hierarchy is presented here:

1. Imagine that you are in your hardest class and the professor announces and discusses a course exam which is to be given in 2 weeks.
2. Imagine that a week has passed and that you are studying hard for the exam.
3. Imagine that you are studying the night before the important exam. You discuss it with some of your classmates. You are having difficulty concentrating on the material in your notes.
4. You are in bed the night before the examination and your mind flashes to the exam. You wonder if you are properly prepared.
5. You wake up and realize that today is the day that you have the final exam that will determine your grade. You leave your room to go to the exam.
6. Imagine that you are entering the exam room. As you take your seat you overhear other students reviewing the material.
7. Imagine that you are sitting in the exam room. The professor arrives and you wait for him to pass out the exam.
8. Imagine that the examination is being handed out now. . . . You get your copy.
9. You are now taking the exam and you come to a question to which you do not know the answer.
10. While trying to think of an answer, you notice that everyone else is busily writing answers.
11. You found that you have taken too much time on the first portion of the exam. You must hurry as you have only 30 minutes to do an hour's worth of work.
12. Imagine that you have only 5 minutes to complete the exam. You have left several questions unanswered. You come to one you prepared carefully for. Your mind goes blank and you freeze up.

Following the discussion of potential items for the test anxiety hierarchy, the subject was hooked up to the physiological apparatus. The EMG and temperature baseline data were collected for 5 min. The subjects in the SSD group were then instructed according to a modified Jacobsonian relaxation training procedure (Bernstein & Borkovec, 1973) that involved brief muscle tension–release relaxation cycles for each muscle group. Physiological data were collected only during relaxation and just before the next tension command was given.

The subjects in the BASD and BACC groups received biofeedback by means of a variable intensity tone produced as described above. Each subject received two 20-min periods of biofeedback training, consisting of four 5-min trials separated by a 1-min pause with the tone off. At the end of each treatment session, the subjects were asked to practice relaxing twice a day on their own, with no biofeedback.

Session 2. At the beginning of this session, the subjects were tested for their ability to visualize, and all were found able to do so. After 5 min of baseline measurement, each subject received relaxation or biofeedback training, following the same procedure as in Session 1. The first hierarchy item was then presented; 10 s later, the subjects were instructed to stop imagining that and continue to relax.

EMG and temperature readings were recorded just before and 2 to 3 s after image presentation. During image presentation, the subjects were asked to indicate any tension they felt by raising the index finger of their dominant hand. If no signal was made, the cycle was repeated until a criterion of three consecutive trials without tension was attained.

If anxiety or tension was signaled, subjects in the SSD and BASD groups were instructed to "stop imagining that and continue to relax"; specific suggestions for relaxation were also made. The image was then presented for 5 s, followed by 30 s of relaxation, and the subject was again asked to signal if anxiety or tension was felt. If tension was not signaled, the cycle was repeated, followed by resumption of the presentation of the next hierarchy item.

The BACC subjects who signaled tension were instructed to "hold on to the image" and to try to develop a strategy for relaxing away tension or anxiety. After the subjects indicated that they were relaxed (by lowering their index finger), they were permitted to continue to relax for 30 s. The hierarchy item was then repeated until the criterion of three trials without tension was achieved. In this session, the experimenters attempted to help all subjects work through the first two hierarchy items to the specified criterion.

Session 3. During this session, which was similar to Session 2, the experimenters attempted to cover Hierarchy Items 2 through 6. The biofeedback-assisted relaxation training for the members of the BASD and BACC groups was limited to one 20-minute segment that corresponded with the time required by the SSD subjects to practice muscle relaxation.

Session 4. The procedure was the same as Session 3 except that biofeedback training was provided only during the first and third trials. To control for the time required for this biofeedback training, the SSD subjects were given two 5-min self-relaxation sessions.

Session 5. The last treatment session was the same as Session 4, except that on completing the 12th and final hierarchy item, the last 4 items (Items 9, 10, 11, and 12) were repeated, with a criterion of one presentation without any indication of stress. On completion of treatment, the subjects were scheduled for post-testing during the following week.

RESULTS

Each self-report measure was evaluated by means of a $4 \times 2 \times 2$ analysis of variance (ANOVA), which revealed highly significant ($p < .001$) pre–post reductions for the TAS and the TAI Total, W and E subscale scores. The pre–post reduction for the STAI T-Anxiety subscale was significant at the $p < .05$ level, whereas there was no change in S-Anxiety. The Treatment $\times$ Pre–Post Testing interaction effects for the TAS; TAI Total, W, and E; and T-Anxiety measures were all significant at $p < .05$.

Conditons by Pre- and Posttesting

Figure 12.2 shows the interaction of treatments by pre- and posttest for the TAI Total scores. Because the findings for the TAI W and E subscales were almost identical to those for the TAI Total, the findings for the subscales are not reported. Using Scheffé tests, the subjects in both the SSD and the BACC conditions were significantly lower in test anxiety at the posttest than were the control subjects ($p < .01$).

The SSD subjects also tended to show a greater reduction in test anxiety than did the subjects in the BASD condition ($p < .10$), whereas subjects in the BACC and BASD conditions did not significantly differ in test anxiety reduction. Moreover, the BASD and NTC conditions did not differ on any of the Scheffé tests. Because the pattern of results in the ANOVA for the TAS were quite similar to those for the TAI, these findings are not reported.

The Treatment Conditions $\times$ Pre–Post Testing interaction for T-Anxiety subscale scores is shown in Figure 12.3. The SSD and BACC conditions both produced significantly greater reductions in trait anxiety than did the NTC condition ($p < .05$). Subjects in the SSD condition also showed a greater reduction than did those in the BASD condition ($p < .01$), whereas subjects in the BACC condition also tended to show a greater reduction than those in the BASD condition ($p < .10$). There was no difference in the amount of reduction in trait anxiety for subjects in the SSD and the BACC conditions; the BASD and NTC groups showed no reductions at all.

ANOVAs were performed on the four physiological measures: EMG and finger temperature during the imagery tape and EMG and finger temperature during completion of the Otis test. The Conditions $\times$ Pre- and Posttesting interaction effects were not significant for any of the physiological variables, indicating that there were no differential changes for the treatment groups as compared with the NTC group. The only statistically significant main effect for the physiological measures involved pre–post changes in finger tempera-

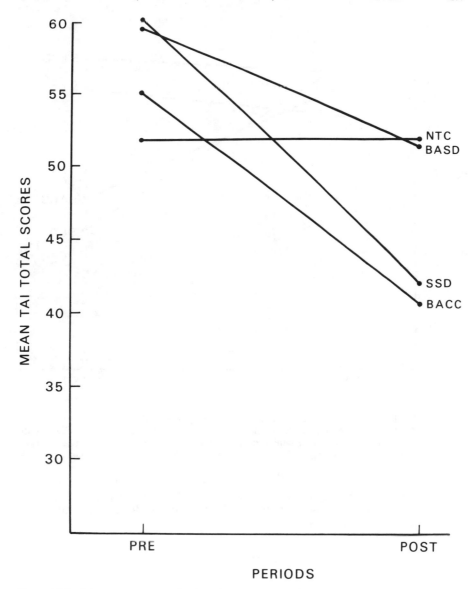

Figure 12.2 Mean pretreatment (Pre) and posttreatment (Post) Test Anxiety Inventory (TAI) Total scores for the subjects in the standard systematic desensitization (SSD) group, biofeedback-assisted systematic desensitization (BASD) group, biofeedback-assisted cognitive coping (BACC) group, and no-treatment control (NTC) group.

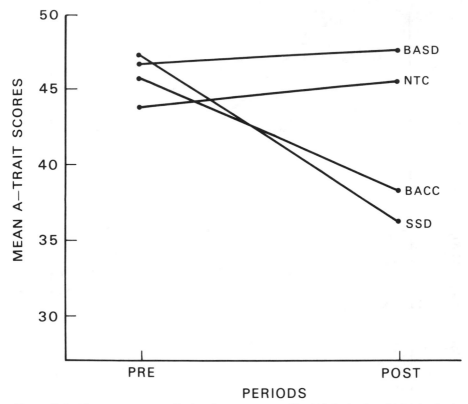

Figure 12.3   Mean pretreatment (Pre) and posttreatment (Post) Trait Anxiety (T-Anxiety) subscale scores for the subjects in the standard systematic desensitization (SSD) group,
biofeedback-assisted systematic desensitization (BASD) group, biofeedback-assisted
cognitive coping (BACC) group, and no-treatment control (NTC) group.

ture. Finger temperatures increased during both the Otis test (there were no
significant pre–post differences between the four groups for the Otis test) and
the imagery tape ($p < .05$).

DISCUSSION

The results of this study indicated consistently greater pre–post reductions
in anxiety for subjects in the SSD and BACC conditions than for those in the
BASD and the NTC conditions. The BASD group did not differ from the NTC
group, whose anxiety appeared not to change appreciably during the period
between pre- and posttesting.

Because the SSD and BACC conditions were equally effective, it appears
that neither progressive relaxation nor cognitive coping are critical in the
treatment of test anxiety, but something common to these two conditions may

be the essential element. Traditional desensitization teaches the client Jacobsonian relaxation techniques and how to relax in the presence of the noxious stimulus. In the cognitive coping approach to desensitization used in this study, the client was forced to work out his or her own verbal cues, which may have involved self-instructions to relax, not to worry about the test, or other appropriate verbal strategies for coping with the stress. Both of these approaches, SSD and BACC, involve strong cognitive cues, and biofeedback does not. In addition, the subjects in both of these groups were taught how to use these cues in the presence of the noxious testing situation. Biofeedback does not appear to provide a cognitive cue that can be similarly used.

Desensitization and cognitive coping were equally effective in reducing test anxiety as measured by the TAI *W* and *E* subscales. These findings were contrary to expectations based on a cognitive model, which would predict that reductions in test anxiety are dependent on decreased worry and relatively independent of emotionality. The counterconditioning (desensitization) model focuses on reducing the emotional or physiological response to stimuli associated with exams. However, as was pointed out earlier, muscle relaxation used in desensitization may also provide verbal cues that can be used to reduce worry during tests. Similarly, the cognitive coping approach to desensitization affects both worry and emotionality about equally. In this study, both muscle relaxation and cognitive coping were associated with substantial reductions in trait anxiety, suggesting that the use of the cognitive cues provided by these techniques within the desensitization paradigm are far reaching and pervasive.

Failure to find any reduction in muscle electromyograph for the treatment groups in this study was contrary to results reported in both the biofeedback and the progressive relaxation literatures. This may have been an artifact of the time-sampling methods used and the lack of automated recording equipment for collecting the physiological data, which made it possible for moment-to-moment fluctuations in the digital readout to influence the data. It is difficult to know to what extent these fluctuations were determined by the clients or by extraneous factors. Because of these limitations, no firm conclusions can be reached with regard to the relation between biofeedback and muscle relaxation.

Although the thermal data were not as subject as the electromyographs to rapid fluctuations, these data provided little additional insight into the relation between biofeedback and relaxation. The only significant thermal result was a pre–post temperature increase during the Otis test, which may be most parsimoniously explained as relaxation due to an adaptation effect. The clients were more relaxed in the final session of the experiment than they were in the initial session.

SUMMARY AND CONCLUSIONS

The effectiveness of three desensitization approaches to the treatment of test anxiety were evaluated. SSD based on Wolpe's (1958) work and BACC desensitization were more effective than BASD in reducing test anxiety and trait anxiety. There were no differential effects of these treatments on electro-myographs recorded from the frontalis muscles and thermal measures taken from the middle finger of the dominant hand.

BASD was not effective alone in reducing anxiety, but this treatment in combination with cognitive coping was effective. These findings suggest that both muscle relaxation and cognitive coping provide verbal or cognitive cues (albeit different cues) that students use in desensitization as a means for reducing anxiety in the face of previously noxious stimuli.

13

Cognitive Therapy, Study Skills Training, and Biofeedback in the Treatment of Test Anxiety

Peter R. Vagg and James D. Papsdorf
University of Michigan, Ann Arbor, Michigan, USA

The emphasis in test anxiety theory and research has recently shifted from emotionality to cognition (e.g., Pekrun, 1992; Schwarzer & Jerusalem, 1992). The research evidence has suggested that both areas must be dealt with if the anxiety experienced in test situations is to be reduced and improved grades are to occur as a result of treatment (Hembree, 1988; Spielberger & Vagg, 1987). This study was concerned with the relative importance of treating either the cognitive or the emotional aspects of test anxiety, as compared with treatments that are directed toward both components.

Early research on test anxiety, as outlined by Spielberger and Vagg in Chapter 1, focused almost exclusively on the emotional reactions experienced during tests. McKeachie (1951) and Mandler and Sarason (1952) were among the first to demonstrate that high test-anxious students showed poorer academic performance than low test-anxious students. The Test Anxiety Questionnaire (TAQ) was developed by Mandler and Sarason to measure self-oriented reactions that inferfered with task-oriented responses in testing situations. Assessment of these "self-oriented responses" marked the first time attention had been directed toward the disruptive task-irrelevant reactions of test-anxious students that interfered with their performance.

I. G. Sarason (1958b, 1972, 1980) placed even greater emphasis on the disruptive cognitions of test-anxious students. He observed that under evaluative conditions high test-anxious students experienced more negative self-centered thoughts and interpreted tests in a more personalized way than did low test-anxious students. The importance of cognitive variables in the treatment of test anxiety was also noted by Meichenbaum (1972), who observed that test-anxious students tended to be distracted by negative self-statements,

The research reported in this chapter is based on the first author's Ph.D. dissertation and was supported by Grant 30133 from the Human Resources Institute at the University of Michigan. The authors would also like to thank Dr. Charles D. Spielberger for his consultation on the preparation of the manuscript and Jess Ghannam for his assistance with the data analysis of this research.

and by Wine (1971), who suggested that test-anxious students had difficulty in focusing their attention on task-relevant stimuli.

Two major components of test anxiety, as detailed in Chapters 1–3, are worry and emotionality. Liebert and Morris (1967) were the first to conceptualize test anxiety as consisting of these two components. They defined worry as cognitive concern over failure and emotionality as the negative feelings and associated autonomic arousal experienced during tests. They identified subsets of TAQ items with worry and emotionality content and derived scales based on these items to assess worry and emotionality. Worry was found to be negatively correlated with academic performance, whereas no relation was found between emotionality and performance.

Spielberger (1972a, 1972b, 1975, 1980) and his colleagues (Spielberger et al., 1978; Spielberger & Vagg, 1987) defined test anxiety as a situation-specific form of trait anxiety. According to Spielberger et al. (1976), high test-anxious students perceive tests as personally more threatening and respond to examination situations with greater increases in state anxiety than do low test-anxious students. The Test Anxiety Inventory (TAI) was constructed to measure test anxiety as a situation-specific trait (Spielberger, 1980), with factorially derived subscales for assessing its worry and emotionality components. Using the TAI to assess worry and emotionality, Spielberger et al. (1978) confirmed Liebert and Morris's (1967) finding that worry was related to performance and emotionality was not. Thus, in both theory and measurement, emphasis has shifted from defining test anxiety as a unitary psychological state toward conceptualizing it as a situation-specific trait with both cognitive and visceral–emotional components.

TREATMENT FOR TEST ANXIETY

Although a number of variations of dynamic psychotherapy have been used in treating test-anxious students, systematic desensitization was the first treatment found to be effective in reducing test anxiety (see studies reported in Gonzalez, Chapter 9, and Parker et al., Chapter 12). According to Wolpe (1958), desensitization is effective in the treatment of anxiety-related disorders by replacing anxiety with relaxation by means of a counterconditioning process. Bedell (1975) has shown that muscle relaxation alone can lead to reductions in test anxiety. However, as Gonzalez (1978a) has pointed out, changes in performance have consistently been found only in studies using desensitization enriched by study skills training or group counseling on how to cope with anxiety during tests (see Gonzalez, Chapter 9).

Cognitive therapy as a treatment for test anxiety focuses on the cognitive or worry aspects of testing experienced by the student as contrasted with the emotional components treated in desensitization. Algaze (see Chapter 10) reviewed the literature on cognitive–behavioral treatments of test anxiety, which included six studies that used rational–emotive therapy (RET) and seven that used Meichenbaum's (1972, 1977) cognitive behavior modification (CBM). He concluded that both RET and CBM were as effective as desensitization.

Like Meichenbaum, Algaze found that cognitive therapy was most effective when used in combination with desensitization. There was little evidence that cognitive treatments by themselves help improve performance. Meichenbaum (1972) found that CBM led to an improvement in grades, but his design included elements of desensitization. Thus, the most effective means of treatment for test anxiety appears to involve desensitization of the emotional component and restructuring of the self-defeating cognitive elements that occur during tests.

Parker et al. (see Chapter 12) attempted to evaluate the effects of different treatments on the worry and emotionality aspects of test anxiety. Biofeedback was used for the emotional component and cognitive coping for the worry component. There were three treatment groups. The treatment for Group 1 involved a standard desensitization approach. The treatment for Group 2 included the standard desensitization procedure used with Group 1, modified by substituting biofeedback of the frontalis muscles for progressive relaxation in order to give the client more direct information about his or her level of muscular tension. The treatment for Group 3 added a cognitive coping approach to the treatment given to Group 2.

There was no improvement in grade point average (GPA) as a result of any of the treatments. The combination of cognitive coping, biofeedback, and modified desensitization in Group 3 was no more effective than standard desensitization in reducing test anxiety, and the treatment involving biofeedback (Group 2) did not differ significantly from a no-treatment control (NTC) group. Parker et al. (Chapter 12) suggested that the reason the traditional desensitization and cognitive coping treatments were effective was because they both provided cognitive cues that could be learned and used in the testing situation to reduce anxiety, whereas biofeedback by itself provided no such cues.

The inability of behavioral treatments to improve performance has been repeatedly reported in the test anxiety literature for some time. Several authors have recently suggested that study skills are essential in the treatment of test anxiety (Gonzalez, 1976; Morris & Liebert, 1973; Spielberger et al., 1976; Wittmaier, 1972). Gonzalez (see Chapter 9) reported that study counseling alone reduced test anxiety in 5 of 10 studies, but led to an increase in GPA in only 1 of the studies.

The complexity of GPA as an index of performance has been pointed out by a number of authors (Allen, 1971; Lin & McKeachie, 1970). This measure confounds academic performance with type of course (e.g., introductory chemistry vs. psychology), number of courses taken (less accurate in early years of college), and student characteristics such as ethnic background, dress, manner, and so on that may influence grades. Nevertheless, Gonzalez, as detailed earlier in Chapter 9, concluded that treatments consisting of a combination of desensitization and discussions about reducing anxiety during tests consistently led to an increase in GPA. Apart from the Algaze study (see Chapter 10), only one prior test anxiety treatment study has attempted to teach study counseling in combination with cognitive therapy. Although test anxiety was reduced in this study, there was no improvement in GPA (Lavigne, 1974).

GOALS OF THIS STUDY

This study used techniques similar to those of Parker et al. in the study reported in Chapter 12, but was designed to compare more directly the effectiveness of biofeedback and cognitive therapy in treating test anxiety. Because Parker et al. combined biofeedback and cognitive coping in a single treatment, it was not known whether only one of these variables or the combination of the two was responsible for the observed reduction in test anxiety. This study was designed to evaluate these factors in a 2×2 experimental design in which the four treatment groups were defined by the presence or absence of biofeedback and the presence or absence of cognitive treatment.

A second goal in this study was to examine the effects of pretreatment study skills on performance. Within each of the four experimental groups, students with high or low study skills were identified on the basis of their scores on the W. F. Brown–Holtzman (1965) Survey of Study Habits and Attitudes (SSHA).

METHOD

Subjects

The subjects in the study were selected from among volunteers who responded to a newspaper story or a poster advertising a test anxiety program at the Reading and Learning Skills Center of the University of Michigan. All subjects who responded were interviewed and administered the Debilitating Anxiety Scale of the Alpert–Haber (1960) Achievement Anxiety Test. The students who participated in the study (18 men and 14 women) scored in the upper 20% on the Debilitating Anxiety Scale, and all but 1 had a GPA of 3.5 or less. They all signed a contract to participate in the study and a release form for their transcripts.

Measures

Five standard tests were administered individually at both the pre- and posttesting sessions. The TAI (Spielberger et al., 1978) provides a total score in addition to Worry (W) and Emotionality (E) subscale scores. The State–Trait Anxiety Inventory (STAI) Form X (Spielberger et al., 1970) measures state and trait anxiety. The Irrational Beliefs Test (IBT) (Jones, 1969) provides a measure of irrationality. The SSHA (W. F. Brown & Holtzman, 1965) evaluates study habits and attitudes. The Wonderlic Personnel Test (Wonderlic, 1975) provides a measure of intellectual ability. Form I was administered at the pretest and Form II at the posttest. Cumulative GPA and GPAs for the semester preceding and the semester during which treatment took place were used as estimates of academic performance.

Electromyographic (EMG) and finger temperature (thermal) psycho-physiological measures were taken before, during, and after treatment. The equipment and method of data collection were essentially the same as those described by Parker et al. in Chapter 12. The EMG recording was 1-20th of the actual voltage; temperature was the degrees deviation (in Celsius) from the baseline established for each client.

Procedure

The students were randomly assigned to one of four experimental groups defined by the presence or absence of biofeedback and cognitive therapy: biofeedback plus cognitive therapy (BCT, $n = 8$), biofeedback (BIO, $n = 8$) only; cognitive therapy only (CTO, $n = 8$), and no-treatment control (NTC, $n = 8$). Within each of these groups, 4 students were assigned to high and low study skills conditions, based on a median split of the sum of the subjects' scores on the SSHA Study Habits and Study Attitudes subscales.

The students were contacted by one of the four therapists (two men and two women), all of whom had experience in behavior therapy, and an appointment was made for pretesting. Each therapist was assigned to work with 2 students in each of the four experimental groups. In the pretreatment testing session, each student was individually tested in a quiet room 1 week before treatment began. The following questionnaires were administered to all subjects in randomized order: STAI, TAI, SSHA, and IBT. After completing the questionnaires, the students were connected to the electrophysiological equipment and EMG and thermal baseline measures were taken. The experimental EMG and thermal data were then obtained during the presentation of the test anxiety hierarchy tape (R. S. Shapiro, 1976) and while the students completed the Wonderlic Personnel Test.

There were five 1-hr treatment sessions for each therapy group. The BIO group received the same biofeedback procedures and session-by-session presentation of the 12-item test anxiety hierarchy items described by Parker et al. in Chapter 12. In addition, a detailed outline of each session was prepared (Vagg & Papsdorf, 1977) to ensure uniformity of the procedures for the subjects receiving biofeedback training. This group received only biofeedback and the counterposing of biofeedback-induced relaxation with the hierarchy items during the treatment sessions. In the first treatment session, the Yerkes–Dodson (1908) law was explained as the rationale for the efficacy of the biofeedback procedures. In the next four sessions, the students were instructed to "attempt to use the biofeedback techniques to reduce any tension that you feel as a result of imagining the item." They were also instructed to practice the biofeedback techniques twice a day at home.

The CTO group also followed a detailed manual (Vagg & Papsdorf, 1977), based on Meichenbaum's (1972) approach, in which the five treatment sessions were outlined. The first treatment session involved training the clients to distinguish between thoughts and feelings and demonstrating how negative self-statements contribute to self-defeating emotions and cause decrements in performance. The second CTO treatment session involved the discussion of three of Ellis and Grieger's (1977) irrational ideologies: approval, perfection, and getting your own way. The discussion centered on the influence of these ideologies in producing negative self-statements during tests and how to formulate positive coping self-statements to counteract them. The students then developed their own coping statements during presentation of the first two hierarchy items.

Treatment Sessions 3–5 involved further discussion of the use of the RET model in dealing with test anxiety, together with the continuation and completion of the test anxiety hierarchy and refinement of coping statements. Clients were also given RET worksheets for homework practice in developing coping statements for any situation in which they felt anxious or tense.

A detailed treatment manual was also developed for the BCT group. Students assigned to this group received a combination of the biofeedback and cognitive therapy procedures that were described above for the BIO and CTO groups.

The posttreatment testing session was conducted 1 week after the final treatment session. The STAI, TAI, SSHA, and IBT were readministered in randomized order, followed by data collection on the same comparable physiological measures that were taken in the pretreatment testing sessions. Finally, the students in the treatment conditions were debriefed about the experiment's purpose. The subjects in the NTC group were informed they would be offered treatment during the following semester.

RESULTS

The students in this study were selected on the basis of high scores on the Debilitating Anxiety Scale of the Achievement Anxiety Test. These students scored approximately 1 standard deviation above the mean (85th percentile) for college students on the STAI State Anxiety (S-Anxiety) and Trait Anxiety (T-Anxiety) subscales (Spielberger et al., 1970) and the TAI Total, W, and E subscales (Spielberger, 1980) given in the pretreatment testing session. Thus, the subjects who participated in this study were highly anxiety-prone and emotionally disturbed before the initiation of treatment.

Before evaluating the treatment effects, possible differences between the experimental and control groups before treatment were examined by comparing the pretest scores of the subjects in the four experimental groups (BIO, BCT, CTO, and NTC). These differences were evaluated in $2 \times 2 \times 2$ analyses of variance (ANOVAs) in which the between-subjects variables were presence or absence of biofeedback, presence or absence of cognitive therapy, and high versus low study skills. In these analyses the BIO group had significantly lower T-Anxiety subscale scores than did the other three treatment groups, and the high study skills students had significantly higher GPAs than the low study skills students. Higher GPAs were expected for the students with better study skills. Because the subjects were randomly assigned to the four experimental conditions, there was no apparent explanation other than chance for the finding that the BIO group was lower in trait anxiety than the other groups.

The treatment programs in this study were conducted by four different experimenters (therapists): two men and two women. Each therapist worked with 8 subjects, 2 from each of the four experimental groups. To determine whether sex of experimenter influenced treatment outcome, $2 \times 2 \times 2 \times 2$ ANOVAs were performed in which biofeedback, cognitive therapy, and sex of the experimenter were the between-subject variables and pre- and posttesting was the within-subjects variable. The results indicated that sex of the experimenter was not significantly related to changes in any of the dependent variables. However, there was a nonsignificant tendency for the students who were treated by the more experienced therapists to show greater reductions in anxiety from pretest to posttest.

Effects of Treatment

The impact of the experimental treatments on students with high or low study skills was evaluated for three different groups of dependent measures. The first group included test anxiety, trait anxiety, and irrational beliefs. The second group involved transient states or processes and included frontalis electromyographs, finger temperature, and self-reports of state anxiety. The third set of variables consisted of two performance measures: scores on the Wonderlic Personnel Test and GPA. The dependent measures were evaluated in $2 \times 2 \times 2 \times 2$ repeated-measures ANOVAs in which biofeedback, cognitive therapy, and study skills were the between-subject variables and pre- and posttesting was the within-subjects variable.

The pre- and posttest means for the TAI Total, W, and E subscale scores are reported in Table 13.1. The results for each of these measures were almost identical. The cognitive therapy by pre–post treatment interactions were significant ($p < .05$) for all three TAI measures. The reductions in the TAI scores were larger for subjects in the cognitive treatment groups (BCT and CTO) than for those in the other groups (BIO and NTC), as can be seen in Table 13.1. The small reductions in the TAI scores of the BIO subjects were not significantly different from those of the NTC subjects. Because the NTC group showed essentially no change in any of the test anxiety measures, the reductions in the TAI scores can be attributed primarily to the effects of cognitive therapy.

The mean STAI trait anxiety scores for the four treatment conditions are reported in Table 13.2. For this measure, the Cognitive Therapy $\times$ Study Skills $\times$ Pretesting and Posttesting triple interaction was statistically significant ($p < .05$). Although all of the cognitive therapy groups showed reductions in trait anxiety, the low study skills–BCT group showed only a small decline. In contrast, the T-Anxiety subscale scores of the BIO groups actually increased, whereas the scores of the NTC groups were essentially unchanged. The Cognitive Therapy $\times$ Pretesting and Posttesting interaction was also statistically significant ($p < .05$). This interaction resulted from the decrease in the T-Anxiety subscale scores of the BCT and CTO groups, which appeared to be due to cognitive therapy, whereas the scores for the BIO and NTC groups showed a slight increase.

The mean scores for the IBT are also reported in Table 13.2. The pre–post main effect was statistically significant ($p < .01$), reflecting the fact that six of

Table 13.1 Pretesting (Pre), posttesting (Post), and difference (Diff) scores for the biofeedback plus cognitive therapy (BCT), cognitive therapy only (CTO), biofeedback only (BIO), and no-treatment control (NTC) groups for Test Anxiety Inventory (TAI) Total, Worry, and Emotionality subscale scores ($n = 32$)

TAI subscale	Low study skills			High study skills		
	Pre	Post	Diff	Pre	Post	Diff
Total						
BCT	62.0	48.3	−11.7	56.3	35.5	−20.8
CTO	67.0	51.8	−15.2	59.0	43.0	−15.0
BIO	55.3	46.5	−8.8	55.5	43.8	−11.7
NTC	45.8	45.3	−0.5	54.0	54.5	0.5
Worry						
BCT	23.3	19.0	−4.3	18.5	12.5	−6.0
CTO	26.0	18.7	−7.3	20.5	15.0	−5.5
BIO	19.3	15.8	−3.5	17.8	14.0	−3.8
NTC	15.5	16.3	0.8	18.5	19.5	−1.0
Emotionality						
BCT	26.0	18.5	−7.5	25.3	15.8	−9.5
CTO	27.5	21.3	−6.2	24.5	19.5	−5.0
BIO	24.5	20.3	−4.2	25.3	19.0	−6.3
NTC	19.0	16.5	−2.5	24.5	23.5	−1.0

Table 13.2 Pretesting (Pre), posttesting (Post), and difference (Diff) scores for the biofeedback plus cognitive therapy (BCT), cognitive therapy only (CTO), biofeedfack only (BIO), and no-treatment control (NTC) groups State–Trait Anxiety Inventory for Trait Anxiety (T-Anxiety) and Irrational Beliefs Test (IBT) Total ($n = 32$)

	Results					
	Low study skills			High study skills		
Subscale	Pre	Post	Diff	Pre	Post	Diff
T-Anxiety						
BCT	52.3	50.8	−1.5	45.5	40.3	−5.2
CTO	54.8	49.5	−5.3	49.8	38.0	−11.8
BIO	26.5	30.5	4.0	31.8	37.8	6.0
NTC	51.0	51.3	0.3	44.0	45.5	1.5
IBT total						
BCT	317	303	−14	298	275	−23
CTO	299	282	−17	318	269	−49
BIO	265	268	3	279	244	−35
NTC	311	297	−14	285	290	5

Table 13.3 Pretesting (Pre), posttesting (Post), and difference (Diff) scores for the biofeedback plus cognitive therapy (BCT), cognitive therapy only (CTO), biofeedfack only (BIO), and no-treatment control (NTC) groups for cumulative and term grade point average (n = 32)

Grade point average	Low study skills			High study skills		
	Pre	Post	Diff	Pre	Post	Diff
Cumulative						
BCT	2.72	2.72	0.00	2.86	2.78	−0.08
CTO	3.04	2.95	−0.09	3.38	3.43	0.05
BIO	2.12	2.31	0.19	2.77	3.01	0.24
NTC	2.55	2.54	−0.01	2.73	2.78	0.05
Term						
BCT	2.95	2.88	−0.07	2.70	2.60	−0.10
CTO	3.04	2.81	−0.23	3.31	3.52	0.22
BIO	2.24	2.31	0.07	2.81	3.43	0.62
NTC	2.38	2.37	−0.01	2.73	2.95	0.22

the eight treatment conditions showed reductions in irrational beliefs. The significant four-way Biofeedback × Cognitive Therapy × Study Skills × Pre–Post interaction effect ($p < .05$) can be most clearly seen in the IBT difference scores in Table 13.2. Students with high study skills showed large reductions in irrational beliefs in the three therapeutic treatment conditions; students with low study skills showed somewhat smaller reductions in the two cognitive therapy and the NTC conditions; scores of students in the low study skills BIO group and the high study skills NTC group were essentially unchanged.

The second group of variables evaluated in this study involved transient individual states or processes. A high significant pre–post reduction ($p < .001$) in S-Anxiety subscale scores was found. All groups, including the NTC group, showed this reduction. The results for the two physiological measures, frontalis electromyographs and finger temperature, were similar to those for state anxiety. The students showed physiological arousal during the pretest imagery and while working on the Wonderlic Personnel Test, but little or no arousal while engaged in these tasks during the posttest.

In the evaluation of the effects of the treatment procedures on the performance measures, the pre–post treatment effect for the Wonderlic Personnel Test was highly significant ($p < .001$). The mean scores on this measure increased substantially from the pretest to the posttest; the amount of increase was about the same for all groups, including the NTC group.

Cumulative GPAs (C-GPAs) and term GPAs (T-GPAs) for the high and low study skills students in the four treatment groups are reported in Table 13.3. The significant Cognitive Therapy × Pre–Post Periods interaction ($p < .05$) for C-GPA reflected the finding that the GPAs for the BIO group showed a small pre–post increase, whereas those for the other groups were essentially unchanged.

In the analysis of the effects of treatment on C-GPA, the significant study skills main effect ($p < .05$) indicated that students with high study skills had higher C-GPAs, as expected. The cognitive therapy main effect indicated that students in the CTO and BCT groups had consistently higher C-GPAs ($p <$ .05) than the students in the BIO and NTC groups. Although the pattern of results for the T-GPA were similar to those for C-GPA, none of these results were statistically significant.

DISCUSSION

The results of this study showed that cognitive therapy was effective in reducing test anxiety. Substantial reductions in TAI Total, W, and E subscale scores were found for the CTO treatment, whereas the effects for the BIO treatment were not significantly different from those for the NTC group in terms of their influence on test anxiety scores.

Cognitive therapy resulted in large reductions in the TAI W subscale scores and was equally effective alone or in combination with biofeedback. Although both biofeedback and cognitive therapy seemed to reduce TAI subscale scores, this effect was not statistically significant. The combination of these treatments produced the greatest reductions in emotionality.

The effective treatment of test anxiety seems to require the development of test-taking and anxiety-modulating skills. Bedell and Weathers (1979) identified two specific requirements for effective skills enhancement: cognitive understanding and practice. In this study, the cognitive therapy treatment readily fulfilled both of these requirements. It provided a skill in developing cognitive coping statements about tests as well as behavioral practice in using these coping statements in an imagined hierarchy of test-relevant situations.

Although cognitive therapy and biofeedback were equated in terms of behavioral practice, biofeedback provided relatively little understanding of the skills involved in its use. Therefore, the superior effectiveness of cognitive therapy can be attributed to a better understanding of the skills provided by this treatment. The finding that biofeedback does not provide students with knowledge of cognitive skills that are easily understood is consistent with the results reported by Parker et al. in Chapter 12.

The importance of cognitive cues was also reflected by the finding that the greatest reductions in emotionality occurred when the physiologically based biofeedback was augmented by cue-based cognitive therapy. However, there was no demonstrable advantage in adding biofeedback to cognitive therapy in reducing cognitive-based worry. The failure of biofeedback to produce significant reductions in test anxiety could have resulted from the insufficient number of biofeedback trials. Even if this explanation was correct, however, one is still left with the fact that in this study cognitive therapy was simpler and more economical and showed better and more rapid results than biofeedback.

A major concern in this study was to evaluate the effects of treatment on two enduring maladaptive personality characteristics: trait anxiety and irrational beliefs. Cognitive therapy resulted in reduced T-Anxiety subscale scores. Moreover, cognitive therapy alone appeared to produce a larger reduction in T-Anxiety subscale scores than the combination of biofeedback with cognitive therapy. These results were consistent with Algaze's finding (see Chapter 9) that the effects of cognitive therapy generalize from testing situations to other stressful situations involving threats to self-esteem that are typically assessed by trait anxiety measures.

Reductions in scores on the IBT were also greatest in the cognitive therapy groups, and students with good study skills showed larger reductions than those with poor study skills. Thus, in addition to modifying the adverse impact of maladaptive personality characteristics by reducing the intensity and frequency of anxiety reactions in test situations, cognitive treatment was also effective in reducing negative self-statements stemming from irrational beliefs.

The therapeutic effects of the cognitive and biofeedback treatments on self-report and physiological anxiety process measures yielded identical results for finger temperature, frontalis electromyographs, and STAI S-Anxiety subscale scores: State anxiety (arousal) was elevated at pretest as compared with baseline measures and did not differ from baseline during posttest. Because the findings for the NTC group were essentially the same as those for the treatment groups, these results suggested that the novelty of the laboratory situation evoked anxiety in the pretest and that subjects adapted to this situation by the posttest.

On the Wonderlic Personnel Test, the treatment and control groups showed large pre–post increases, indicating a substantial practice effect even though parallel forms of this test were administered. Given the magnitude of this practice effect, the Wonderlic Personnel Test would seem to be unsuitable as a performance outcome measure in test anxiety research. The results for GPA, the second performance measure, were much more difficult to interpret. Surprisingly, the BIO treatment, which had no influence on test anxiety, led to an improvement in cumulative GPA. Because the pretest mean C-GPA for students with low study skills who received this treatment was very low, the GPA for these students probably increased at posttest because of regression to the mean. There is no ready explanation for the C-GPA increase for the high study skills–BIO group.

This study's results provide evidence that test-anxious students with good study skills perform relatively well in examinations and have significantly better GPAs than students with poor study skills. Those students nevertheless feel uncomfortable and anxious when they think about or take tests, and they generally seek treatment for their anxiety, not because of poor grades. Cognitive therapy produced the desired treatment effects for these students, leading to large reductions in test anxiety, trait anxiety, and irrational beliefs.

Treatment of students with poor study skills is generally more difficult. Cognitive therapy can reduce the anxiety of these students, as was demonstrated in this study, but it cannot help them to improve their grades because they do not know how to study. Although it is possible to remedy their study skills deficits by training in study methods (Gonzales, 1976; Spielberger et al., 1978), it remains to be demonstrated that significant gains in study skills lead to improvement in GPA. Recent research findings suggest that study counseling improves students' motivation to study (see Algaze, Chapter 10) and that group discussion of study techniques facilitates academic achievement (see Gonzalez, Chapter 9).

SUMMARY

This study compared the effectiveness of biofeedback and cognitive therapy in the treatment of test anxiety. The treatment outcome measures were the TAI with its *W* and *E* subscales, the STAI S-Anxiety and T-Anxiety subscales, the IBT, the Wonderlic Personnel Test, GPAs, and frontalis EMG and finger temperature. Cognitive therapy produced significant reductions in TAI Total, *W*, and *E* scores, STAI T-Anxiety scores, and irrational beliefs. The effects of biofeedback on these same variables were generally not distinguishable from the control group.

Significant pre–post reductions in state anxiety and EMG scores were found for all treatment groups, as well as for the NTC group. Scores on the Wonderlic Personnel Test and finger temperature increased from pretest to posttest for all groups. These results suggested that all subjects responded with increased anxiety to the novelty and unfamiliarity of the testing situation and were less anxious at the posttest, presumably because they had adapted to the testing situation.

Students with good study skills had significantly higher GPAs at both pretest and posttest than did students with poor study skills, but no significant improvement resulted from treatment. However, students with good study skills showed substantial reductions in irrational beliefs in all of the treatment conditions, as compared with the NTC group.

The effectiveness of cognitive therapy in this study can be attributed to the fact that it provided a clear understanding of how to develop and use cognitive coping techniques in test situations. Although the cognitive therapy and biofeedback groups were equated in terms of behavioral practice, the biofeedback training provided relatively little understanding of the skills required to use this technique outside the treatment situation.

IV

THEORY-BASED TREATMENT OF TEST ANXIETY

14

Treatment of Test Anxiety: Application of the Transactional Process Model

Peter R. Vagg
University of Michigan, Ann Arbor, Michigan, USA

Charles D. Spielberger
University of South Florida, Tampa, Florida, USA

New developments in the treatment of test anxiety have essentially mirrored the evolution of the behavioral therapies. Beginning in the mid-1960s, research on the treatment of test anxiety focused primarily on relaxation training and systematic desensitization. Over the past two decades, increasing emphasis has been given to cognitive techniques in test anxiety treatment studies (e.g., Kreitler & Kreitler, 1987; Spielberger & Vagg, 1987; Sud & Sharma, 1990). In addition, biofeedback and study skills training have been used in a number of studies, either as separate treatment conditions or in combination with desensitization or cognitive therapies.

Most test anxiety treatment studies have primarily been concerned with evaluating the relative effectiveness of specific treatment components in reducing test anxiety and improving academic performance (Hembree, 1988; Meichenbaum & Butler, 1980; van der Ploeg et al., 1986; N. Wilson & Rotter, 1986; see Part III, Chapters 9–13). In contrast to the large number of outcome studies, relatively little attention has been directed toward identifying the internal mechanisms that mediate the effects of treatment on the emotional and cognitive (worry) processes now generally recognized as the major components of test anxiety. It is our conviction that test anxiety treatment research should be based on a careful analysis of the intrapersonal processes of test-anxious students that evoke worry and emotionality and that contribute to their adverse effects on test performance.

In Chapter 1, we examined the emotional and cognitive processes that mediate the effects of test anxiety on intellectual performance. Research findings have convincingly demonstrated that test-anxious students perceive examinations as highly threatening and that they experience more intense emotional reactions and more numerous self-derogatory worry conditions during examinations than students who are low in test anxiety. Emotionality activates task-irrelevant thoughts and behaviors that interfere with attention and concentration, whereas worry cognitions negatively affect information processing and retrieval of information from storage.

In evaluating the efficacy of a test anxiety treatment program, it is essential to identify both the specific locus of therapeutic impact and the particular treatment components that contribute to its effectiveness. The Transactional Process Model proposed in Chapter 1 identifies the major components and correlates of test anxiety and provides a framework for analyzing and evaluating the effectiveness of diverse treatment approaches. Treatments can be placed along a cognitive–emotionality continuum on the basis of the intended locus of impact of the therapeutic techniques that comprise a particular treatment program, and they can then be evaluated within the conceptual framework provided by the Transactional Process Model, which was described in Chapter 1 (see Figure 1.1).

COGNITIVE–EMOTIONALITY TREATMENT CONTINUUM

Some test anxiety treatments are directed primarily toward reducing students' emotional reactions during examinations, and others focus on eliminating or modifying worry cognitions. In Figure 14.1, the therapeutic interventions that have been used most frequently in test anxiety treatment research are placed on a cognitive–emotionality treatment continuum and then linked to one or more of the elements and processes that are specified in the Transactional Process Model. The emotionality pole of this continuum is anchored by treatments that consist primarily of biofeedback and relaxation training, whereas cognitive therapy defines the opposite pole. Test anxiety treatments that include both cognitive and emotionality-focused therapeutic components are placed at intermediate points on the continuum, depending on the extent to which a particular treatment component focuses on modifying the worry cognitions or the emotional reactions experienced by test-anxious students.

In the treatment of test anxiety, biofeedback (BIO) training has been used alone, and in combination with other treatment approaches, to help students become more aware of, and sensitive to, their own internal physiological states of tension and arousal (see Parker, Vagg, & Papsdorf, Chapter 12, and Vagg & Papsdorf, Chapter 13). Used by itself, BIO teaches students to monitor and modify the physiological processes associated with their emotional reactions. Thus, BIO is primarily emotionality-focused and can be placed in Figure 14.1 at the emotionality end of the treatment continuum, linked by a single solid-line vector to the emotional state experienced by test-anxious students. However, in some BIO treatments, instructions provide information on how to develop and use cognitive cues to facilitate the effects of BIO in reducing anxiety. These types of BIO treatment are represented in Figure 14.1 by the solid-line vector that links BIO to other emotionality-focused treatments that also include cognitive instruction. Because the intended locus of impact of BIO is on emotionality, there is no vector shown relating these treatments to worry.

Like BIO, relaxation training (RT) is directed primarily toward modifying the emotional reactions of test-anxious students during examinations. Thus, RT is also placed near the emotionality end of the cognitive–emotionality treatment continuum, but somewhat more toward the center of this continuum

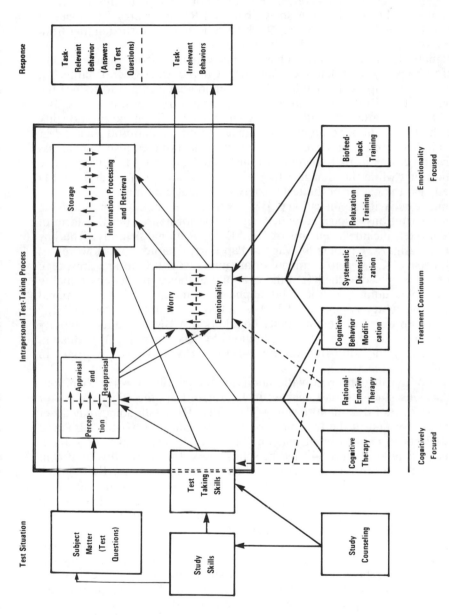

Figure 14.1 Test-anxiety treatments are placed on a cognitive–emotionality treatment continuum and linked by solid- or dotted-line vectors to one or more of the elements or processes specified in the Transactional Process Model. Study counseling has been added to the model because of its frequent use in test-anxiety treatment studies and its demonstrated impact on processes that influence test anxiety, its worry and emotionality components, and academic achievement.

because RT instructions generally provide information and directions that involve cognitive activity. However, as RT does not attempt to modify worry cognitions directly, no relation is shown between RT and worry. The locus of impact of RT is indicated in Figure 14.1 by a solid-line vector extending from RT to emotionality.

Systematic desensitization (SD) has been investigated more than any other form of test anxiety treatment (see Gonzalez, Chapter 9; Algaze, Chapter 10; Parker, Vagg, & Papsdorf, Chapter 12). The main goal of SD is to reduce the negative emotional reactions that are experienced during examinations. Because SD does not attempt to alter worry cognitions, it falls on the emotionality side of the treatment continuum and is linked to emotionality in Figure 14.1 by a solid-line vector. However, desensitization techniques also encompass cognitive processes in that students are instructed to attend to and rehearse relaxation cues while they imagine they are in a test situation. Therefore, SD is placed near the center of the test anxiety treatment continuum.

Cognitive behavior modification (CBM) focuses on eliminating or modifying the worry cognitions associated with poor test performance, but this form of treatment often includes elements of RT, SD, or Rational–Emotive Therapy (RET) (see Algaze, Chapter 10; Vagg & Papsdorf, Chapter 13). However, as the main goal of CBM is to eliminate or attenuate worry cognitions, this type of treatment is placed to the left of the midpoint of the cognitive–emotionality treatment continuum. Given its dual emphasis on modifying both emotional processes and worry cognitions, CBM is linked in Figure 14.1 by solid-line vectors to both worry and emotionality. In addition, CBM attempts to modify the perception and appraisal of test situations to make them less threatening, as indicated by the solid-line vectors linking CBM to these processes in Figure 14.1.

RET is primarily concerned with modifying the irrational worry cognitions of test-anxious students, as indicated in Figure 14.1 by the solid-line vector linking this form of treatment to worry. Therefore, RET falls somewhat closer to the cognitive end of the treatment continuum than does CBM. RET also helps students to identify, confront, and refute their irrational beliefs about tests, as indicated in Figure 14.1 by the solid-line vector linking this treatment to the model's perception, appraisal, and reappraisal processes. By reducing the threat associated with irrational appraisals, RET also indirectly influences emotionality, as shown by the dotted-line vector in Figure 14.1. Fletcher and Spielberger (Chapter 11) and Vagg and Papsdorf (Chapter 13) used RET components in their test anxiety treatment studies.

Cognitive therapy (CT) is primarily concerned with modifying or eliminating worry cognitions, for example, negative ideas and derogatory self-statements. In essence, the goal of CT is to eliminate or reduce negative thoughts during examinations and replace them with cognitions that facilitate test performance. Hence, as previously noted, CT anchors the cognitive end of the treatment continuum; its focus on reducing worry is indicated in Figure 14.1 by the solid-line vector linking CT to worry. As with CBM and RET, CT also positively influences perception and appraisal and is linked to these processes by a solid-line vector in Figure 14.1. Although CT therapists generally acknowledge the adverse effects of intense levels of state anxiety on performance, there is little effort in this form of treatment to deal directly with emotional factors. Algaze (Chapter 10) and Fletcher and Spielberger (Chapter 11) used CT in their studies, and Parker et al. (Chapter 12) helped clients develop their own CT approach.

A major goal of most test anxiety treatments that include cognitive components, such as CT, RET, and CBM, is to help test-anxious students appraise examinations as less threatening. This treatment goal is reflected in the solid-line vectors in Figure 14.1 from all three cognitively focused treatments to perception, appraisal, and reappraisal. In addition, CT and CBM treatments help students to organize and more effectively structure their activities in test situations, thus contributing indirectly to improved test-taking skills. The dotted-line vectors in Figure 14.1, from CT and CBM to test-taking skills, represent the indirect impact of these treatments on how students organize such behaviors during examinations.

Test-anxious students typically have poor study skills, along with negative, nonproductive attitudes toward academic work. Consequently, in the treatment of test anxiety, study counseling (SC) is often used in combination with other treatment components that focus on reducing worry and emotionality. Although SC is directed toward improving a variety of cognitive activities that affect the organization, processing, and retrieval of information (e.g., study habits and test-taking skills), training in study skills does not directly address the reduction of test anxiety. Therefore, SC procedures do not logically fall on the test anxiety treatment continuum but rather augment other cognitive interventions. Hence, SC has been placed to the left of the cognitive pole of the continuum.

In most SC programs, there are two related components: teaching students how to study for tests and training students in test-taking skills. Study skills training involves helping students to (a) structure their study time more efficiently, (b) systematically review the material to be learned, and (c) organize information so that it can be more effectively and easily retrieved and clearly communicated. Training in test-taking skills typically involves techniques that help students to comprehend and follow test instructions and interpret test questions in a manner that enhances their understanding of what is being asked. Thus, in Figure 14.1 the solid-line vectors from SC to both study skills and test-taking skills recognizes the cognitive focus of these types of training while also reflecting the influence of study skills training on the cognitive activities involved in appraisal and reappraisal and on information processing and retrieval.

The evidence that a variety of cognitive techniques are effective in reducing test anxiety is impressive. It should be noted, however, that the term *cognitive* in test anxiety treatment research is conceptually ambiguous and has been used in at least four different ways. The most frequent descriptive usage refers to students' worries about personal shortcomings and limitations that dispose them to failure. *Cognitive* has also been used to describe students' worries about how others will react to their poor test performance (e.g., how disappointed one's parents will feel if the student is not accepted into medical school). In CT and CBM, treatment is directed toward reducing these two types of test-related worries.

A third usage of *cognitive* in test anxiety treatment research is in reference to the irrational beliefs that contribute to students' negative appraisals of themselves and to their expectations of poor performance or failure. The appraisal of a test as threatening, though in part realistic, often stems from irrational worry cognitions in which the consequences of test performance are exaggerated (e.g., "My entire future depends on how well I do on this test"). RET focuses on eliminating irrational beliefs, reducing the emotional discomfort associated with such appraisals, and developing more accurate and appropriate appraisals of threatening situations.

A fourth meaning of *cognitive* in test anxiety treatment research pertains to the instructions that are given to students to help them use and benefit from the training procedures in ways that will facilitate their test performance. In SD and RET, cognitive instructions provide information on when and how to use relaxation techniques during examinations. In study skills training, cognitive instructions focus attention on coding, rehearsal and retrieval processes, and test-taking skills (e.g., how to analyze and respond to various types of test questions).

It should be noted that the four meanings of *cognitive* in test anxiety research are not mutually exclusive. Moreover, *cognitive* is often used to refer simultaneously to one or more of these meanings. The specific conceptual meaning that is intended in describing a particular cognitive intervention should be specified in test anxiety treatment studies, along with the experimental operations for defining this meaning. Only then can the locus of impact and the efficacy of different forms of cognitive treatment be meaningfully analyzed and evaluated.

ANALYSIS OF THE PROCEDURES AND FINDINGS IN THE TEST ANXIETY TREATMENT STUDIES REPORTED IN PART III

The procedures and findings in the five test anxiety treatment studies reported in Part III of this volume are examined in this section. Each study is evaluated in the context of the Transactional Process Model introduced in Chapter 1, with particular reference to the cognitive and emotional underpinnings of the treatment procedures. We also examine the efficacy of each treatment component in reducing test anxiety, as well as its impact on trait anxiety, irrational beliefs, study habits and attitudes, and academic performance. Also, the treatment procedures and major findings in each study are further evaluated and compared. (Hereinafter, all references are to chapters in this volume, unless otherwise noted.)

Although the treatment components and procedures differed markedly from study to study, cognitive treatments were implemented and evaluated in all five studies and some form of desensitization was used in four of the five studies. To clarify the actual procedures used in each study, the 14 treatment conditions that were investigated in the five studies, along with the therapeutic components comprising each treatment, are summarized in Table 14.1. The treatment conditions and components that were evaluated in each study are then described in detail, and each treatment condition is placed on the cognitive–emotionality continuum.

Study 1

Gonzalez (Chapter 9) compared the relative effectiveness of a treatment that included both systematic desensitization and study counseling (D + SC) with desensitization (D) and no-treatment control (NTC) groups. In Gonzalez's D + SC treatment, the SC component was designed to enhance the students' ability to organize and process relevant information associated with their course work. To control for the time required to provide study counseling, students in the D treatment were given an opportunity to discuss their use of relaxation training in coping with anxiety during examinations. Hence, this treatment condition was labeled desensitization plus anxiety-coping training (D + ACT). Gonzalez's D + SC and D + ACT treatments are both described in Table 14.1.

The D component in Gonzalez's D + SC and D + ACT treatment conditions was concerned primarily with reducing emotionality in test situations. However, the desensitization procedures in this study also instructed students on how to use relaxation skills in test situations, and may thus have had a secondary impact on perceptual and cognitive appraisal processes. Because Gonzalez's D + SC and D + ACT treatments both included explicit cognitive and emotionality-focused components in the Transactional Process Model presented in Figure 14.1, these treatments fall near the middle of the cognitive–emotionality treatment continuum.

Contrary to expectation, no reduction in test anxiety was found in Gonzalez's D + SC condition, nor in worry, emotionality, or trait anxiety. Moreover, students who received this treatment showed no improvement in study habits and a slight though nonsignificant decline in GPA. Apparently, students who received Gonzalez's SC treatment were required to learn so much new material that information overload occurred, producing an increase in state anxiety, which counteracted the anxiety-reducing effects of desensitization.

In Gonzalez's D + ACT treatment condition, significant reductions in test anxiety and in its worry and emotionality components were found, but there was no reduction in trait anxiety. Contrary to expectation, students receiving this treatment showed a significant improvement in academic performance. Although included primarily to control treatment time, the ACT component of Gonzalez's D + ACT treatment seems to have had a beneficial impact on grade point average (GPA). This surprising finding is discussed in greater detail in the following section.

In further analyses of his data, Gonzalez divided the participants who received treatment in his study into two groups. One group consisted of students with moderate to large reductions in test anxiety; the second group consisted of students for whom there was little or no reduction. Students with good pretreatment study skills who obtained large reductions in test anxiety showed

Table 14.1 Therapeutic components included in each of the treatment conditions evaluated in the five test anxiety treatment studies

Authors(s)	Chapter	Therapeutic components	Treatment condition[a]
Gonzalez	9	D + SC D + ACT	Desensitization plus study counseling Desensitization plus anxiety-coping training
Algaze	10	CT CT + SC CBM CBM + SC	Cognitive therapy alone Cognitive therapy plus study counseling Cognitive therapy plus desensitization[b] Cognitive therapy plus desensitization[b] plus study counseling
Spielberger & Fletcher	11	CT′ + SC RET + SC	Modified cognitive therapy plus study skills training Rational–emotive therapy plus study skills training
Parker, Vagg, & Papsdorf	12	D D′ + BIO D′(CI) + BIO	Desensitization alone Modified desensitization with biofeedback Modified desensitization with cognitive instructions plus biofeedback
Vagg & Papsdorf	13	D′ + BIO D′(CT + RET) D′(CT + RET) + BIO	Modified desensitization with biofeedback Modified desensitization with cognitive therapy and rational–emotive therapy Modified desensitization with cognitive therapy and rational–emotive therapy plus biofeedback

[a]No-treatment control conditions included in all five studies are not listed.
[b]Cognitive therapy plus systematic desensitization (CT + SD) in these treatments was essentially the same as the procedures used in cognitive behavior modification (CBM).

a substantial improvement in GPA. In contrast, students with good study habits and little or no reduction in test anxiety and those with poor study habits showed essentially no change in GPA as a result of treatment.

Study 2

Algaze (Chapter 10) investigated the effects of cognitive therapy, desensitization, and study counseling on test anxiety and academic achievement for test-anxious university students. His four treatment groups received cognitive therapy (CT) alone or CT in combination with study counseling (CT + SC), with systematic desensitization (CT + SD), or with both (CT + D + SC). Because the CT and D treatment components in Algaze's study were similar to Meichenbaum's (1972) cognitive behavior modification (CBM) procedures, Algaze's CT + D and CT + D + SC treatments are referred to, respectively, as the CBM and CBM + SC conditions. Algaze's four treatment conditions and the components in each of his treatments are summarized in Table 14.1.

The CT treatment in Algaze's study focused primarily on altering perceptual and appraisal processes and worry cognitions and thus falls at the cognitive extreme of the test anxiety treatment continuum. Adding the SC treatment component, which was essentially the same as that used by Gonzalez (Chapter 9), the resulting CT + SC condition also falls near the cognitive pole of the treatment continuum. The CBM treatments used by Algaze focused mainly on modifying perceptual and appraisal processes and worry cognitions, whereas the D component of these treatments was directed at reducing students' emotional reactions. Therefore, Algaze's CBM treatment falls near the midpoint of the cognitive–emotionality treatment continuum, and his CBM + SC condition can be placed slightly more toward the cognitive pole.

When compared with his NTC group, all four of Algaze's treatment conditions were effective in reducing test anxiety and its emotionality and worry components, except CT alone, for which the treatment effect approached significance ($p < .10$). Improved study habits were also found in all four of Algaze's treatment conditions, whereas study attitudes improved only in the two treatment conditions with an SC component (CT + SC and CBM + SC). No significant reduction in trait anxiety, or improvement in GPA, were found for any of Algaze's treatment conditions as compared with his NTC group. However, when the data for Algaze's two CBM treatments (CBM and CBM + SC) were combined, a significant improvement in GPA was found in comparison with the two treatments that did not include a desensitization component (CT and CT + SC).

Study 3

Spielberger and Fletcher (Chapter 11) compared the relative effectiveness of RET and CT when these therapeutic components were combined with SC in the treatment of test-anxious university students. The CT conditions in this study were similar to Algaze's CT treatment, except that all elements of RET were eliminated. The combination of this "pure" form of cognitive treatment

(CT') with SC (CT' + SC) falls at the extreme left pole of the cognitive–emotionality treatment continuum. Although the RET treatment component in Spielberger and Fletcher's RET + SC treatment condition focused primarily on eliminating irrational beliefs, RET is also concerned with reducing the emotional reactions that are typically associated with such beliefs. Therefore, in Figure 14.1 the RET + SC treatment is placed to the left of center on the cognitive–emotionality treatment continuum.

Spielberger and Fletcher's two treatment conditions are summarized in Table 14.1. They found that both RET and CT', in combination with SC, were equally as effective in reducing test anxiety, its worry and emotionality components, and trait anxiety. Students in both treatment conditions also had significantly improved study habits after treatment, but no changes were found in study attitudes. The RET + SC condition reduced the strength of irrational beliefs, whereas irrational beliefs were not influenced by the CT' + SC condition. Neither treatment was effective in helping students to improve their academic performance.

Study 4

Parker, Vagg, and Papsdorf (Chapter 12) investigated the effects of systematic desensitization combined with frontalis electromyographic biofeedback in the treatment of test-anxious university students. In contrast to the group treatment procedures used in Studies 1, 2, and 3, the students who participated in the three treatment conditions of this study were all seen individually. Parker et al.'s traditional D treatment was similar to Gonzalez's D condition. In Parker et al.'s second treatment condition, BIO was substituted for relaxation training in the D procedure, resulting in a modified D (D') plus BIO condition (D' + BIO).

Parker et al.'s third treatment condition was similar to their second condition, except that students were told to "hold on to the image" during D and to think about practical strategies for using BIO to reduce their tension and anxiety. Because this treatment condition included BIO and incorporated cognitive instruction (CI) in the modified desensitization program (D'), it is referred to as D'(CI) + BIO. Parker et al.'s three treatment conditions are summarized in Table 14.1.

D was a major treatment component in all three of Parker et al.'s conditions. Therefore, these treatments fall to the right of the midpoint of the cognitive–emotionality treatment continuum. However, the D'(CI) + BIO condition also included self-instructions and information to facilitate cue utilization, which may be regarded as elements of cognitive therapy. Therefore, this condition falls nearer the middle of the treatment continuum than do either the D or the D' + BIO treatments. The D' + BIO treatment is placed nearest the emotionality pole of the treatment continuum because the BIO component is concerned exclusively with reducing emotionality.

When compared with his NTC group, Parker et al.'s D and D'(CI) + BIO treatments were equally as effective in reducing test anxiety, its worry and emotionality components, and trait anxiety. In contrast, the D' + BIO condition failed to reduce either test anxiety or trait anxiety. None of Parker et al.'s treatments were effective in helping students to improve either their test performance or their grades.

Study 5

Vagg and Papsdorf (Chapter 13) investigated the relative effectiveness of a modified desensitization procedure combined with cognitive components, BIO training, or both for reducing the test anxiety of university students. The modified D + BIO treatment in this study, which was essentially the same as Parker et al.'s D' + BIO condition, can be placed at the emotionality end of the treatment continuum in Figure 14.1. Vagg and Papsdorf substantially strengthened the cognitive intervention used in Parker et al.'s D'(CI) + BIO condition by adding both CT and RET components. The resulting treatments, referred to as the D'(CT + RET) and D'(CT + RET) + BIO, fall close to the cognitive pole of the cognitive–emotionality treatment continuum. Although the D'(CT + RET) + BIO treatment consists primarily of cognitive components, the inclusion of BIO training places it nearer the midpoint of the continuum. Vagg and Papsdorf's three treatment conditions are summarized in Table 14.1.

The two cognitive treatments in the Vagg and Papsdorf study, which included CT and RET, were equally effective in reducing test anxiety, its worry and emotionality components, trait anxiety, and irrational beliefs. However, the cognitive treatment that included the BIO component was no more effective than the otherwise identical cognitive treatment. Thus, BIO did not augment the effectiveness of the cognitive treatment procedures and was no more effective in the modified D condition than was the NTC group in reducing test anxiety, trait anxiety, or irrational beliefs.

Paradoxically, a significant increase in academic performance was found for the D' + BIO treatment condition, whereas the cognitive treatments failed to improve performance. However, the pretreatment mean GPA for students in the D' + BIO condition was quite low as compared with those for the other treatment groups and the NTC group, suggesting that the GPA improvement in the D' + BIO condition was probably an artifact of regression to the mean.

EVALUATION OF THE TEST ANXIETY TREATMENT STUDIES

The primary objective in the test anxiety treatment studies reported in this volume was to evaluate the relative effectiveness of specific therapeutic treatment interventions in reducing test anxiety and in improving test performance, academic achievement, or both. Consistent with this emphasis on treatment outcome, indicators of reduced test anxiety and improved performance were the most important dependent variables in these studies. To further assess treatment outcome, measures of individual differences in trait anxiety, irrational beliefs, and pre- and postmeasures of physiological process, such as muscle tension and finger temperature, were also obtained in several studies.

The findings for four different sets of outcome measures are summarized in Table 14.2 for each of the 14 treatment conditions in the five treatment studies described in the previous section. The results for the cognitively focused treatment conditions are grouped in the top half of Table 14.2; findings for the emotionality-based treatments appear in the lower half. However, the treatment conditions within each study are grouped together, except for the Vagg and Papsdorf study in which treatment conditions are assigned to different places in Table 14.2. The D' + BIO treatment in the Vagg and Papsdorf study is placed at the emotionality pole; the other two treatment conditions, which have a predominantly cognitive focus, are placed nearer the cognitive end of the continuum.

The effects of each treatment condition on test anxiety and on its worry and emotionality components are reported in the first three columns of Table 14.2. Findings for trait anxiety and irrational beliefs are reported in the next two columns. The findings for the third major category of outcome measures, study habits and attitudes, are presented in columns 6 and 7. The results for the intellectual performance measures (e.g., academic grades and tests of achievement) are reported in the last two columns.

Test anxiety was significantly reduced by all of the predominantly cognitively focused treatment conditions, as can be noted in Table 14.2. Both worry and emotionality were also significantly reduced by various cognitive treatments, with the single exception of Algaze's CT treatment in which the reduction in worry approached significance ($p < .10$). Emotionality-focused treatments with explicit cognitive instructions on how to reduce emotionality during tests were also successful in reducing test anxiety and its worry and emotionality components in Gonzalez's D + ACT and Parker et al.'s D and D'(CI) + BIO treatment conditions.

Biofeedback combined with modified desensitization (D' + BIO) was not effective in reducing test anxiety, or its worry or emotionality components, in the Parker et al. and Vagg and Papsdorf studies. Surprisingly, Gonzalez's D + SC condition also failed to reduce test anxiety even though this treatment included a D component that had been successful in reducing test anxiety in previous studies. The explanation for this finding seems to lie in the complex nature of Gonzalez's SC condition that overloaded the students and increased their anxiety. This increased anxiety appeared to counteract the anxiety-reducing effects of the desensitization procedure.

The cognitively focused treatments in the Spielberger and Fletcher and Vagg and Papsdorf studies also reduced trait anxiety. Although trait anxiety scores also declined substantially in all three of Algaze's cognitively focused treatment conditions, these scores also declined in his NTC group. Consequently, the difference between Algaze's cognitively focused treatments and his control group were not statistically significant.

In the Parker et al. study, two of the three emotionality-focused treatments were effective in reducing trait anxiety. However, both of these treatments included strong cognitive elements (e.g., instructions about when and how to use relaxation or biofeedback to reduce emotionality during examinations). Although Gonzalez's emotionality-focused D + ACT and D + SC treatment

Table 14.2 Summary of findings of the effects of the 14 treatment conditions on outcome measures in the five test anxiety treatment studies

Treatment condition	Test anxiety			Trait-beliefs		Study skills		Performance	
	Total	Worry	Emotionality	Anxiety	Irrational beliefs	Habits	Attitudes	Grades	Tests
Cognitively focused[a]									
Spielberger & Fletcher									
CT' + SC	**	**	**	**	—	**	—	—	—
RET + SC	**	**	**	**	**	**	—	—	—
Algaze									
CT + SC	**	**	**	—		**	**	—	—
CT	**	*	**	—		**	—	—	—
CBM + SC	**	**	**	—		**	**	**	—
CBM	**	**	**	—		**	—	—	—
Vagg & Papsdorf									
D'(CT+RET)	**	**	**	**	**	—	—	—	—
D'(CT+RET)+BIO	**	**	**	**	**	—	—	—	—
Gonzalez									
D + ACT	**	**	**	—		—		**	
D + SC	—	—	—	—		*			
Parker et al.									
D'(CI) + BIO	**	**	**	**				—	—
D	**	**	**	**				—	—
D' + BIO	—	—	—	—					—
Emotionality focused									
Vagg & Papsdorf									
D' + BIO	—	—	—	—	*	—	—	**	—

Note. Each treatment condition was compared with a no-treatment control condition. Dashes indicate that a condition was evaluated, but not significant. CT' = modified cognitive therapy; SC = study counseling; RET = rational–emotive therapy; CBM = cognitive behavior modification; D' = modified desensitization; BIO = biofeedback; ACT = anxiety-coping training; CI = cognitive instruction.

[a]Refers to the two poles of the cognitive–emotionality treatment continuum. The placement of each treatment condition on this continuum is approximate.

*$p < .10$. **$p < .05$.

conditions also included a cognitive intervention, these treatments did not reduce trait anxiety. An important difference between the Gonzalez and Parker et al. studies was that Gonzalez ran his students in groups, whereas Parker et al. treated students individually. Thus, the increased student–therapist interaction in Parker et al.'s treatment sessions may have facilitated greater cognitive restructuring, which resulted in the observed reduction in trait anxiety.

The treatment conditions in the Spielberger and Fletcher and the Vagg and Papsdorf studies that included an RET component were successful in reducing irrational beliefs. In contrast, the CT' treatment in the Spielberger and Fletcher study, which was designed to eliminate only test-related worry cognitions, failed to reduce irrational beliefs. Because RET is the only treatment that attempts to modify or eliminate irrational beliefs (e.g., "It is important that others approve of me" and "I want everyone to like me"), these findings were consistent with theoretical expectations and provide evidence of a special benefit of RET in the treatment of test anxiety.

The treatment groups in the Gonzalez and the Spielberger and Fletcher studies that received study counseling (study skills training) showed significant improvement in study habits. Improvement in study habits was also found in all four of Algaze's treatment conditions, including the two treatments in which no study skills training was given. In explaining this unexpected finding, Algaze suggested that the students who received no study skills training shared significant information about their study habits during the placebo discussions, which may have helped some of them to improve their study skills.

Algaze also found that students who received study skills training showed improvement in study attitudes. In contrast, study counseling had no effect on study attitudes in the Spielberger and Fletcher study. Although Gonzalez provided study counseling in his D + SC treatment, he did not evaluate study attitudes; neither Parker et al. nor Vagg and Papsdorf provided study skills training. Given the limited research on the effects of study skills training on study attitudes, it seems premature to attempt to draw any conclusions with regard to the effects of study counseling (or other test anxiety treatment components) on the study attitudes of test-anxious students.

In the four studies in which tests of ability were used as outcome measures, improved performance was found for all treatment conditions. However, the control groups in these studies also showed improvement comparable to the treatment groups, suggesting that the observed gains in performance can be attributed to practice effects. Substantial practice effects were found even when parallel forms of the ability measures were used. Thus, ability and aptitude tests appear to be of limited value as outcome measures in test anxiety treatment research because large practice effects may mask and obscure the effects of treatment.

Of the five studies reviewed in this chapter, in which a total of 14 different treatment conditions were evaluated, only Gonzalez's D + ACT treatment was effective in both reducing test anxiety and improving grades. In this treatment, Gonzalez provided an opportunity for students to share information about how they studied for tests and their test-taking behavior. This feedback from peers seemed to enhance cognitive restructuring and build confidence, which had a positive impact on students' grades. Gonzalez also found that only students with good pretreatment study habits who experienced large reductions in test anxiety showed improved performance. A significant increase in GPA was also found by Algaze when he combined his two CBM treatment groups and compared them with his CT and NTC conditions. Although Vagg and Papsdorf found an increase in GPA in their D' + BIO treatment condition, this improvement in grades seemed to be an artifact resulting from regression to the mean, as was previously noted.

The treatment conditions that produced a nonartifactual improvement in grades appear to have two elements in common: a desensitization component and a cognitive component that emphasized either reducing test-related worry cognitions or using newly acquired anxiety-reduction skills. Neither desensitization alone in the Parker et al. and Gonzalez studies, nor cognitive therapy alone in the Algaze study, produced an increase in GPA. Therefore, in treating test anxiety, both cognitive and desensitization treatment components appear to be required to enhance academic achievement. Feedback on how to study and training in test-taking skills may also facilitate academic achievement when combined with desensitization.

On the basis of his review and meta-analysis of 562 test anxiety treatment studies, Hembree (1988) observed that systematic desensitization, cognitive–behavioral treatments, and study counseling reduced test anxiety and that such "treatments provided gains in test performance and GPA" (p. 70). We concur with Hembree's observation that many different treatments are effective in reducing test anxiety, but his conclusion concerning improvement in GPA is contradicted by the results of the five studies reported in Part III of this volume. They also differ from the conclusions in earlier reviews of this research literature (Allen et al., 1980; Tryon, 1980). Although Hembree's meta-analysis was methodologically rigorous in rating studies as to their adequacy and in excluding those judged to be deficient, in combining diverse groups of study participants who were treated with vastly different therapeutic techniques, Hembree has moved far from the actual data. Moreover, given his methodology, it is not possible to evaluate the efficacy of specific components of the various treatments, or to identify the locus of impact of the therapeutic interventions on the intrapersonal processes of those receiving the treatment.

In summary, cognitively focused treatments were consistently more successful than emotionality-focused treatments in reducing test anxiety and its worry and emotionality components in the test anxiety treatment studies reported in Part III of this volume. Cognitively focused treatments were also more effective in reducing trait anxiety apparently because the components of these treatments seem to generalize more readily to a wider range of school-related, social–evaluative situations (e.g., giving talks in class and interacting with instructors). Emotionality-focused treatments (including BIO) were only effective in reducing test anxiety if these treatments also included specific cognitive elements, such as instructions on how to use relaxation or biofeedback techniques to reduce emotionality in test situations.

Other investigators have also reported that cognitive treatments are generally more effective than emotionality-focused treatments in reducing test anxiety (e.g., Cooley & Spiegler, 1980; Goldfried et al., 1978). Studies using RET (Barabasz & Barabasz, 1981) or variants of Meichenbaum's CBM (McCordick et al., 1981) have also reported reductions in test anxiety for these cognitively focused treatments. However, group counseling, when used alone with no specific anxiety-reducing treatment component, failed to have a significant impact in Hembree's (1988) meta-analysis of six studies that used this type of cognitive treatment.

Although both cognitive and emotionality-focused treatments are generally effective in reducing test anxiety, it should be noted that systematic desensitization combined with a comprehensive, multifaceted study skills training program did not reduce test anxiety in Gonzalez's study. Students receiving this treatment appeared to experience severe information overload, which interfered with the efficacy of a desensitization treatment that had proved successful in reducing test anxiety in a number of earlier studies (e.g., Anton, 1975; Bedell, 1975) and in Gonzalez's D + ACT treatment. Thus, excessive cognitive demands may counteract otherwise successful anxiety-reducing treatment effects.

STUDY HABITS, TEST-TAKING SKILLS, AND MODELING IN THE TREATMENT OF TEST ANXIETY

Test-anxious students tend to have poor study habits (Culler & Holahan, 1980; Hembree, 1988; Naveh-Benjamin et al., 1987) and inadequate test-taking skills (Tobias, 1985; Topman & Jansen, 1984). Therefore, even when a treatment is successful in reducing test anxiety, lowering anxiety may have little impact on the performance of students with poor study habits. However, reducing test anxiety does facilitate improved academic performance for students with adequate study skills (Gonzalez, 1978a; also see Chapter 9).

Clearly, different types of treatment seem to be needed for test-anxious students with poor study habits than for those with adequate study skills, who often do well in their academic work even though they may experience intense anxiety during examinations (S. D. Brown & Nelson, 1983; Vagg & Papsdorf, Chapter 13). In his meta-analysis and review of test-anxiety treatment studies, Hembree (1988) found that, by itself, study skills training was not effective in reducing test anxiety or in improving performance, but when combined with other treatments, study skills training had a positive impact on test performance. Unfortunately, Hembree's review of test anxiety treatment studies did not examine how different treatments might be adapted to meet the diverse needs of students with good or poor study habits.

Although study skills training can improve study habits (Annis, 1986), test anxiety treatments that lead to better study skills do not generally result in higher grades. It seems unrealistic to expect students to benefit immediately from study counseling because time is required for improved study skills to influence academic performance. Because there are few investigations of the long-term effects of study skills training on academic performance, it is not clear how long it takes for improved study skills to produce better grades.

However, reducing test anxiety does seem to facilitate academic performance if students are encouraged to practice and improve the study skills they possess. This was demonstrated in Gonzalez's D + ACT and Algaze's CT and CBM treatments, which did not include a study counseling component.

Topman and Jansen (1984) maintained that, in addition to helping test-anxious students to improve their study habits, it is important to teach them more effective test-taking skills. Although poor study habits contribute to the failure of students to master the subject matter, inadequate test-taking skills interfere with a clear understanding of test questions and effective retrieval of relevant information, thus undermining students' ability to organize and report what they know. Naveh-Benjamin et al. (1981) have observed that poor test-taking skills appear to be a major determinant of the worry cognitions that contribute to the performance decrements of test-anxious students largely to the adverse effects of worrying during examinations. According to Covington, "during testing, anxious students worry that they are falling behind, scold themselves for forgetting the answers, and fearfully recall similar, previous test situations that ended in disaster. Such intrusive worry inhibits all but the simplest, automatic responses" (p. 39).

Modeling procedures have been used extensively to help clients and patients develop effective skills for coping with a variety of behavioral problems (Bandura, 1977), including test anxiety (Dykeman, 1989; King et al., 1991). For example, O'Neil and Richardson (1980) presented test-anxious students with videotapes of models who initially failed on a test and then succeeded after mastering anxiety-reducing techniques. In addition to helping test-anxious students identify and eliminate self-defeating worry cognitions and ineffective test-taking behaviors, modeling also provides a powerful approach for teaching effective study habits and test-taking skills.

The most effective programs for the treatment of test-anxious students have included both cognitively focused and emotionality-focused treatment components. Such treatments facilitate the development of coping strategies for reducing anxiety during examinations and encourage students to practice these strategies. They also train students in cognitive coping techniques that can be used effectively in a wide range of stressful evaluative situations. Feedback from a therapist regarding newly acquired anxiety-reducing and cognitive coping skills, or from other students, also provides information for refining and improving study and test-taking skills and helps students prepare for and take examinations. In addition, specific instructions on how to take tests and the use of models to demonstrate effective test-taking skills appears to be effective in reducing test anxiety and enhancing the performance of test-anxious students.

Given the deficiencies in the study habits and test-taking skills of test-anxious students, it would seem desirable for treatment programs to include components for remediating these problems. There are limits, however, to how much can be included in a test anxiety treatment program without overwhelming the participants. As previously noted, the excessive cognitive demands in Gonzalez's D + SC treatment counteracted the anxiety-reducing effects of systematic desensitization, thus precluding any improvement in grades (see Table

14.2). In contrast, the same desensitization procedures that were ineffective in Gonzalez's D + SC treatment were highly effective in reducing test anxiety in his D + ACT treatment. Moreover, the group counseling component of his D + ACT treatment seemed to facilitate cognitive restructuring in that students receiving this treatment experienced fewer self-depreciating doubts about personal shortcomings and were thus able to concentrate more on studying and taking examinations. In essence, the D + SC treatment in Gonzalez's study was analogous to trying to teach students who were drowning in test anxiety how to swim, whereas the group discussion in his D + ACT treatment was equivalent to throwing these students a life preserver.

SUMMARY AND CONCLUSIONS

In evaluating the efficacy of different approaches to the treatment of test anxiety, it is important to examine the locus of therapeutic impact of various treatment components on the intrapersonal mechanisms that mediate the adverse effects of test anxiety on information processing, the retrieval of information from storage, and the activation of task-irrelevant thoughts and behaviors that interfere with attention and concentration. Consistent with this goal, diverse approaches to the treatment of test-anxious students were examined in this chapter within the framework of a Transactional Process Model that identifies the major components and correlates of test anxiety.

The therapeutic procedures used in the test anxiety treatment studies that are reported in Part III of this volume were evaluated and classified according to their relative emphasis on cognitive or emotionality-focused anxiety reduction techniques. Each treatment was placed on a cognitive–emotionality treatment continuum and linked to one or more of the elements specified in the Transactional Process Model. The emotionality pole of the cognitive–emotionality continuum is anchored by test anxiety treatments that consist primarily of biofeedback and relaxation training; the cognitive pole of this continuum is defined by treatments that focus on eliminating or attenuating worry and other interfering cognitive processes.

The findings in the treatment studies reported in Part III of this volume suggest that cognitively focused treatments are generally more effective than emotionality-focused treatments in reducing test anxiety (see Table 14.2). Cognitive treatments were also more effective in stimulating the development of coping strategies that reduce trait anxiety, and thus seem to generalize more readily to a wider range of the evaluative situations typically encountered by test-anxious students. It should be noted, however, that the most effective treatments included both cognitive and emotionally focused components and provided an opportunity for students to discuss and practice their newly learned coping skills.

It is more efficient and generally more effective to provide treatment for groups of test-anxious students rather than to work with these students on an individual basis. Group counseling also enables students to discuss the effectiveness of different approaches to studying and stimulates them to try out new anxiety-reducing techniques during examinations and in other stressful situations. It should be noted, however, that group counseling that does not focus specifically on reducing anxiety during tests, or on improving study and test-taking skills, is generally ineffective in the treatment of test-anxious students.

Most students whose performance is impaired by test anxiety need instruction in how to study and in effective test-taking skills. Care must be taken, however, not to overwhelm students with too much information during treatment as this can be counterproductive. Consequently, a two-stage treatment program would seem to produce the best long-term results. The first stage should focus on reducing test anxiety during examinations and helping students use their existing coping skills more effectively. By analogy, this would involve supplying a life preserver for students drowning in their test anxiety. The second stage would then focus on improving study skills and test-taking skills, thus teaching the students to swim while not overwhelming them with cognitive demands that increase anxiety and interfere with test performance.

REFERENCES

-A-

Alexander, S., & Husek, T. R. (1962). The Anxiety differential: Initial steps in the development of measures of situational anxiety. *Educational and Psychological Measurement, 22,* 325–348.

Algaze, B. (1980). Combination of cognitive therapy with systematic desensitization and study counseling in the treatment of test anxiety (Doctoral dissertation, University of South Florida, 1979). *Dissertation Abstracts International, 40,* 3376B. (University Microfilms No. 8002196)

Allen, G. J. (1971). Effectiveness of study counseling and desensitization in alleviating test anxiety in college students. *Journal of Abnormal Psychology, 77,* 282–289.

Allen, G. J. (1972). The behavior treatment of anxiety: Recent research and future trends. *Behavior Therapy, 3,* 253–262.

Allen, G. J. (1973). Treatment of test anxiety by group-administered and self-administered relaxation and study counseling. *Behavior Therapy, 4,* 349–360.

Allen, G. J., Elias, M. J., & Zlotlow, S. F. (1980). Behavioral interventions for alleviating test anxiety: A methodological overview of current therapeutic practices. In J. G. Sarason (Ed.), *Test anxiety: Theory, research and applications.* Hillside, NJ: Erlbaum.

Allen, G. J., Lerner, W. M., & Hinrichsen, J. J. (1972). Study behaviors and their relationships to test anxiety and academic performance. *Psychological Reports, 30,* 407–410.

Alpert, R., & Haber, R. N. (1960). Anxiety in academic achievement situations. *Journal of Abnormal and Social Psychology, 61,* 207–215.

Anastasi, A. (1976). *Psychological testing* (4th ed.). New York: Macmillan.

Anderson, S. B., Ball, S., & Murphy, R. T. (1975). *Encyclopedia of educational evaluation.* San Francisco: Jossey-Bass.

Anderson, S. B., Katz, M., & Shimberg, B. (1965). *Meeting the test.* New York: Four Winds Press.

Anderson, S. B., Messick, S., & Hartshorne, N. (1972). *Priorities and directions for research and development related to measurement of young children* (OCD Grant No. H-2993 A/H/O). Princeton, NJ: Educational Testing Service.

Annis, L. F. (1986). Improving study skills and reducing test anxiety in regular and low achieving college students: The effects of a model course. *Techniques, 2,* 115–125.

Anton, W. D. (1975). An evaluation of process and outcome variables in the systematic desensitization of test anxiety (Doctoral dissertation, University of South Florida, 1975). *Dissertation Abstracts International, 36,* 900B. (University Microfilms No. 7517830)

Anton, W. D. (1976). An evaluation of outcome variables in the systematic desensitization of test anxiety. *Behavior Research and Therapy, 14,* 217–224.

Aponte, J. F., & Aponte, C. (1971). Group preprogrammed systematic desensitization without the simultaneous presentation of aversive scenes with relaxation training. *Behavior Research and Therapy, 9,* 337–346.

Atkinson, J. W., & Litwin, G. H. (1960). Achievement motive and test anxiety conceived as motive to approach success and motive to avoid failure. *Journal of Abnormal and Social Psychology, 60,* 52–64.

Atkinson, J. W., & O'Connor, P. (1966). Neglected factors in studies of achievement-oriented performance. In J. W. Atkinson & N. T. Feather (Eds.), *A theory of achievement motivation.* New York: Wiley.

Auerbach, S. M. (1973). Effects of orienting instructions, feedback-information, and trait-anxiety level on state anxiety. *Psychological Reports, 33,* 779–786.

-B-

Bail, P. L. (1979). Therapy components in the management of test anxiety: Cerebral lateralization correlates (Doctoral dissertation, University of Michigan, 1979). *Dissertation Abstracts International, 40,* 902B. (University Microfilms No. 791661)

Bajtelsmit, J. W. (1977). Test-wiseness and systematic desensitization programs for increasing adult test-taking skills. *Journal of Educational Measurement, 14,* 335–341.

Ball, S. (1977). A postscript: Thoughts toward an integrated approach to motivation. In S. Ball (Ed.), *Motivation in education.* New York: Academic Press.

Bandura, A. (1977). Self-efficacy: Toward a unifying theory of behavior change. *Psychological Review, 84,* 171–215.

Barabasz, A. F., & Barabasz, M. (1981). Effects of rational-emotive therapy on psychophysiological and reported measures of test anxiety arousal. *Journal of Clinical Psychology, 37,* 511–514.

Bedell, J. R. (1975). The role of suggestion in the desensitization and relaxation treatments of test anxiety (Doctoral dissertation, University of South Florida, 1975). *Dissertation Abstracts International, 36,* 2458B. (University Microfilms No. 24028)

Bedell, J. R. (1976). Systematic desensitization, relaxation-training and suggestion in the treatment of test anxiety. *Behavior Research and Therapy, 14,* 309–311.

Bedell, J. R. & Weathers, L. R. (1979). A psychoeducational model of skills training: Therapist-facilitated and game-facilitated applications. In D. Upper & S. M. Koss (Eds.), *Behavioral group therapy 1979: An annual review.* Champaign, IL: Research Press.

Bem, D. J., & Allen, A. (1975). On predicting some of the people some of the time: The search for cross-situational consistencies in behavior. *Psychological Review, 81,* 506–520.

Bendig, A. W. (1956). The development of a short form of the Manifest Anxiety Scale. *Journal of Consulting Psychology, 20,* 384.

Beneke, W. M., & Harris, M. B. (1972). Teaching self-control of study behavior. *Behavior Research and Therapy, 10,* 35–42.

Benson, J., & Bandalos, D. L. (1992). Second-order confirmatory factor analysis of the reactions to Tests Scale with cross-validation. *Multivariate Behavioral Research, 27,* 459–487.

Benson, J., & El-Zahhar, N. (1994). Further refinement and validation of the Revised Test Anxiety Scale. *Structural Equation Modeling, 1,* 203–221.

Benson, J., Moulin-Julian, M., Schwarzer, C., Seipp, B., & El-Zahhar, N. (1992). Cross-validation of a revised test anxiety scale using multi-national samples. In K. A. Hagtvet & T. B. Johnsen (Eds.), *Advances in test anxiety research* (Vol. 7). Lisse, The Netherlands: Swets & Zeitlinger.

Benson, J., & Tippets, E. (1990). A confirmatory factor analysis of the Test Anxiety Inventory. In C. D. Spielberger & R. Diaz-Guerrero (Eds.), *Cross-cultural anxiety* (Vol. 4). New York: Hemisphere/Taylor & Francis.

Bergler, E. (1933). Psychoanalysis of a case of examination anxiety. *Zentbl. f. Psychotherap., 6,* 65–83. (From *Psychological Abstracts,* 1933, 7, Abstract No. 471)

Berkun, M. M., Bialek, H. M., Kern, R. P., & Yagi, K. (1962). Experimental studies of psychological stress in man. *Psychological Monographs, 76*(15, Whole No. 534).

Bernstein, D. A., & Borkovec, T. D. (1973). *Progressive relaxation training: A manual for the helping professions.* Champaign, IL: Research Press.

Betz, N. E. (1978). Prevalence, distribution, and correlates of math anxiety in college students. *Journal of Counseling Psychology, 25,* 441–448.

Birenbaum, M., & Gutvirtz, Y. (1993). The relationship between test anxiety and seriousness of errors in algebra. *Journal of Psychoeducational Assessment, 11,* 12–19.

Bloxom, B. (1968). *Test dimensions, test anxiety, and test performance* (RB-68-30). Princeton, NJ: Educational Testing Service.

Boudewyns, P. A. (1976). A comparison of the effects of stress vs. relaxation instruction on the finger temperature response. *Behavior Therapy, 7,* 54–67.

Brown, C. H. (1938a). Emotional reactions before examinations: II. Results of a questionnaire. *The Journal of Psychology, 5,* 11–26.

Brown, C. H. (1938b). Emotional reactions before examinations: III. Interrelations. *The Journal of Psychology, 5,* 27–31.

Brown, C. H., & Gelder, D. V. (1938). Emotional reactions before examinations: I. Physiological changes. *The Journal of Psychology, 5,* 1–9.

Brown, M. A. (1969). *A set of eight parallel forms of the digit symbol test.* Unpublished sets of tests, University of Waterloo, Waterloo, Ontario, Canada.

Brown, S. D., & Nelson, T. L. (1983). Beyond the uniformity myth: A comparison of academically successful and unsuccessful test-anxious college students. *Journal of Counseling Psychology, 30,* 367–374.

Brown, W. F. (1964). *Effective study test: Manual of directions.* San Marcos, TX: Effective Study Materials.

Brown, W. F., & Holtzman, W. (1965). *Survey of study habits and attitudes: College level.* New York: Psychological Corporation.

Bruch, M. A., Bernardy, W. P., & Coon, K. L. (1974). *Comparison of cognitive modeling and rehearsal with desensitization in the treatment of test anxiety.* Unpublished manuscript, Bradley University.

Brunig, J. L., & Kintz, B. L. (1968). *Computation handbook of statistics.* Glenview, IL: Scott, Foresman.

Budyzinski, T. H., & Stoyva, J. M. (1969). An instrument for producing deep muscle relaxation by means of analogue information feedback. *Journal of Applied Behavior Analysis, 2,* 231–237.

Buglione, S. A., Devito, A. J., & Mulloy, J. M. (1990). Traditional group therapy and computer-administered treatment for test anxiety. *Anxiety Research, 3,* 33–39.

Bull, R. H. C., & Gale, M. A. (1975). Electrodermal activity recorded concomitantly from the subject's two hands. *Psychophysiology, 12,* 94–97.

-C-

Calvo, M. G., Ramos, P. M., & Estevez, A. (1992). Test anxiety and comprehension efficiency: The role of prior knowledge and working memory deficits. *Anxiety, Stress and Coping, 5,* 125–138.·

Cannon, W. B. (1929). *Bodily changes in pain, hunger, fear, and rage.* New York: Appleton.

Castaneda, A., McCandless, B. T., & Palermo, D. S. (1956). The children's form of the Manifest Anxiety Scale. *Child Development, 27,* 317–326.

Cattell, R. B., & Scheier, I. H. (1961). *The meaning and measurement of neuroticism and anxiety.* New York: Ronald Press.

Chang-Liang, R., & Denny, D. R. (1976). Applied relaxation as training in self-control. *Journal of Counseling Psychology, 23,* 183–189.

Chestnut, W. J. (1965). The effects of structured and unstructured group counseling on male students' underachievement. *Journal of Counseling Psychology, 12,* 388–394.

Christie, R., & Budnitzky, S. (1957). A short forced-choice anxiety scale. *Journal of Counseling Psychology, 21,* 501.

Cohen, R. (1969). The effects of group interaction and progressive hierarchy presentation on desensitization of test anxiety. *Behavior Research and Therapy, 7,* 15–26.

Cole, C. W., Oetting, E. R., & Sharp, B. (1969). Measurement of stimulus-specific anxiety. *Psychological Reports, 25,* 49–50.

Cooley, E. J. (1977). Cognitive versus emotional coping skills as alternative responses for the high test anxious college student (Doctoral dissertation,

University of Texas, Austin, 1976). *Dissertation Abstracts International, 37,* 4133B. (University Microfilms No. 7703882)

Cooley, E. J., & Spiegler, M. D. (1980). Cognitive versus emotional coping responses as alternatives to test anxiety. *Cognitive Therapy and Research, 4,* 159–166.

Cornish, R. D., & Dilley, J. S. (1973). Comparison of three methods of reducing test anxiety: Systematic desensitization, implosive therapy, and study counseling. *Journal of Counseling Psychology, 20,* 499–503.

Counts, D. K., Hollandsworth, J. G., Jr., & Alcorn, J. D. (1978). Use of electromyographic, biofeedback and cue-controlled relaxation in the treatment of test anxiety. *Journal of Counseling and Clinical Psychology, 46,* 990–996.

Covington, M. V. (1984). Anxiety management via problem-solving instruction. In H. M. van der Ploeg, R. V. Schwarzer, & C. D. Spielberger (Eds.), *Advances in test anxiety research* (Vol. 3). Lisse, The Netherlands/Hillsdale, NJ: Swets & Zeitlinger/Erlbaum.

Covington, M. V. (1992). *Making the grade. A self-worth perspective on motivation and school reform.* Cambridge, England: Cambridge University Press.

Crawford, O. G., Friesen, D. D., & Tomlinson-Keasey, C. (1977). Effects of cognitively induced anxiety on hand temperature. *Biofeedback and Self-Regulation, 2,* 139–146.

Crighton, J., & Jehu, D. (1969). Treatment of examination anxiety by systematic desensitization or psychotherapy in groups. *Behavior Research and Therapy, 7,* 245–248.

Cronbach, L. J. (1975). Beyond the two disciplines of scientific psychology. *American Psychologist, 30,* 116–127.

Culler, R. E., & Holahan, C. J. (1980). Test anxiety and academic performance: The effects of study-related behaviors. *Journal of Educational Psychology, 72,* 16–20.

-D-

D'Ailly, H., & Bergering, A. (1992). Mathematics anxiety and mathematics avoidance behavior: A validation of two MARS factor-derived subscales. *Educational and Psychological Measurement, 52,* 369–377.

Darwin, C. (1965). *Expression of emotions in men and animals.* Chicago: University of Chicago Press. (Original work published 1872)

Davidson, R. J., & Schwartz, G. E. (1976). Patterns of cerebral lateralization during cardiac biofeedback vs. the self-regulation of emotion: Sex differences. *Psychophysiology, 13,* 62–74.

Deffenbacher, J. L. (1977). Relationships of worry and emotionality to performance on the Miller Analogies Test. *Journal of Educational Psychology, 69,* 191–195.

Deffenbacher, J. L. (1980). Worry and emotionality in test anxiety. In I. G. Sarason (Ed.), *Test anxiety: Theory, research, and application.* Hillsdale, NJ: Erlbaum.

Deffenbacher, J. L., & Snyder, A. L. (1976). Relaxation as self-control in the treatment of test and other anxieties. *Psychological Reports, 39,* 379–385.

Denny, D. R. (1974). Active, passive and vicarious desensitization. *Journal of Counseling Psychology, 21,* 369–375.

Denny, J. P. (1966). Effects of anxiety and intelligence on concept formation. *Journal of Experimental Psychology, 72,* 596–602.

Denny-Brown, D., Meyer, J. S., & Horenstein, S. (1952). The significance of perceptual rivalry resulting from parietal lesions. *Brain, 75,* 433–471.

Desiderato, O., & Koskinen, P. (1969). Anxiety, study habits and academic achievement. *Journal of Counseling Psychology, 16,* 162–165.

Diekhoff, G. M., Garland, J., Damereau, D. F., & Walker, C. A. (1978). Muscle tension, skin conductance and finger pulse volume. Asymmetries as a function of cognitive demands. *Acta Psychologica, 42,* 83–93.

Dimond, S. J., & Farrington, L. (1977). Emotional response to films shown to the right or left hemisphere of the brain measured by heart rate. *Acta Psychologica, 41,* 255–260.

Doctor, R. M., & Altman, F. (1969). Worry and emotionality as components of test anxiety: Replication and further data. *Psychological Reports, 24,* 563–568.

Doctor, R. M., Aponte, J., Burry, A., & Welch, R. (1970). Group counseling versus behavior therapy in treatment of college underachievement. *Behavior Research and Therapy, 8,* 87–89.

Donner, L., & Guerney, B. G. (1969). Automated group desensitization for test anxiety. *Behavior Research and Therapy, 7,* 1–13.

Doris, J., & Sarason, S. B. (1955). Test anxiety and blame assignment in a failure situation. *Journal of Abnormal and Social Psychology, 50,* 335–338.

Driscoll, R. (1976). Anxiety reduction using physical exertion and positive images. *The Psychological Record, 26,* 87–94.

Dunn, J. A. (1968). The theoretical rationale underlying the development of the School Anxiety Questionnaire. *Psychology in the Schools, 5,* 204–210.

Dunn, J. A. (1970). *The School Anxiety Questionnaire: Theory, instrument and summary of results* (ED 045 700). Princeton, NJ: ERIC Clearinghouse on Tests, Measurement, & Evaluation.

Dusek, J. B. (1980). The development of test anxiety in children. In I. G. Sarason (Ed.), *Test anxiety: Theory, research, and applications.* Hillsdale, NJ: Erlbaum.

Dykeman, B. (1989). A social-learning perspective of treating test-anxious students. *College Student Journal, 23,* 123–125.

-E-

Ebel, R. L. (1972). *Essentials of educational measurement.* Englewood Cliffs, NJ: Prentice Hall.

Ehrlichman, H., & Weinberger, A. (1978). Lateral eye movements and hemispheric asymmetry: A critical review. *Psychological Bulletin, 85,* 1080–1101.

Ekehammer, B., & Magnusson, D. (1972). A method to study stressful situations. *Reports from the Psychological Laboratories, University of Stockholm, Sweden, 343,* 7.

Ellis, A. (1962). *Reason and emotion in psychotherapy.* New York: Lyle Stuart.

Ellis, A. (1973). *Humanistic psychotherapy: The rational-emotive approach.* New York: Julian Press.

Ellis, A., & Grieger, R. (1977). *Handbook of rational-emotive therapy.* New York: Springer.

Ellis, A., & Harper, R. A. (1975). *A new guide to rational living.* Englewood Cliffs, NJ: Prentice Hall.

Emery, J. R., & Krumboltz, J. D. (1967). Standard versus individualized hierarchies in desensitization to reduce test anxiety. *Journal of Counseling Psychology, 14,* 204–209.

Endler, N. S. (1974). A person-situation interaction model for anxiety. In C. D. Spielberger & I. G. Sarason (Eds.), *Stress and anxiety* (Vol. 1). Washington, DC: V. H. Winston.

Endler, N. S., Edwards, J. M., & Vitelli, R. (1991). *Endler Multidimensional Anxiety Scales: Manual.* Los Angeles: Western Psychological Services.

Endler, N. S., & Hunt, J. McV. (1969). Generalizability of contributions from sources of variance in the S-R inventories of anxiousness. *Journal of Personality, 37,* 1–24.

Endler, N. S., Hunt, J., & Rosenstein, A. J. (1962). An S-R inventory of anxiousness. *Psychology Monograph, 76*(17, Whole No. 536).

Endler, N. S., & Okada, N. A. (1975). A multidimensional measure of trait anxiety: The S-R Inventory of General Trait Anxiousness. *Journal of Consulting and Clinical Psychology, 43,* 319–329.

Engle, P. L., & Sieber, J. E. (1969). *The relation between human figure drawing and test anxiety in children.* (Research and Development Memorandum No. 52). Palo Alto, CA: Stanford University Center for Research and Development in Teaching.

Everson, H. T., Tobias, S., Hartman, H., & Gourgey, A. (1993). Test anxiety and the curriculum: The subject matters. *Anxiety, Stress, and Coping: An International Journal, 6,* 1–8.

-F-

Fabick, S. D. (1976). The relative effectiveness of systematic desensitization, cognitive modification, and mantra meditation in the reduction of test anxiety (Doctoral dissertation, West Virginia University, 1976). *Dissertation Abstracts International, 37,* 4862A. (University Microfilms No. 7702548)

Feather, N. T. (1965). The relationship of expectation of success to need achievement and test anxiety. *Journal of Personality and Social Psychology, 1,* 118–126.

Feld, S., & Lewis, J. (1969). The assessment of achievement anxieties in children. In C. P. Smith (Ed.), *Achievement-related motives in children.* New York: Russell Sage Foundation.

Felsen, R. E., & Tarudeau, L. (1991). Gender differences in mathematics performance. *Social Psychology Quarterly, 54,* 113–126.

Fennema, E., & Sherman, J. (1976). Fennema-Sherman Mathematics Attitudes Scales: Instruments designed to measure attitudes toward the learning of mathematics by males and females. *JSAS Catalog of Selected Documents in Psychology, 6,* 31. (Ms. No. 1225)

Fennema, E., & Sherman, J. A. (1977). Sex-related differences in mathematics achievement, spatial visualization, and affective efforts. *American Educational Research Journal, 14,* 51–71.

Fiedler, F. E. (1949). An experimental approach to preventive psychotherapy. *Journal of Abnormal and Social Psychology, 44,* 386–393.

Fincham, F. D., Hokoda, A., & Sanders, R. (1989). Learned helplessness, test anxiety, and academic achievement: A longitudinal study. *Child Development, 60,* 138–145.

Finger, R., & Galassi, J. P. (1977). Effects of modifying cognitive versus emotionality responses in the treatment of test anxiety. *Journal of Consulting and Clinical Psychology, 45,* 280–287.

Folin, O., Demis, W., & Smillie, W. G. (1914). Some observations on emotional glycosuria in man. *Journal of Biological Chemistry, 17,* 519–520.

Fox, C., Davidson, K. S., Lighthall, F. F., Waite, R. R., & Sarason, S. B. (1958). Human figure drawing of high and low anxious children. *Child Development, 29,* 297–301.

Freeling, N. W., & Shemberg, K. M. (1970). The alleviation of test anxiety by systematic desensitization. *Behavior Research and Therapy, 8,* 293–299.

French, J. W. (1961). *A study of emotional states aroused during examinations* (RE-61-6). Princeton, NJ: Educational Testing Service.

French, J. W. (1962). Effect of anxiety on verbal and mathematical examination scores. *Educational and Psychological Measurement, 22,* 553–564.

Freud, S. (1924). *Collected papers* (Vol. 1). London: Hogarth Press. (Original work published 1895)

Freud, S. (1936). *The problem of anxiety.* New York: W. W. Norton.

-G-

Gainotti, G. (1972). Emotional behavior and hemispheric side of the lesion. *Cortex, 8,* 41–55.

Galin, D. (1974). Implications for psychiatry of left and right cerebral specialization. *Archives of General Psychiatry, 31,* 572–583.

Galin, D. (1977). Lateral specialization and psychiatric issues: Speculations on development and the evaluation of consciousness. *Annals of the New York Academy of Sciences, 299,* 397–408.

Galin, D., Diamond, R., & Braff, D. (1977). Lateralization of conversion systems: More frequent on the left. *American Journal of Psychiatry, 134,* 578–580.

Garcia, J. (1975). *The comparison of two methods of treating test anxiety: Group systematic desensitization and group study counseling.* Unpublished doctoral dissertation, Nova University, Ft. Lauderdale.

Gaudry, E. (1977). Studies of the effects of experimentally induced experiences of success or failure. In C. D. Spielberger & I. G. Sarason (Eds.), *Stress and anxiety* (Vol. 4). Washington, DC: Hemisphere.

Gazzaniga, M. S. (1970). *The bisected brain.* New York: Appleton-Century-Crofts.

Geer, J. H. (1965). The development of a scale to measure fear. *Behavior Research and Therapy, 3,* 45–53.

Gerlach, V. S., Schutz, R. E., Baker, R. L., & Mazer, G. E. (1964). Effects of variations in test direction on originality of test response. *Journal of Educational Psychology, 55,* 79–83.

Glanzmann, P. (1985). Anxiety, stress, and performance. In B. D. Kirkcaldy (Ed.), *Individual differences in movement.* Lancaster: MTP Press.

Goldfried, M. R. (1971). Systematic desensitization as training in self-control. *Journal of Consulting and Clinical Psychology, 37,* 228–234.

Goldfried, M. R., Linehan, M. M., & Smith, J. L. (1978). Reduction of test anxiety through cognitive restructuring. *Journal of Consulting and Clinical Psychology, 46,* 32–39.

Goldfried, M. R., & Sobocinski, D. (1975). Effect of irrational beliefs on emotional arousal. *Journal of Consulting and Clinical Psychology, 43,* 504–510.

Goldfried, M. R., & Trier, C. S. (1974). Effectiveness of relaxation as an active coping skill. *Journal of Abnormal Psychology, 83,* 348–355.

Goldstein, K. (1939). *The organism: A holistic approach to biology, derived from pathological data in man.* New York: American Books.

Gonzalez, H. P. (1976). *The effects of three treatment approaches on test anxiety, study habits and academic performance.* Unpublished master's thesis, University of South Florida.

Gonzalez, H. P. (1978a). Effect of systematic desensitization, study counseling, and anxiety coping training in the treatment of test anxious students with good and poor study habits (Doctoral dissertation, University of South Florida, 1978). *Dissertation Abstracts International, 39,* 1955B. (University Microfilms No. 7818997)

Gordon, H. W., & Sperry, B. W. (1969). Lateralization of olfactory perception in the surgically separated hemispheres of man. *Neuropsychologia, 7,* 111–120.

Gorsuch, R. L. (1966). The general factor in the Test Anxiety Questionnaire. *Psychological Reports, 19,* 308.

Grooms, S. R., & Endler, N. S. (1960). The effect of anxiety on academic achievement. *Journal of Educational Psychology, 51,* 299–304.

Groveman, A. M., Richards, C. S., & Caple, R. B. (1975). Literature review, treatment manuals, and bibliography for study skills counseling and behavioral self-control approaches to improving study behavior. *Catalog of Selected Documents in Psychology, 5,* 342.

Gur, R. E., & Gur, R. C. (1975). Defense mechanisms, psychosomatic symptomatology, and conjugate lateral eye movements. *Journal of Consulting and Clinical Psychology, 43,* 416–420.

-H-

Haggard, M. P., & Parkinson, A. M. (1971). Stimulus and task factors as determinants of ear advantages. *Quarterly Journal of Experimental Psychology, 23,* 168–177.

Hagtvet, K. (1984). Fear of failure, worry, and emotionality. Their suggestive causal relationship to mathematical performance and state anxiety. In H. M. van der Ploeg, R. Schwarzer, & C. D. Spielberger (Eds.), *Advances in test anxiety research* (Vol. 3). Lisse, The Netherlands: Swets & Zeitlinger.

Hagtvet, K. A., & Backer-Johnsen, T. (1992). *Advances in test anxiety research* (Vol. 7). Lisse, The Netherlands: Swets & Zeitlinger.

Hagtvet, K. A., & Min, Y. R. (1992). Changing impact of ability, motivation, and anxiety in cognitive performance: A process analysis. In D. G. Forgays, T. Sosnowski, & K. Wrzesniewski (Eds.), *Anxiety: Recent developments in cognitive, psychophysiological, and health research.* Washington, DC: Hemisphere.

Hahnloser, R. M. (1974). A comparison of cognitive restructuring and progressive relaxation in test anxiety reduction (Doctoral dissertation, University of Oregon, 1974). *Dissertation Abstracts International, 35,* 1444A. (University Microfilms No. 74-18, 897)

Hansen, R. A. (1977). Anxiety. In S. Ball (Ed.), *Motivation in education.* New York: Academic Press.

Harleston, B. W. (1962). Test anxiety and performance in problem-solving situations. *Journal of Personality, 30,* 557–573.

Harris, L. J. (1976). Sex differences in spatial ability: Possible environmental, genetic, and neurological factors. In M. Kinsbourne, *Hemispheric asymmetries of function.* Cambridge, England: Cambridge University Press.

Hastings, J. T. (1944). Tensions and school achievement examinations. *Journal of Experimental Education, 12,* 143–164.

Hecaen, H., Ajuriaguerra, J., & Massonet, J. (1951). Les troubles visuo-constructifs par lesion parietoccipitale droite: Role des perturbations vestibulaires. *Encephale, 1,* 122–179.

Heckhausen, H. (1975). Fear of failure as a self-reinforcing motive system. In I. G. Sarason & C. D. Spielberger (Eds.), *Stress and anxiety* (Vol. 2). Washington, DC: Hemisphere.

Heckhausen, H. (1977). Achievement motivation and its constructs: A cognitive model. *Motivation and Emotion, 1,* 283–329.

Heckhausen, H. (1982). Task-irrelevant cognitions during an exam. In H. W. Krohne & L. Laux (Eds.), *Achievement, stress, and anxiety.* Washington, DC: Hemisphere.

Heckhausen, H. (1991). *Motivation and action.* Berlin: Springer-Verlag.

Heineman, C. W. (1953). A forced-choice form of the Taylor Anxiety Scale. *Journal of Counseling Psychology, 17,* 447–454.

Hembree, R. (1988). Correlates, causes, effects, and treatment of test anxiety. *Review of Educational Research, 58,* 47–77.

Hendel, D. D. (1977). *The Math Anxiety Program: Its genesis and development in continuing education for women.* Minneapolis: University of Minnesota, Measurement Services Center.

Hendel, D. D., & Davis, S. O. (1978). Effectiveness of an intervention strategy for reducing mathematics anxiety. *Journal of Counseling Psychology, 25,* 429–434.

Heston, J. C. (1953). *How to take a test.* Chicago: Science Research Associates.

Hill, K. T. (1972). Anxiety in the evaluative context. In W. Hartrup (Ed.), *The young child* (Vol. 2). Washington, DC: National Association for the Education of Young Children.

Hill, K. T., & Eaton, W. O. (1977). The interaction of test anxiety and success-failure experiences in determining children's arithmetic performance. *Developmental Psychology, 13,* 205–211.

Hill, K. T., & Sarson, S. B. (1966). The relation of test anxiety and defensiveness to test and school performance over the elementary-school years: A further longitudinal study. *Monographs of the Society for Research in Child Development, 31* (2, Serial No. 104).

Hodapp, V. (1982). Causal inference from non-experimental research on anxiety and educational achievement. In H. W. Krohne & L. Laux (Eds.), *Achievement, stress, and anxiety.* Washington, DC: Hemisphere.

Hodapp, V. (1989). Anxiety, fear of failure, and achievement: Two path analytical models. *Anxiety Research, 1,* 301–312.

Hodapp, V. (1991) Das Prüafimgsängststlichkeitsinventar TAI-G: Eine erweiterte und modifizierte Version mit vier Komponenten [The Test Anxiety Inventory TAIG-G: An expanded and modified version with four components]. *Zeitschrift für Pädagogisch Psychologie, 5,* 121–130.

Hodapp, V. (1994). Theorien, Meßethoden and Interventionstechniken in der Prüfungsangstforschung. In F.-J. Hehl, V. Ebel, & W. Ruch (Hrsg.), *Bericht über den 12. Kongreß für Angewandte Psychologie, Berufsverband Deutscher Psychologen,* 21.-25.9.93 Universität Düsseldorf (Band 6) München.

Hodapp, V., & Henneberger, A. (1982). Test anxiety, study habits, and academic performance. In H. M. van der Ploeg, R. Schwarzer, & C. D. Spielberger (Eds.), *Advances in test anxiety research* (Vol. 2). Lisse, The Netherlands: Swets & Zeitlinger.

Hodapp, V., Laux, L., & Spielberger, C. D. (1982). Theorie und Messung der emotionalen und kognitiven Komponente der Prüfungsangst. *Zeitschrift für Differentielle und Diagnostische Psychologie, 13,* 169–184.

Hodges, W. F. (1968). Effects of ego threat and threat of pain on state anxiety. *Journal of Personality and Social Psychology, 8,* 364–372.

Hodges, W. F., & Felling, J. P. (1970). Types of stressful situations and their relations to trait anxiety and sex. *Journal of Consulting and Clinical Psychology, 34,* 333–337.

Hodges, W. F., & Spielberger, C. D. (1966). The effects of threat of shock on heart rate for subjects who differ in manifest anxiety and fear of shock. *Psychophysiology, 2,* 287–294.

Holroyd, K. A. (1976). Cognition and desensitization in the group treatment of test anxiety. *Journal of Consulting and Clinical Psychology, 44,* 991–1001.

Holroyd, K. A., Westbrook, T., Wolf, M., & Badhorn, E. (1978). Performance, cognition, and physiological responding and test anxiety. *Journal of Abnormal Psychology, 87,* 442–451.

Hopkins, K. D., & Chambers, A. C. (1966). *Anxiety, physiologically and psychologically measured, and its consequences on mental test performance* (HEW Contract No. OE-5-10-324). Los Angeles: University of Southern California.

Horn, A. M., & Matson, J. L. (1977). A comparison of modeling, desensitization, flooding, study skills, and control groups for reducing test anxiety. *Behavior Therapy, 8,* 1–8.

-J-

Jacobs, B., & Strittmatter, P. (1979). *Der schulängstliche Schüler. Eine empirische Untersuchung über mögliche Ursachen und Konsequenzen der Schulangst.* Munich, Germany: Urban & Schwarzenberg.

Jacobs, P. D., & Munz, D. C. (1968). An index for measuring perceived stress in a college population. *Journal of Psychology, 70,* 9–15.

Jacobson, E. (1938). *Progressive relaxation.* Chicago: University of Chicago Press.

Jamieson, J., Ghannun, J., & Papsdorf, J. D. (1978, March). Test anxiety imagery and differential autonomic reactivity. In C. D. Spielberger (Chair), *The nature and treatment of test anxiety.* Symposium presented at the meeting of the Southeastern Psychological Association, Atlanta.

Jerusalem, M. (1985). A longitudinal field study with trait worry and trait emotionality: Methodological problems. In H. M. van der Ploeg, R. Schwarzer, & C. D. Spielberger (Eds.), *Advances in test anxiety research* (Vol. 4). Lisse, The Netherlands: Swets & Zeitlinger.

Johnson, S. M., & Sechrest, L. (1968). Comparison of desensitization and progressive relaxation in treating test anxiety. *Journal of Consulting and Clinical Psychology, 32,* 280–286.

Jones, R. G. (1969). A factor measure of Ellis' irrational belief system with personality and maladjustment correlates (Doctoral dissertation, Texas Technological College, 1969). *Dissertation Abstracts International, 29,* 4379B. (University Microfilms No. 6906443)

Jöreskog, K. G., & Sörbom, D. (1978) *LISREL IV: Analysis of linear structural relationships by the method of maximum likelihood. User's guide.* Chicago: National Educational Resources.

Jöreskog, K. G., & Sörbom, D. (1988). *LISREL 7: A guide to the program and applications.* Chicago: SPSS.

-K-

Kanfer, F. H., & Phillips, J. S. (1969). A survey of current behavior therapies and a proposal for classification. In C. M. Franks (Ed.), *Behavior therapy: Appraisal and status.* New York: McGraw-Hill.

Kanfer, F. H., & Phillips, J. S. (1970). *Learning foundations of behavior therapy.* New York: Wiley.

Kass, W., & Gilner, F. H. (1974). Drive level, incentive conditions and systematic desensitization. *Behavior Research and Therapy, 12,* 99–101.

Katahn, M., Strenger, S., & Cherry, N. (1966). Group counseling and behavior therapy with test anxious college students. *Journal of Consulting and Clinical Psychology, 30,* 544–549.

Katkin, E. S. (1965). Relationship between manifest anxiety and two indices of autonomic response to stress. *Journal of Personality and Social Psychology, 2,* 324–333.

Kerle, R. H., & Bialek, H. M. (1958). *The construction, validation, and application of a subjective stress scale* (staff memorandum). Monterey, CA: U.S. Army Leadership Human Research Unit.

Kerres, M. (1988). Prüfungsangst und-bewältigung. *Eine Untersuchung zu selbstregulativen Aktivitäten im Prüfungsgeschehen.* Frankfurt/M., Germany: Lang.

Ketterer, M. W., & Smith, B. D. (1977). Bilateral electrodermal activity, lateralized cerebral processing and sex. *Psychophysiology, 14,* 513–516.

King, F. J., Heinrich, D. L., Stephenson, R. S., & Spielberger, C. D. (1976). An investigation of the causal influence of trait and state anxiety on academic achievement. *Journal of Educational Psychology, 68,* 330–334.

King, N. J., Ollendick, T. H., & Gullone, E. (1991). Test anxiety in children and adolescents. *Australian Psychologist, 26,* 25–32.

Kinsbourne, M. (1972). Eye and head turning indicate cerebral lateralization. *Science, 176,* 532–541.

Klein, S. P., Frederiksen, N., & Evans, F. R. (1968). *Anxiety and learning to formulate hypotheses* (RB-68-63). Princeton, NJ: Educational Testing Service.

Kogelman, S., & Warren, J. (1978). *Mind over math.* New York: Dial Press.

Kostka, M. P., & Galassi, J. P. (1974). Group systematic desensitization vs. covert positive reinforcement in the reduction of test anxiety. *Journal of Counseling Psychology, 21,* 464–468.

Kreitler, S., & Kreitler, H. (1987). Modifying anxiety by cognitive means. *Advances in Test Anxiety Research, 5,* 195–206.

Krohne, H. W. (1992). Developmental conditions of anxiety and coping: A two-process model of child-rearing effects. In K. A. Hagtvet & T. B. Johnsen (Eds.), *Advances in test anxiety research* (Vol. 7). Amsterdam/Lisse, The Netherlands: Swets & Zeitlinger.

Kukla, A. (1972). Formulations of an attributional theory of performance. *Psychological Review, 79,* 454–470.

-L-

Lam, D. J., & Hong, Y. (1992). Strategies and dimensions of coping with examination stress. In K. A. Hagtvet & T. B. Johnsen, *Advances in test anxiety research* (Vol. 7). Lisse, The Netherlands: Swets & Zeitlinger.

Lamb, D. H. (1972). Speech anxiety: Towards a theoretical conceptualization and preliminary scale development. *Speech Monographs, 39,* 62–67.

Landy, F. J., & Trumbo, D. A. (1976). *Psychology of work behavior.* Homewood, IL: Dorsey.

Lang, P. J. (1969). The mechanics of desensitization and the laboratory study of human fear. In C. M. Franks (Ed.), *Behavior therapy: Appraisal and status.* New York: McGraw-Hill.

Laux, L., Glanzmann, P., & Schaffner, P. (1985). General versus situation-specific traits as related to anxiety in ego-threatening situations. In C. D. Spielberger, I. G. Sarason, & P. B. Defares (Eds.), *Stress and anxiety* (Vol. 9). Washington, DC: Hemisphere/McGraw Hill.

Lavigne, J. V. (1974). *The relative efficacy of cognitive-behavior rehearsal and systematic desensitization in the treatment of test anxiety* (Unpublished doctoral dissertation, University of Texas at Austin, 1974). *Dissertation Abstracts International, 35,* 2437-2438B.

Lawrence, S. W., Jr. (1962). The effects of anxiety, achievement motivation, and task importance upon performance on an intelligence test. *Journal of Educational Psychology, 53,* 150–156.

Lazarus, R. S. (1966). *Psychological stress and the coping process.* New York: McGraw-Hill.

Lazarus, R. S., & Averill, J. R. (1972). Emotions and cognitions: With special references to anxiety. In C. D. Spielberger (Ed.), *Anxiety: Current trends in theory and research* (Vol. 2). New York: Academic Press.

Lazarus, R. S., & Eriksen, C. W. (1952). Effects of failure stress upon skilled performance. *Journal of Experimental Psychology, 43,* 100–105.

Lens, W. (1983). Fear of failure and performance on ability tests. In S. B. Anderson & J. S. Helmick (Eds.), *On educational testing* (pp. 175–190). San Francisco: Jossey-Bass.

Levinson, D., & Klisch, M. (1978). *A mathematics anxiety treatment program.* Unpublished manuscript, University of South Florida.

Levitt, E. E. (1967). *The psychology of anxiety.* Indianapolis, IN: Bobbs-Merrill.

Levy, N. (1958). A short form of the Children's Manifest Anxiety scale. *Child Development, 29,* 153–154.

Lick, J., & Bootzin, R. (1975). Expectancy factors in the treatment of fear: Methodological and theoretical issues. *Psychological Bulletin, 82,* 917–931.

Liebert, R. M., & Morris, L. W. (1967). Cognitive and emotional components of test anxiety: A distinction and some initial data. *Psychological Reports, 20,* 975–978.

Liepman, D., Marggraf, C., Felfe, J., & Hosemann, A. (1992). Anxiety, action orientation, subjective state and situational aspects: A study of tank-lorry drivers. In K. A. Hagtvet & T. B. Johnsen (Eds.), *Advances in test anxiety research* (Vol. 7). Amsterdam/Lisse, The Netherlands: Swets & Zeitlinger.

Lin, Y. G., & McKeachie, W. J. (1970). Aptitude, anxiety, study habits, and academic achievement. *Journal of Counseling Psychology, 17,* 306–309.

Liss, E. (1944). Examination anxiety. *American Journal of Orthopsychiatry, 14,* 345–348.

Lomont, J. F., & Sherman, L. J. (1971). Group systematic desensitization and group insight therapies for test anxiety. *Behavior Therapy, 2,* 511–518.

London, P. *The modes and morals of psychotherapy.* New York: Holt, Rinehart & Winston.

Luria, A. R. (1932). *The nature of human conflicts* (W. H. Gantt, Trans.). New York: Liveright.

-M-

Manchetti, A., McGlynn, F. D., & Patterson, A. S. (1977). Effects of cue-controlled relaxation, a placebo treatment, and no treatment on changes in self-reported and psychophysiological indices of test anxiety among college students. *Behavior Modification, 1,* 47–72.

Mandler, G., & Sarason, S. B. (1952). A study of anxiety and learning. *Journal of Abnormal and Social Psychology, 47,* 166–173.

Mandler, G., & Sarason, S. B. (1953). The effects of prior experience and subjective failure on the evocation of test anxiety. *Journal of Personality, 21,* 338–341.

Mathis, A. G. (1978). *Interpretive manual, Inner Child Inventory.* Unpublished manuscript.

May, R. (1977). *The meaning of anxiety.* New York: W. W. Norton. (Original work published 1950)

McCordick, S. M., Kaplan, R. M., Smith, S., & Finn, M. E. (1981). *Psychotherapy: Theory, Research, & Practice, 18,* 170–178.

McKeachie, W. J. (1951). Anxiety in the college classroom. *Journal of Educational Research, 45,* 153–160.

McManus, M. (1971). Group desensitization of test anxiety. *Behavioral Research and Therapy, 9,* 51–56.

McMillan, J. R. (1974). The effects of desensitization treatment, rational emotive therapy, and a combination treatment program for test anxious students with high and moderate levels of generalized anxiety (Doctoral dissertation, University of Maryland, 1974). *Dissertation Abstracts International, 34,* 6217B. (University Microfilms No. 13184)

Meece, J. L., Wigfield, A., & Eccles, J. S. (1990). Predictors of math anxiety and its influence on young adolescents' course enrollment intentions and performance in mathematics. *Journal of Educational Psychology, 82,* 60-70.

Meichenbaum, D. H. (1972). Cognitive modification of test anxious college students. *Journal of Consulting and Clinical Psychology, 39,* 370–380.

Meichenbaum, D. H. (1977). *Cognitive behavior modification: An integrative approach.* New York: Plenum.

Meichenbaum, D., & Butler, L. (1980). Toward a conceptual model for the treatment of test anxiety: Implications for research and treatment. In I. G. Sarason (Ed.), *Test anxiety: Theory, research, and applications*. Hillsdale, NJ: Erlbaum.

Meyer, W. U. (1973). *Leistungsmotiv und Ursachenerklärung von Erfolg und Mißerfolg*. Stuttgart, Germany: Klett.

Millman, J., Bishop, C. H., & Ebel, R. (1965). An analysis of test-wiseness. *Educational and Psychological Measurement, 25*, 707–726.

Millman, J., & Pauk, W. (1969). *How to take tests*. New York: McGraw-Hill.

Mitchell, K. R. Hall, R. F., & Piatkowska, O. E. (1975). A group program for the treatment of failing college students. *Behavioral Therapy, 6*, 324–336.

Mitchell, K. R., & Ingram, R. J. (1970). The effects of general anxiety and group desensitization on test anxiety. *Behavior Research and Therapy, 69*, 1–13.

Mitchell, K. R., & Ng, K. T. (1972). Effects of group counseling and behavior therapy on the academic achievement of test anxious students. *Journal of Counseling Psychology, 19*, 491–497.

Montgomery, A. G. (1971). Comparison of the effectiveness of systematic desensitization, rational-emotive therapy, implosive therapy, and no therapy, in reducing test anxiety in college students (Doctoral dissertation, Washington University, St. Louis, 1971). *Dissertation Abstracts, 32*, 1861B. (University Microfilms No. 7127337)

Montgomery, G. K. (1977). Effects of performance evaluation and anxiety on cardiac response in anticipation of difficult problem solving. *Psychophysiology, 14*, 251–257.

Moore, J. C. (1968). Manipulating the effectiveness of a self-instructional program. *Journal of Educational Psychology, 59*, 315–319.

Moore, J. C., Schutz, R. E., & Baker, R. L. (1966). The application of a self-instructional technique to develop a test-taking strategy. *American Educational Research Journal, 3*, 13–17.

Morris, L. W., Davis, M. A., & Hutchings, C. H. (1981). Cognitive and emotional components of anxiety: Literature review and revised worry-emotionality scale. *Journal of Educational Psychology, 73*, 541–555.

Morris, L. W., & Liebert, R. M. (1969). Effects of anxiety on timed and untimed intelligence tests: Another look. *Journal of Consulting and Clinical Psychology, 33*, 240–244.

Morris, L. W., & Liebert, R. M. (1970). Relationship of cognitive and emotional components of test anxiety to physiological arousal and academic performance. *Journal of Consulting and Clinical Psychology, 35*, 332–337.

Morris, L. W., & Liebert, R. M. (1973). Effects of negative feedback, threat of shock, and level of trait anxiety on the arousal of two components of anxiety. *Journal of Counseling Psychology, 20*, 321–326.

Morris, L. W., & Perez, T. L. (1972). Effects of test-interruption on emotional arousal and performance. *Psychological Reports, 31*, 559–564.

Morris, L. W., Smith, L. R., Andrews, E. S., & Morris, N. C. (1975). The relationships of emotionality and worry components of anxiety to motor skills performance. *Journal of Motor Behavior, 7*, 121–130.

Mueller, J. H. (1992). Anxiety and Performance. In A. P. Smith & D. M. Jones (Eds.), *Handbook of human performance* (Vol. 3). London: Academic Press.

Myslobodsky, M. S., & Rattok, J. (1975). Asymmetry of electrodermal activity in man. *Bulletin of the Psychonomic Society, 6,* 501–502.

Myslobodsky, M. S., & Rattok, J. (1977). Bilateral electrodermal activity in waking man. *Acta Psychologica, 41,* 273–282.

-N-

Naveh-Benjamin, M. (1991). A comparison of training programs intended for different types of test-anxious students: Further support for an information-processing model. *Journal of Educational Psychology, 83,* 134–139.

Naveh-Benjamin, M., McKeachie, W. J., & Lin, Y. G. (1987). Two types of test-anxious students: Support for an information processing model. *Journal of Educational Psychology, 79,* 131–136.

Naveh-Benjamin, M., McKeachie, W. J., Lin, Y., & Halinger, D. P. (1981). Test anxiety: Deficits in information processing. *Journal of Educational Psychology, 73,* 816–824.

Neumann, J. (1933). *Anxiety and illness before examination.* Gutersloh: Bertels.

Nicholls, J. C. (1976). When a scale measures more than its name denotes: The case of the Test Anxiety Scale for Children. *Journal of Consulting and Clinical Psychology, 44,* 976–985.

-O-

Oldfield, R. C. (1971). The assessment and analysis of handedness: The Edinburgh Inventory. *Neuropsychologia, 9,* 97–113.

O'Neil, H. F., Baker, E. L., & Matsuura, S. (1992). Reliability and validity of Japanese children's trait and state worry and emotionality scales. *Anxiety, Stress and Coping: An International Journal, 5,* 225–239.

O'Neil, H. F., Jr., & Richardson, F. C. (1980). Test anxiety reduction and computer-based learning environments. In I. G. Sarason (Ed.), *Test anxiety: Theory, research, and applications.* Hillsdale, NJ: Erlbaum.

Osarchuck, M. M. (1976). A comparison of a cognitive, a behavior therapy, and a cognitive and behavior therapy treatment of test anxious college students (Doctoral dissertation, Adelphi University, Garden City, NY, 1976). *Dissertation Abstracts International, 36,* 3619B. (University Microfilms No. 7601425)

Osipow, S. H., & Kreinbring, I. (1971). Temporal stability of an inventory to measure test anxiety. *Journal of Counseling Psychology, 18,* 152–154.

Osterhouse, R. A. (1972). Desensitization and study-skills training as treatment for two types of test-anxious students. *Journal of Counseling Psychology, 19,* 301–307.

Otis, S., & Lennon, R. T. (1965). *Otis Quick-Scoring Mental Ability Tests.* Orlando, FL: Harcourt Brace Jovanovich.

-P-

Paivio, A., Baldwin, A., & Berger, A. (1961). Measurement of children's sensitivity to audiences. *Child Development, 32,* 721–730.

Paivio, A., & Lambert, W. E. (1959). Measures and correlates of audience anxiety ("stage fright"). *Journal of Personality, 27,* 1–17.

Pallone, N. (1961). Effects of short- and long-term developmental reading courses upon S.A.T. verbal scores. *Personnel and Guidance Journal, 39,* 654–657.

Papsdorf, J. D., Ghannum, J., Kuzma, T., & Jamieson, J. (1979). Operant eye movements and stress: Implications for EEG biofeedback training. In N. Birbaum & H. D. Kimmel (Eds.), *Biofeedback and self regulation.* Hillsdale, NJ: Erlbaum.

Parker, J. C., IV. (1977). *Biofeedback assisted relaxation training for the reduction of test anxiety.* Unpublished doctoral dissertation, University of Michigan.

Paul, G. L. (1969). Outcome of systematic desensitization I: Background, procedures, and uncontrolled reports of individualized treatment. In C. M. Franks (Ed.), *Behavior therapy: Appraisal and status.* New York: McGraw-Hill.

Paul, G. L., & Ericksen, C. W. (1964). Effects of test anxiety on "real-life" examinations. *Journal of Personality, 32,* 480–494.

Pekrun, R. (1991). Prüungsangst und Schulleistung: Eine Längsschnittanalyse [Test anxiety and academic achievement: A longitudinal analysis]. *Zeitschrift für Pädagogische Psychologie, 5,* 99–109.

Pekrun, R. (1992). The impact of emotions on learning and achievement: Towards a theory of cognitive/motivational mediators. *Applied Psychology: An International Review, 41,* 359–376.

Pervin, L. A. (1967). Aptitude, anxiety and academic performance: A moderator variable analysis. *Psychological Reports, 20,* 215–221.

Phillips, B. N. (1966). *An analysis of causes of anxiety among children in school* (Final Report, HEW Grant No. OE-5-10-012). Austin: University of Texas.

Pike, L. W. (1978). *Short-term instruction, testwiseness, and the Scholastic Aptitude Test: A literature review with research recommendations.* (College Entrance Examination Board Research and Development Report, RDR 77-78, No. 2). Princeton, NJ: Educational Testing Service.

Pike, L. W., & Evans, F. R. (1972). *Effects of special instruction for three kinds of mathematics aptitude items* (Research Rep. No. 1). New York: College Entrance Examination Board.

Prochaska, J. O. (1971). Symptom and dynamic cues in the implosive treatment of test anxiety. *Journal of Abnormal Psychology, 77,* 133–142.

-R-

Redl, F. (1933). We teachers and the fear of examinations. *Z. Psychoanal. Padag., 7,* 378–400.

Reed, M., & Saslow, C. A. (1980). The effects of relaxation instructions and EMG biofeedback on test anxiety, general anxiety, and locus of control. *Journal of Clinical Psychology, 36,* 683–690.

Reed, R., & Meyer, R. G. (1974). Reduction of test anxiety via autogenic therapy. *Psychological Reports, 35,* 649–650.

Reister, B. W. (1975). A treatment outcome study: Two group treatments and their outcomes in relation to state and trait anxiety (Doctoral dissertation, Indiana University, 1975). *Dissertation Abstracts International, 36,* 5835A. (University Microfilms No. 7606292)

Richardson, F. (1971). Unpublished survey, University of Texas at Austin.

Richardson, F. (1976). Anxiety management training: A multimodal approach. In A. Lazarus (Ed.), *Multimodal behavior therapy.* New York: Springer.

Richardson, F., O'Neill, H., Whitmore, S., & Judd, W. (1977). Factor analysis of the Test Anxiety Scale and evidence concerning the components of test anxiety. *Journal of Consulting and Clinical Psychology, 45,* 704–705.

Richardson, F., & Suinn, R. (1972). The Mathematics Anxiety Rating Scale: Psychometric data. *Journal of Counseling Psychology, 19,* 551–554.

Richardson, F., & Suinn, R. (1971). *The Mathematics Anxiety Rating Scale: Normative data.* Unpublished manuscript, University of Texas at Austin.

Richardson, F., & Suinn, R. (1973). A comparison of traditional systematic desensitization, accelerated massed desensitization, and anxiety management training in the treatment of mathematics anxiety. *Behavior Therapy, 4,* 212–218.

Richardson, F. C., & Suinn, R. M. (1974). Effects of two short term desensitization methods in the treatment of test anxiety. *Journal of Counseling Psychology, 21,* 457–458.

Ryan, V. L., Krall, C. A., & Hodges, W. F. (1976). Self-concept change in behavior modification. *Journal of Consulting and Clinical Psychology, 44,* 638–645.

-S-

Salamé, R. F. (1984). Test anxiety: Its determinants, manifestations, and consequences. In H. M. van der Ploeg, R. Schwarzer, & C. D. Spielberger (Eds.), *Advances in test anxiety research* (Vol. 3). Lisse, The Netherlands: Swets & Zeitlinger.

Sarason, I. G. (1958a). The effects of anxiety, reassurance and meaningfulness of material to be learned, on verbal learning. *Journal of Experimental Psychology, 56,* 472–477.

Sarason, I. G. (1958b). Interrelationships among individual differences variables, behavior in psychotherapy, and verbal conditioning. *Journal of Abnormal and Social Psychology, 56,* 339–344.

Sarason, I. G. (1959). Intellectual and personality correlates of test anxiety.
Journal of Abnormal and Social Psychology, 59, 272–275.

Sarason, I. G. (1960). Empirical findings and theoretical problems in the use
of anxiety scales. *Psychological Bulletin, 57,* 403–415.

Sarason, I. G. (1961). A note on anxiety, instructions, and word association
performance. *Journal of Abnormal and Social Psychology, 62,* 153–154.

Sarason, I. G. (1965). The human reinforcer in research on verbal behavior.
In L. Krassner & L. Ullman (Eds.), *Research in behavior modification.* New
York: Holt, Rinehart & Winston.

Sarason, I. G. (1968). Test anxiety and the observation of models. *Journal of
Personality, 36,* 493–511.

Sarason, I. G. (1972). Experimental approaches to test anxiety: Attention and
the uses of information. In C. D. Spielberger (Ed.), *Anxiety: Current trends
in theory and research* (Vol. 2). New York: Academic Press.

Sarason, I. G. (1975a). Test anxiety, attention and general problem of anxiety.
In C. D. Spielberger & I. G. Sarason (Eds.), *Stress and anxiety* (Vol. 1).
Washington, DC: Hemisphere/Wiley.

Sarason, I. G. (1975b). Anxiety and self-preoccupation. In I. G. Sarason &
C. D. Spielberger (Eds.), *Stress and anxiety* (Vol. 2). Washington, DC:
Hemisphere.

Sarason, I. G. (1978). The Test Anxiety Scale: Concept and research. In C. D.
Spielberger & I. G. Sarason (Eds.), *Stress and anxiety* (Vol. 5). New York:
Hemisphere/Wiley.

Sarason, I. G. (Ed.). (1980). *Test anxiety: Theory, research and applications.*
Hillsdale, NJ: Erlbaum.

Sarason, I. G. (1983). Understanding and modifying test anxiety. In S. B.
Anderson & J. S. Helmick (Eds.), *On educational testing.* San Francisco:
Jossey-Bass.

Sarason, I. G. (1984). Stress, anxiety, and cognitive interference: Reactions to
tests. *Journal of Personality and Social Psychology, 46,* 929–938.

Sarason, I. G. (1988). Anxiety, self-preoccupation and attention. *Anxiety Research: An International Journal, 1,* 3–8.

Sarason, I. G., & Ganzer, V. J. (1962). Anxiety, reinforcement and experimental instructions in a free verbal situation. *Journal of Abnormal and
Social Psychology, 65,* 303–307.

Sarason, I. G. & Ganzer, V. J. (1963). Effects of test anxiety and reinforcement
history on verbal behavior. *Journal of Abnormal and Social Psychology, 67,*
513–519.

Sarason, I. G., & Harmatz, M. G. (1965). Test anxiety and experimental
conditions. *Journal of Personality and Social Psychology, 1,* 499–505.

Sarason, I. G. & Koenig, K. P. (1965). The relationship of test anxiety and
hostility to description of self and parents. *Journal of Personality and Social
Psychology, 2,* 617–621.

Sarason, I. G., & Mandler, G. (1952). Some correlates of test anxiety. *Journal of Abnormal and Social Psychology, 47,* 810–817.

Sarason, I. G., Peterson, A. M., & Nyman, B. A. (1968). Test anxiety and the observation of models. *Journal of Personality, 36,* 493–511.

Sarason, I. G., & Sarason, B. R. (1990). Test anxiety. In H. Leitenberg (Ed.), *Handbook of social and evaluation anxiety.* New York: Plenum.

Sarason, I. G., Sarason, B. R., Keefe, D., Hayes, B. E., & Shearin, E. N. (1986). Cognitive interference: Situational determinants and traitlike characteristics. *Journal of Personality and Social Psychology, 51,* 215–226.

Sarason, S. B., Davidson, K. S., Lighthall, F. F., & Waite, R. R. (1958). Rorschach behavior and performance of high and low anxious children. *Child Development, 29,* 227–285.

Sarason, S. B., Davidson, K. S., Lighthall, F. F., Waite, R. R., & Ruebush, B. K. (1960). *Anxiety in elementary school children.* New York: Wiley.

Sarason, S. B., Hill, K., & Zimbardo, P. G. (1964). A longitudinal study of the relation of test anxiety to performance on intelligence and achievement tests. *Child Development Monograph,* (98).

Sarason, S. B., Mandler, G., & Craighill, P. G. (1952). The effect of differential instruction on anxiety and learning. *Journal of Abnormal and Social Psychology, 47,* 561–565.

Sassenrath, J. M. (1964). A factor analysis of rating-scale items on the Test Anxiety Questionnaire. *Journal of Counseling Psychology, 28,* 371–377.

Sassenrath, J. M., Kight, H. R., & Kaiser, H. F. (1965). Relating factors from anxiety scales between two samples. *Psychological Reports, 17,* 407–416.

Saunders, D. R. (1955). *Some preliminary interpretive materials for the PRI* (RM 55-15). Princeton, NJ: Educational Testing Service.

Schaffner, P., & Laux, L. (1979). Der Einfluß der kognitiven und emotionalen Angstkomponente auf die Prüfungsleistung bei Studenten. In L. H. Eckensberger (Ed.), *Berich über den 31. Kongreß der DGfP in Mannheim 1978* (Bd. 2). Göttingen, Germany: Hogrefe.

Scherer, M. W., & Nakamura, C. Y. (1968). A fear survey schedule for children (FSS-FC): A factor analytic comparison with manifest anxiety (CMAS). *Behavior Research and Therapy, 6,* 173–182.

Schwartz, G. E., Davidson, R. J., & Maer, F. (1975). Right hemisphere lateralization for emotion in the human brain: Interactions with cognition. *Science, 190,* 286–288.

Schwarzer, R. (1979). *Schulangst und Schulunlust in Gesamt- und Realschulen.* Forschungsbericht im Auftrag des Instituts für Theorie und Praxis der Schule des Landes Schleswig-Holstein, Aachen.

Schwarzer, R. (1984). Worry and emotionality as separate components in test anxiety. *International Review of Applied Psychology, 33,* 205–220.

Schwarzer, R., & Jerusalem, M. (1992). Advances in anxiety theory: A cognitive process approach. In H. M. van der Ploeg, R. Schwarzer, & C. D. Spielberger (Eds.), *Advances in test anxiety research* (Vol. 7). Lisse, The Netherlands: Swets & Zeitlinger.

Schwarzer, R., & Quast, H.-H. (1985). Multidimensionality of the anxiety experience. Evidence for additional components. In H. M. van der Ploeg,

R. Schwarzer, & C. D. Spielberger (Eds.), *Advances in test anxiety research* (Vol. 4). Lisse, The Netherlands: Swets & Zeitlinger.

Schwarzer, R., van der Ploeg, H. M., & Spielberger, C. D. (Eds.). (1987). *Advances in test anxiety research* (Vol. 5). Lisse, The Netherlands: Swets & Zeitlinger.

Schwarzer, R., van der Ploeg, H. M., & Spielberger, C. D. (Eds.). (1989). *Advances in test anxiety research* (Vol. 6). Lisse, The Netherlands: Swets & Zeitlinger.

Scrivner, R. W. (1974). Systematic desensitization and cognitive modification with high emotionality and high worry subjects. (Unpublished doctoral dissertation, The University of Texas at Austin, 1974). *Dissertation Abstracts International, 35,* 2447B. (University Microfilms No. 7424933)

Seipp, B. (1991). Anxiety and academic performance: A meta-analysis of findings. *Anxiety Research, 4,* 27–41.

Shapiro, D. H., Sr., Zifferblatt, S. M. (1976). Zen meditation and behavioral self-control: Similarities, differences and clinical applications. *American Psychologist, 31,* 519–532.

Shapiro, R. S. (1976). *Study skills training versus study skills training plus cue controlled relaxation in the alleviation of test-anxiety in college students.* Unpublished senior honors thesis, University of Michigan.

Shedletsky, R., & Endler, N. S. (1974). Anxiety: The state-trait model and the interaction model. *Journal of Personality, 42,* 511–527.

Sheffield, F. D., & Temmer, H. W. Relative resistance to extinction of escape training and avoidance training. *Journal of Experimental Psychology, 40,* 287–298.

Shipley, R. H., Mock, L. A., & Levis, D. J. (1970). Effects of several response prevention procedures on activity, avoidance responding, and conditioned fear in rats. *Journal of Comparative Physiological Psychology, 77,* 256–270.

Showalter, J. M. (1974). Test anxiety reduction: A comparison of three approaches (Doctoral dissertation, Ohio State University, 1974). *Dissertation Abstracts International, 35,* 828A. (University Microfilms No. 7417807)

Sidman, M. (1955). On the persistance of avoidance behavior. *Journal of Abnormal and Social Psychology, 50,* 217–220.

Slatker, M. J., Koehler, R. A., & Hampton, S. H. (1970). Learning test-wiseness by programmed texts. *Journal of Educational Measurement, 7,* 247–254.

Smith, R. E., & Nye, S. L. (1973). A comparison of implosive therapy and systematic desensitization in the treatment of test anxiety. *Journal of Consulting and Clinical Psychology, 41,* 37–42.

Smith, W. F., & Rockett, F. C. (1958). Test performance as a function of anxiety, instructor and instructions. *Journal of Educational Research, 52,* 138–141.

Snieder, J. G., & Oetting, E. R. (1966). Autogenic training and the treatment of examination anxiety in students. *Journal of Clinical Psychology, 22,* 111–114.

Solomon, R. L., Kamin, L. J., & Wynne, L. C. (1953). Traumatic avoidance learning: The outcomes of several extinction procedures with dogs. *Journal of Abnormal and Social Psychology, 48,* 291–295.

Solomon, R. L., & Wynne, L. C. (1953). Traumatic avoidance learning: Acquisition in normal dogs. *Psychological Monographs: General and Applied, 67,* 1–19.

Solomons, R. S. (1974). The role of expectation in the desensitization of test anxiety (Doctoral dissertation, University of Colorado, 1974). *Dissertation Abstracts International, 35,* 524–525B. (University Microfilms No. 7412408)

Spence, K. W., Farber, I. E., & McFann, H. H. (1956). The relation of anxiety in (drive) level to performance in competitional and non-competitional paired associates learning. *Journal of Experimental Psychology, 52,* 296–305.

Sperber, Z. (1961). Test anxiety and performance under stress. *Journal of Counseling Psychology, 25,* 226–233.

Spiegler, M. D., Cooley, E. J., Marshall, G. J., Prince, H. T., II, Puckett, S. P., & Skenazy, J. A. (1976). A self-control versus a counter conditioning paradigm for systematic desensitization: An experimental comparison. *Journal of Counseling Psychology, 23,* 83–86.

Spiegler, M. D., Morris, L. W., & Liebert, R. M. (1968). Cognitive and emotional components of test anxiety temporal factors. *Psychological Reports, 22,* 451–456.

Spielberger, C. D. (1962). The effects of manifest anxiety on the academic achievements of college students. *Mental Hygiene, 46,* 420–425.

Spielberger, C. D. (1966a). Theory and research on anxiety. In C. D. Spielberger (Ed.), *Anxiety and behavior.* New York: Academic Press.

Spielberger, C. D. (1966b). The effects of anxiety on complex learning and academic achievement. In C. D. Spielberger (Ed.), *Anxiety and behavior.* New York: Academic Press.

Spielberger, C. D. (1972a). Anxiety as an emotional state. In C. D. Spielberger (Ed.), *Anxiety: Current trends in theory and research* (Vol. 1). New York: Academic Press.

Spielberger, C. D. (1972b). Conceptual and methodological issues in anxiety research. In C. D. Spielberger (Ed.), *Anxiety: Current trends in theory and research* (Vol. 2). New York: Academic Press.

Spielberger, C. D. (1975). Anxiety: State-trait process. In C. D. Spielberger & I. G. Sarason (Eds.), *Stress and anxiety.* Washington, DC: Hemisphere/Wiley.

Spielberger, C. D. (1976). The nature and measurement of anxiety. In C. D. Spielberger & R. Diaz-Guerrero (Eds.), *Cross-cultural research on anxiety.* Washington, DC: Hemisphere/Wiley.

Spielberger, C. D. (1979). *Understanding stress and anxiety.* London: Harper & Row.

Spielberger, C. D. (1980). *Preliminary professional manual for the Test Anxiety Inventory.* Palo Alto, CA: Consulting Psychologists Press.

Spielberger, C. D., Anton, W. D., & Bedell, J. (1976). The nature and treatment of test anxiety. In M. Zuckerman & C. D. Spielberger (Eds.), *Emo-*

tions and anxiety: New concepts, methods, and applications. New York: Erlbaum.

Spielberger, C. D. (1983). *Manual for the State-Trait Anxiety Inventory (STAI).* Palo Alto, CA: Consulting Psychologists Press.

Spielberger, C. D., Edwards, C. D., Lushene, R. E., Montuori, J., & Platzek, D. (1973). *STAIC preliminary manual for the State-Trait Anxiety Inventory for Children.* Palo Alto, CA: Consulting Psychologists Press.

Spielberger, C. D., Gonzalez, H. P., & Fletcher, T. (1979). Test anxiety reduction, learning strategies and academic performance. In H. F. O'Neil & C. D. Spielberger (Eds.), *Cognitive and affective learning strategies.* New York: Academic Press.

Spielberger, C. D., Gonzalez, H. P., Taylor, C. J., Algaze, B., & Anton, W. D. (1978). Examination stress and test anxiety. In C. D. Spielberger and I. G. Sarason (Eds.), *Stress and anxiety* (Vol. 5). Washington, DC: Hemisphere/Wiley.

Spielberger, C. D., Gorsuch, R. L., & Lushene, R. E. (1970). *Manual for the State-Trait Anxiety Inventory.* Palo Alto, CA: Consulting Psychologists Press.

Spielberger, C. D., O'Neil, H. F., & Hansen, D. N. (1972). Anxiety, drive theory, and computer assisted learning. In B. A. Maher (Ed.). *Progress in experimental personality research* (Vol. 6). New York: Academic Press.

Spielberger, C. D., & Smith, L. H. (1966). Anxiety (drive), stress, and serial-position effects in serial-verbal learning. *Journal of Experimental Psychology, 72,* 589–595.

Spielberger, C. D., & Vagg, P. (1987). The treatment of test anxiety: A transactional process model. In R. Schwarzer, H. M. van der Ploeg, & C. D. Spielberger (Eds.), *Advances in test anxiety research* (Vol. 5). Lisse, The Netherlands: Swets & Zeitlinger.

Spielberger, C. D., & Weitz, H. (1964). Improving the academic performance of anxious college freshmen: A group-counseling approach to the prevention of underachievement. *Psychological Monographs, 78* (13, Whole No. 590).

Spielberger, C. D., Weitz, H., & Denny, J. P. (1962). Group counseling and the academic performance of anxious college freshmen. *Journal of Counseling Psychology, 9,* 195–204.

Stanford, D., Dember, W., & Stanford, L. (1963). A children's form of the Alpert-Haber Achievement Anxiety Scale. *Child Development, 34,* 1027–1032.

Stengel, E. (1936). Examination fear and examination neuroses. *Z. Psychoanalitical Pedagogy, 10,* 300–320.

Stent, A. (1977). Can math anxiety be conquered? *Change, 9,* 40–43.

Stephan, E., Fischer, S., & Stein, F. (1983). Self-related cognitions in test anxiety research: An empirical study and critical conclusions. In R. Schwarzer, H. M. van der Ploeg, & C. D. Spielberger (Eds.), *Advances in test anxiety research* (Vol. 2). Lisse, The Netherlands: Swets & Zeitlinger.

Stern, D. B. (1977). Handedness and the lateral distribution of conversion reactions. *The Journal of Nervous and Mental Disease, 164,* 122–128.

241

Suberi, M., & McKeever, W. F. (1977). Differential right hemisphere memory storage of emotional and non-emotional faces. *Neuropsychologia, 15,* 757–767.

Sud, A., & Sharma, S. (1990). Two short-term, cognitive interventions for the reduction of test anxiety. *Anxiety Research, 3,* 131–147.

Suinn, R. M. (1968). The desensitization of test anxiety by group and individual treatment. *Behavior Research and Therapy, 6,* 64–65.

Suinn, R. M. (1969). The STABS: A measure of test anxiety for behavior therapy: Normative data. *Behavior Research and Therapy, 7,* 335–339.

Suinn, R. (1970). *The application of short-term videotape therapy for the treatment of test anxiety of college students.* Progress report, Colorado State University.

Suinn, R. (1972). *Mathematics Anxiety Rating Scale (MARS).* Ft. Collins, CO: RMBSI.

Suinn, R., Edie, C., Nicoletti, J., & Spinelli, P. (1973). The MARS, a measure of mathematics anxiety: Psychometric data. *Journal of Clinical Psychology, 38,* 373–374.

Suinn, R., Edie, C., & Spinelli, P. (1970). Accelerated massed desensitization: Innovation in short-term treatment. *Behavior Therapy, 1,* 303–311.

Suinn, R. M., & Hall, R. (1970). Marathon desensitization groups: An innovation. *Behavior Research and Therapy, 8,* 97–98.

Suinn, R., & Richardson, F. (1971). Anxiety management training: A nonspecific behavior therapy program for anxiety control. *Behavior Therapy, 2,* 498–510.

Sullivan, E. T., Clark, W. W., & Tiege, E. W. (1957). *Manual for the California Test of Mental Maturity* (Advanced Ed.). Palo Alto, CA: Consulting Psychologists Press.

-T-

Taylor, J. A. (1953). A personality scale of manifest anxiety. *Journal of Abnormal and Social Psychology, 48,* 285–290.

Taub, E. (1975). Self regulation of human tissue temperature. In G. E. Schwartz & J. Beatty (Eds.), *Biofeedback: Theory and research.* New York: Academic Press.

Thompson, J. W. (1976). *A comparison of four behavior therapies in the treatment of test anxiety in college students* (Doctoral dissertation, University of Arkansas, 1976). *Dissertation Abstracts International, 36,* 3631B. (University Microfilms No. 7600478)

Tobias, S. (1978). *Overcoming math anxiety.* New York: Norton.

Tobias, S. (1985). Test anxiety: Interference, defective skills, and cognitive capacity. *Educational Psychologist, 20,* 135–142.

Tobias, S. (1992). The impact of test anxiety on cognition in school learning. In K. A. Hagtvet & T. B. Johnsen (Eds.), *Advances in test anxiety research* (Vol. 7). Amsterdam/Lisse, The Netherlands: Swets & Zeitlinger.

Tobias, S., & Hedl, J. J., Jr. (1972, June). *Test anxiety: Situationally specific or general?* (Tech. Memo No. 49, Office of Naval Research Grant No. N00014-68-A-4094). Tallahassee: Florida State University, CAI Center.

Topman, R. M., Kleijn, W. C., van der Ploeg, H. M., & Masset, E. A. (1992). In K. A. Hagtvet & T. B. Johnsen (Eds.), *Advances in test anxiety research* (Vol. 7). Amsterdam/Lisse, The Netherlands: Swets & Zeitlinger.

Topman, R. M., & Janson, T. (1984). "I really can't do it, anyway": The treatment of test anxiety. In H. M. van der Ploeg, R. Schwarzer, & C. D. Spielberger (Eds.), *Advances in test anxiety research* (Vol. 3). Hillsdale, NJ: Erlbaum.

Trexler, L. D., & Karst, T. O. (1972). Rational-emotive therapy, placebo, and no treatment effects on public speaking anxiety. *Journal of Abnormal Psychology, 79*, 60–67.

Tryon, G. S. (1980). The measurement and treatment of test anxiety. *Review of Educational Research, 50*, 343–372.

Tucker, D., Roth, R. S., Arneson, B. A., & Buckingham, V. (1977). Right hemisphere activation during stress. *Neuropsychologia, 15*, 697–700.

-V-

Vagg, P. R. (1978). *The treatment of test anxiety: A comparison of biofeedback and cognitive coping strategies.* Unpublished doctoral dissertation, University of Michigan, 1977. (Comprehensive Dissertation Index 149p. 38/118, p. 5599.565)

Vagg, P. R., & Papsdorf, J. (1977). *Test anxiety therapy manual.* Unpublished manuscript, Department of Psychology, University of Michigan.

van der Ploeg, H. M., Stapert, J. D., & van der Ploeg, J. (1986). Behavioral group treatment of test anxiety: An evaluation study. *Journal of Behavior Therapy and Experimental Psychiatry, 10*, 255–259.

Varni, J. G., Doerr, H. O., & Franklin, J. R. (1971). Bilateral differences in skin resistance and vasomotor activity. *Psychophysiology, 8*, 390–400.

-W-

Wagaman, G. L. (1975). Effects of self-instructional video modeling tape on cognitive modification of test anxious students (Doctoral dissertation, West Virginia University, 1975). *Dissertation Abstracts International, 36*, 2039A. (University Microfilms No. 7521935)

Wahlstrom, M., & Boersma, F. J. (1968). The influence of test-wiseness upon achievement. *Educational and Psychological Measurement, 28*, 413–420.

Waite, W. H. (1942). The relationship between performance on examinations and emotional responses. *The Journal of Experimental Education, 11*, 88–96.

Walsh, R. P., Engbretson, R. O., & O'Brien, B. A. (1968). Anxiety and test-taking behavior. *Journal of Counseling Psychology, 15*, 572–575.

Ware, W. B., Galassi, J. P., & Dew, K. M. H. (1990). The Test Anxiety Inventory: A confirmatory factor analysis. *Anxiety Research, 3,* 205–212.

Weber, C. (1934). Examination anxiety in taking information tests. *Industrial Psychotechnology, 11,* 53–55.

Wechsler, D. (1955). *Manual for the Wechsler Adult Intelligence Scale.* New York: Psychological Corporation.

West, C. K., Lee, J. F., & Anderson, T. H. (1969). The influence of test anxiety on the selection of relevant from irrelevant information. *Journal of Educational Research, 63,* 51–52.

Wilson, J. W., Cahen, L. S., & Begle, E. G. (Eds.). (1968). *NLSMA Report No. 4: Descriptive and statistical properties of X-population scales.* Stanford, CA: School of Mathematics Study Group.

Wilson, N., & Rotter, J. C. (1986). Anxiety management training and study skills counseling for students on self esteem and test anxiety and performance. *School Counselor, 34,* 18–31.

Wine, J. (1971). Test anxiety and direction of attention. *Psychological Bulletin, 76,* 92–104.

Wine, J. D. (1982). Evaluation anxiety: A cognitive-attentional construct. In H. W. Krohne & L. Laux (Eds.), *Achievement, stress, and anxiety.* Washington, DC: Hemisphere.

Wisocki, P. A. (1973). A covert reinforcement program for the treatment of test anxiety: Brief report. *Behavior Therapy, 4,* 264–266.

Wittmaier, B. C. (1972). Test anxiety and study habits. *Journal of Educational Research, 65,* 352–354.

Wolpe, J. (1958). *Psychotherapy by reciprocal inhibition.* Stanford, CA: Stanford University Press.

Wolpe, J., & Lange, P. J. (1964). A fear survey schedule for use in behavior therapy. *Behavior Research and Therapy, 2,* 27–30.

Wolpe, J., Salter, A., & Reyna, J. (1964). *The conditioning therapies: The challenge in psychotherapy.* New York: Holt, Rinehart & Winston.

Wonderlic, E. F. (1975). *Wonderlic personnel test manual.* Northfield, IL: E. F. Wonderlic.

-Y-

Yerkes, R. M., & Dodson, J. D. (1908). The relationship of strength of stimulus to rapidity of habit formation. *Journal of Comparative and Neurological Psychology, 18,* 459–482.

-Z-

Zimmer, J., Hocevar, D., Bachelor, P., & Meinke, D. L. (1992). An analysis of the Sarason (1984) four-factor conceptualization of test anxiety. In K. A. Hagtvet & T. B. Johnsen (Eds.), *Advances in test anxiety research* (Vol. 7). Lisse, The Netherlands: Swets & Zeitlinger.

Zoller, U., & Ben-Chaim, D. (1990). Gender differences in examination-type preferences, test anxiety, and academic achievements in college science education: A case study. *Science Education, 74,* 597–608.

Zuckerman, M. (1960). The development of an affect adjective check list for the measurement of anxiety. *Journal of Counseling Psychology, 24,* 457–462.

Zuckerman, M., & Lubin, B. (1965). *Manual for the Multiple Affect Adjective Check List.* San Diego, CA: Educational and Industrial Testing Service.

Author Index

Subject Index

Subjective Stress Scale, 32
Suinn Test Anxiety Behavior Scale, 32
Survey of Study Habits and Attitudes, 186
Systematic desensitization (*see*
    Desensitization)

TAI (*see* Test Anxiety Inventory)
T-Anxiety (*see* Trait anxiety)
TAQ (*see* Test Anxiety Questionnaire)
TAS (*see* Test Anxiety Scale)
TASC (*see* Test Anxiety Scale for Children)
Test anxiety
    ability-achievement tests, 20, 110
    academic performance, 49
    anxiety measures, 20–21
    awareness of, 17
    cognitive interpretations of, 44, 51, 167–169
    cognitive treatment of, 135–169, 183–196
    components of, 134, 184
    concept of, 48
    definitions of, 6
    early research on, 3–4
    effect on academic performance, 4, 132
    emotionality and, 7
    feedback loops, 50–53
    general trait anxiety (T-anxiety), 7–8, 48
    impact on cognitive processes, 13
    influencing factors, 24–25
    LEM preference, 92
    literature on, 21, 26
    math and, 94–96, 100
        (*See also* Math anxiety)
    measurement of, 13–18, 35–37, 47–59
    new developments in treatment, 197
    performance and, 111–112
    psychological antecedents of, 79
    research on, 62, 109–111, 183
    reduction of, 117–118, 128, 149–150, 167–
        169, 211–212
    right hemisphere utilization, 79
    self-report measures, 25
    situation-specific anxiety trait, 58
    state-trait anxiety, 6–7, 193–194
    test-wiseness, 23
    theoretical positions, 36, 47–59, 62
    Transactional Process Model, 11–13
    treatment of
        anxiety-coping training, 118
        behavioral approaches, 118–121
        biofeedback and, 171–194
        cognitive coping, 171–194
        cognitive elements, 154–156

effectiveness of, 123–125, 141–149,
    207–212
procedures for, 202–207
progressive relaxation, 180–181
Rational-Emotive Therapy, 153–169
results of, 202–207
study counseling, 125–127, 137
systematic desensitization, 171–194
trait anxiety, 141–149
women and, 87
worry and, 7, 111
Test Anxiety Inventory (TAI), 9, 32, 48, 62,
    84, 121, 173–174
    posttreatment scores, 125, 142
    pretreatment scores, 122, 142
Test Anxiety Questionnaire (TAQ), 9, 32, 38,
    183
Test Anxiety Scale (TAS), 9, 33, 36, 121, 137,
    173,
    A-Trait Subscale, 42
    convergent validity, 41–42
    divergent validity, 43
    evaluation of, 35–46
    pre- and posttreatment results, 142
    predictive validity of, 42
Test Anxiety Scale for Children (TASC), 17,
    33
Test-anxious students, 63
    case studies of, 61–78
    characteristics of, 61
    desensitization and, 121–123, 130
    irrelevant thinking, 22
Test-taking skills, 212–213
Test-wiseness, principles of, 23
Trait Anxiety (T-anxiety), 6–7, 38, 47–48, 63,
    84, 137
Trait Anxiety Inventory (TAI), 138, 150
Trait Anxiety Scale (TAS), 42–44, 138, 150
Trait-State anxiety, 48, 96–98
Transactional Process Model, 11–14, 202, 214

WEQ (*see* Worry-Emotionality
    Questionnaire)
Wide Range Achievement Test, 106
Wonderlic Personnel Test, 186, 187, 193–194
Worry cognitions, 7–8, 13, 33, 51, 95, 134, 181
    transactional model and, 12
    emotionality and, 21–23, 137, 141–142
    factorial relations, 22
    pre- and posttreatment scores, 161
Worry-Emotionality Questionaire (WEQ),
    137, 141, 142

Of similar interest . . .

**Academic journals
in the social sciences
published by
Taylor & Francis:**

SOCIAL EPISTEMOLOGY
Steve Fuller, Editor

Social Epistemology provides a forum for
philosophical and social scientific enquiry that
incorporates the work of scholars from a variety
of disciplines who share a concern with the
production, assessment, and validation of
knowledge. The journal covers both empirical
research into the origination and transmission of
knowledge and normative considerations which
arise as such research is implemented, serving as
a guide for directing contemporary
knowledge enterprises.

ISSN: 0269-1728 • Quarterly

ISSUES IN
MENTAL HEALTH NURSING
Mary Swanson Crockett, R.N., Editor

With emphasis on innovative approaches to
client care, analyses of current issues, and
nursing research findings, this journal provides
information vital to psychological and
mental health nursing.

ISSN: 0161-2840 • Bimonthly

*For more
information and ordering,
please write or call toll-free:*

Taylor & Francis
1900 Frost Road
Suite 101
Bristol, PA 19007-1598
United States
1-800-821-8312